BUSINESS COMMUNICATIONS

BUSINESS COMMUNICATIONS

Khushboo Manoj

CENTRUM PRESS
NEW DELHI-110002 (INDIA)

CENTRUM PRESS
H.O.: 4360/4, Ansari Road, Daryaganj,
New Delhi-110002 (India)
Tel: 23278000, 23261597, 23255577, 23286875
B.O.: No. 1015, Ist Main Road, BSK IIIrd Stage,
IIIrd Phase, IIIrd Block, Bangalore-560085 (INDIA)
Tel: 080-41723429
Email: centrumpress@gmail.com
Visit us at: www.centrumpress.com

Business Communications

First Edition, 2011

ISBN 978-93-80921-21-1

PRINTED IN INDIA

Printed at Mehra Offset Press, Delhi.

Contents

Preface

In business, the term communications encompasses several channels of communication, including the Internet, Print, Radio, Television, Ambient media, Outdoor, and Word of mouth. Business Communication can also refer to internal communication.

A communications director will typically manage internal communication and craft messages sent to employees. It is vital that internal communications are managed properly because a poorly crafted or managed message could foster distrust or hostility from employees.

Business Communication is a common topic included in the curricula of Masters of Business Administration (MBA) programmes of many universities. As well, many community colleges and universities offer degrees in Communications. The content of the information was not compromised in any way, but was condensed to focus on key elements.

The systematic approach provides students with a practical plan for solving communication problems and creating successful communication products. The nine-stage approach of analysing-anticipating-adapting, researching-organizing-approaching, and revising-proofreading-evaluating makes the process understandable.

Author

1

Communication in a Corporate

AN OVERVIEW

To understand communication in a corporate setting, one can explore any of several defining characteristics. One characteristic has to do with time: Communicative acts are embedded within a flow of prior and subsequent interaction. Indeed, in a business setting, a document may not have any more intrinsic importance to that community than the process that created it; that is, the real value in the process may come from negotiating a consensus for the final text. Another characteristic relates to form, as the ideas constructed over time may move through many communicative forms: Informal discussion may lead to an agenda item in a meeting, which may result in a request for a document, which may in turn be presented orally in another meeting.

An almost endless variety of forms are possible — from formal documents to review comments, from hallway conversations to lengthy presentations, from scrawled notes to multimedia. Not only is the relationship between oral and written texts important, but also the plethora of technology-mediated forms that confound traditional definitions of text. Even with so many possibilities, form is a relatively straightforward characteristic in describing communication after the fact.

Form, on the other hand, is considerably more complex for the individual doing the communicating. In a business setting, individuals choosing the form of a communicative performance must balance a whole range of contextual factors from access to timeliness to appropriateness. In short, the flow of communication over time and the form communicators choose to give it are embedded within a social framework a set of cultural expectations — that largely define how the individuals within a particular setting interact.

CONTEXT AND NONACADEMIC WRITING

The connection between context and nonacademic writing has been fruitful territory for research. Nonetheless, it is a difficult concept to generalize.

Witte presents a useful definition of context not tied to a specific research site, which (to paraphrase mightily) focuses on the writer's projected self in light of the writer's understanding of external reality. Context and the social perspective have much to offer in understanding the role of texts in constructing meaning, but they also raise challenging questions when applied to nonacademic research sites. The essential difficulty can be stated briefly: How can we know an unfamiliar context?

Returning to the ideas of flow and form help emphasize this difficulty. As a researcher, we can fairly easily characterize the form of a text; we can also, through various means, explore its flow in terms of precedents and antecedents. Thus, we can describe what a communicative performance is and where it fits into the overall conversation. But context, in one simple word, embraces the localized social complexity of communication and all that suggests in terms of what is knowable and what transformations take place in representation.

The crux of the difficulty may lie in moving from the familiar to the unfamiliar. In researching writing in the classroom, a familiar setting for many researchers, the barriers to understanding context may not be insurmountable to the extent that we can really understand the context of classroom communication from external points of view. But in many nonacademic settings, writing researchers may find themselves on alien turf. Context in a business setting may involve anything from the competitive climate for an entire industry to relations among employees assigned to the same project; from the formal power relationships defined by organizational charts to informal power hierarchies based on information distribution; from managerial attempts to create unified corporate cultures to the unique aspirations of individual employees. Context, in any setting, is layered: The difficulties in its characterization are exacerbated by unfamiliar value systems and distinctly different institutional goals. Yet context can charge texts-even fairly mundane business texts such as memos and meeting minutes — with subtle ironies, implied put-downs, challenges, celebrations, and humour — all difficult to detect for the cultural outsider. For the purposes of this study, however, we chose to impose some boundaries on the idea of context.

Nonacademic writing researchers have most often used qualitative research methods to understand context, generally focusing on individuals or relatively small groups of employees. My own approach is similar but perhaps foregrounds the sources of contextual knowledge to a greater extent in that we asked employees specific questions about context (defined as three layers of corporate culture), supplemented with research into the history of the corporation, where the research took place, and the industry in which it competes. It may be that making explicit the sources of contextual knowledge and relying where possible on the words of cultural insiders to describe their perceptions of context reduces some of the difficulties with representing an unfamiliar culture.

This approach, of course, has its limitations: Perceptions of context will differ among any set of cultural informants so that any claim for an overall characterization of context becomes suspect; the selection of which details to present, although in informants' own words, reflect the researcher's institutional biases.

Still, as cultures are dynamic, context may be best described as a phenomenon based in individual perception. Construction of meaning ultimately begins in the interaction among and between individuals and small groups.

TECHNOLOGY AND CONTEXT

The balance focuses on the relationship between context and technology (a major influence on both form and flow), providing a socio technological perspective on communication at a specific site. We chose this focus for several reasons. First, as noted earlier, connections between text and context are well established, as are links between context and texts over time. Connections between context and use of technology — from a communications point of view — are not as well understood. Third, choice of technology provides a useful site to emphasize a relationship between context defined as perceptions of corporate culture and decision making about communication. Many decisions about communication are fleeting, recoverable only through means such as protocol analysis.

Decisions about choice of technology, on the other hand, are observable and recordable, and other means of gathering information still apply. Finally, like understanding context in unfamiliar settings, understanding the use of technology in a corporate setting presents its own challenges.

In composition and other fields concerned with communication, researchers have tended to study technologies as discrete entities, starting with a focus on personal computers and word processing software in the early and mid-1980s, through recent scholarship focusing on new or emerging technologies such as electronic mail over local area networks, hypertext, and multimedia. In many workplaces, and in contrast to the college or university computer lab, employees often choose among many available computer-based technologies to communicate a particular message. In terms of technology, then, this research had two goals: first, to explore how people chose among many technological options; and second, to investigate links between employees' perceptions of their context and their use of technology to interact with other employees. And there were links. At the corporate site where we conducted my research, social factors defined the use of communication technologies. Specifically,

- Communication technology options were determined by contextual factors at the organizational level. That is, technology deployment echoed the organization's goals, values, and conflicts.

- Choice among the options reflected local culture. For example, widely held perceptions of uncertainty or distrust of management affected which technologies employees used to communicate.
- Not surprisingly, individual factors, such as an employee's interest in new technology, a need for control, or a dislike of writing further affected choice among communication media.

RESEARCH METHODOLOGY

Research for this study took place at the NetCon Division of Computer Corporation. (All names are fictitious at the request of the corporation.)

The research site within NetCon Division was a project team that had just begun working on the development of a new product (Product X), which was based on a technology in which NetCon had little expertise. The purpose of this project team, like other teams at NetCon, was to coordinate the various departments that took part in the product development effort.

Team members included representatives from the areas of software, hardware, and performance engineering, product management, marketing, technical publications, technical customer support, and manufacturing. With Product X, coordination was particularly important, as the product combined hardware and software components. Most products at NetCon are one or the other: These two development areas within NetCon have rarely collaborated directly in developing a new product.

Within the project, several individual participants were selected as "cases." They represented a range of job descriptions, departments, and levels in the corporate hierarchy. It is important to note that the research results emphasize the relationships of context and technology among these individuals at this particular site; we do not intend them to be generalizable to all corporate settings.

Techniques for Gathering Information

I used a multiphase, qualitative research design, similar to that employed by Spilka in her study, "Orality and Literacy in the Workplace: Process and Text-Based Strategies for Multiple-Audience Adaptation." Like Spilka, we used several information gathering strategies, allowing for both methodological triangulation and the broadest coverage of group and individual communicative activities within the 6-month period of the study.

Project Team Meetings

With one exception, we attended all project team meetings over a 6-month period. We particularly noted any discussions that related to the activities of my participants, particularly any "texts" (presentations, memos, formal reports, manuals, etc.) they were involved in preparing, any comments about the work environment, and any discussion concerning technology use.

Questionnaire and Initial Interview

We administered a detailed questionnaire to the four research participants to meet several goals. First, we used it to collect simple demographic information about the participants. Second, we asked them through a series of questions to assess their communicative behaviour. We included these questions to establish a baseline of their own perceptions; we later collected information on the same topics through other means. Questions in this series asked them:

- How much of their time at work they spent writing, what kinds of documents they produced, and how they felt about writing;
- How much of their time at work they spent reading, and how much they read as a reviewer, how much for their own information;
- How much of their time at work they spent in meetings, formal and informal; and
- How they used different communication technologies (including e-mail, voice mail, telephone, and fax).

Another set of questions asked them to describe the corporate culture of their department, of NetCon Division, and of Computer Corporation as a whole. These were general questions and provided a useful springboard for questions in a follow-up, audiotaped interview with each participant.

Logging and Shadowing

Two weeks after the initial interview, We asked each participant to keep a log of their communicative activities for one week. The goal was to capture a snapshot of their communicative activities that could be compared to their self-assessment and to gain insight into each participant's mix of oral, written, and technology-mediated communicative activity.

Detailed log forms were provided to each participant to record and describe acts of reading, writing, and speaking, noting start and end times for each event. However, the logs proved impractical for two of the participants. For these participants, we supplemented their log entries with additional interviews and "shadowing," where we followed these participants as they performed their jobs, asking questions and taking notes.

Writing Samples

I collected writing samples from each participant, which we used for analysis and discourse-based interviews. However, nearly all of the samples we received contained proprietary information. This is a very sensitive issue in the computer industry; thus, we have had to use samples with care as we present them in the discussion that follows.

CORPORATE CULTURE AND TECHNOLOGY USE AT NETCON DIVISION

The follow provide a description and commentary on the use of communications technologies by the four cases. To put this use in its organizational context-and to explore the impact of context on use. We provide a brief historical description of NetCon based on articles in the trade press, reviews of company archives (including company newsletters and press releases), and interviews with public relations employees. This description sheds some light on the current work climate and value system at NetCon.

The second, presents results from the cases, first presenting summaries of perceptions of corporate culture and then examining each person's use of communication technologies, as reported in interviews and as observed through logging/ shadowing.

The Layered Cultures of NetCon Division

NetCon Division, at one time an independent company in the computer industry, had been acquired a number of years previous to the study by Computer Corporation. Shortly after the takeover, like many companies in the computer industry, Computer Corporation laid off significant numbers of employees.

These reductions hit NetCon particularly hard. In addition to the impact of takeover, it appears that significant cultural shifts have taken place during the 20 years or so of NetCon's existence. Its initial entrepreneurial culture was, in Morgan's terms, solidly "organic". The organizational chart was relatively flat (by later standards), and work was accomplished in a project-oriented environment that consisted of teams from many departments. It appears from internal company publications that product innovation and achieving aggressive development schedules were highly valued.

However, the culture of Computer Corporation, as evidenced after the purchase, was quite different. Computer Corporation, although viewing itself as an innovative, adaptable organization, was larger, more bureaucratic — and to use Morgan's terms — more "mechanistic" than NetCon. What followed the acquisition was a difficult mix of Computer Corporation's dominantly mechanistic culture overlaying NetCon's organic one.

Although daily work continued to follow established patterns (*i.e.*, project-oriented work teams), a pervasive atmosphere of process control and budgetary accountability began to change interactions within those groups. This conflict is quite apparent in information gathered from research participants.

CASE ONE: KENT

Corporate Cultures

Kent did not offer strong opinions about the parent company, Computer Corporation. He described it simply as "conservative": "I guess they do things the way that you expect. Pretty hierarchical. People have been here a long time, have done things a certain way.

They listen to the same things." Kent had more to say about the culture of NetCon Division. Although he thought current upper management were more "upbeat" than the other participants, he noted that the workforce at NetCon was "mature, dominated by old-timers," and that the division was "struggling to find a new road to travel."

Although fairly consistent with the other participants in his views on culture at the corporate and division levels, Kent described a more positive departmental culture, noting the mood of the group that he manages as "fairly loose and upbeat." He said that *"it's better than it was. I think people are interested in the [current] project," and in comparing that to recent history at NetCon, noted that, "it's rather bizarre, actually."*

Technology Use: Disparate Networks and Voice Mail

Kent's department uses a sophisticated CASE (computer-aided software engineering) system. This system, beside providing an online environment for writing, compiling, integrating, and testing computer programmes, offers an e-mail facility.

But this e-mail system has limited usefulness. Kent explained: "There are a lot of e-mail systems here, but they aren't connected. We're on the Internet side of the house. Then there's the Novell side. Basically, I e-mail stuff to my people. I can't, like, e-mail stuff to hardware engineering."

Question: "Do you ever converse over e-mail?" Kent: "No. It's one-ended. We don't even get a message every day. It's not as important as voice mail for me. We don't have any surveillance anyway." As Kent noted, he makes heavy use of voice mail: "I hate the telephone. We really do. So voice mail frees me a lot. We can pick up messages when we want, and we can leave messages for people when they aren't there. we love voice mail, but we hate the telephone. One I'm in control, the other I'm not in control."

NetCon's voice mail system, unlike the disparate e-mail systems, is company-wide, requires very little effort to learn, and for those who are interested, offers a fairly wide range of features, including broadcasting to a specified user list, forwarding messages with comments, and storage of up to an hour's worth of messages.

In many ways, it offers all of the advantages of e-mail without the effort of entering text on a keyboard. Kent's comments about "surveillance" and "control" are interesting in this context. He indirectly associated e-mail with surveillance.

By contrast, the idea that he was in control of the voice mail system makes it appear a more comfortable site for Kent to communicate, and more effective when compared to the ordinary telephone and the limited connectivity of his departmental e-mail system. In composing voice mail messages, Kent was observed to follow generally the same pattern:

- Establish the purpose ;
- Provide context and background (e.g., reason for request; allusion to a previous call, conversation, or document);
- Give his own perspective (e.g., a guess about the answer to his question, a possible source for the answer, a possible procedure); and
- Request an action (typically, a return call). This pattern is similar to inductive memo formats where the text builds towards a request for an action. Revision also had a role in Kent's use of voice mail.

He noted: "I guess if I'm doing a group delivery, we think about what I'm going to say, and then I record it. I listen to it, and then do it again. About one out of four times I record it again."

Analysis

The communication technology options facing Kent reflect recent history at NetCon. At the time of the study, Kent could not communicate electronically with Computer Corporation, highlighting the slow integration of NetCon into Computer Corporation and, perhaps, the latter's conservative approach to conducting business.

The lack of e-mail connectivity among departments is more puzzling. Given NetCon's tradition of interdepartmental project teams, one would expect that management would facilitate cooperation among departments with universal e-mail. Yet e-mail system installation occurred after NetCon's acquisition; thus, its insular configuration may not reflect tradition but more recent influences — specifically Computer Corporation's more hierarchical culture.

Connecting workers across (not up) the hierarchy -enabling workers to communicate without managerial mediation — may not have seemed desirable to management. That left voice mail, at least for Kent, as the communication technology that best fit his professional and personal needs (*i.e.*, the need to communicate asynchronously and the need to feel in control of his own communicative activities). It is interesting that for someone who indicated that he did not like writing, his composition of voice mail messages almost appeared to be writing in a different medium.

Use of Technology: Traditional Text and Voice Mail

Mary spends about half of a typical work day in meetings, about a quarter of her time reading and writing, and the final quarter on the phone. Her responses to questions about communications technologies were very similar to Kent's not surprising in that they worked in the same department for many years and have similar professional profiles. While working in software development, Mary used the same e-mail system as Kent. However, the product management department, after years of repeated requests from its workers, had just recently installed a departmental local area network with e-mail capabilities. Like the system in development, the product management system is supposed to communicate with the Computer Corporation system, but otherwise fits NetCon's pattern of incompatible networks. Mary noted: *"It [the system] does go to other departments, but I couldn't tell you who right now."*

Mary expressed the opinion that this defeated the purpose of e-mail: *"I think we should have a company system. I should be able to send a memo to anybody in this building, you know. To a janitor if I want to. The phone's a lot easier right now."* Mary's use of the phone includes both the traditional, including at least one conference call a week, and voice mail. To Mary, the major benefit of voice mail is its convenience for asynchronous communication. She described composing a voice mail message in the same language she used to describe composing a memo: *"For me, it's like a little letter. I think that is the format that people go through mentally."*

Analysis

Overall, Mary spends most of her work time in meetings, in verbal interaction, not with computer-based communications technologies. Even her use of voice mail is somewhat limited. And outside of meetings, most of her communicative activity centres on traditional texts. This reflects her job duties, which focus on the production of planning, marketing, and competitive analysis documents and the fact that product management has been slow in adopting e-mail.

Yet, Mary's responses highlight the "ease of use" factor for the different technologies. With technical difficulties in installing the local area network, with procedural difficulties in sending e-mail to anyone outside of the department, the default technology for distance communication becomes the familiar telephone and the relatively straightforward enhancement of voice mail. Also, one senses in Mary's responses, as in the other cases, a certain reluctance to pursue electronic communication with Computer Corporation. This has its roots in the cultural context, in NetCon Division's sense of separate identity. It is likely that in a more culturally integrated company, the technical obstacles in establishing company-wide e-mail connectivity would seem less significant.

CASE THREE: SCOTT

Corporate Cultures

Like Kent, Scott found the culture of Computer Corporation conservative, but also commented on the power structure. He described Computer Corporation as "a very bureaucratic feudal oligarchy, prone to high level re-orgs that reflect shifts in power." In terms of the culture of NetCon Division, Scott contrasted the current culture with that of NetCon Division in the past: "It's different than it was. There used to be certain movers and shakers who, whether you agreed with them or not, they certainly put their stamp on things. And now that they are gone.... People have a strong notion that [business] is declining. Being part of something declining is really a bummer."

Scott described his own department as one that used to be very cohesive, but because he and other technical communicators had been "colocated" with product development groups instead of being located with other technical communicators, Scott thought much of this had changed: *"It is easy to see how our own practices have gotten diffuse, when people don't use the same tools, or use them in the same way. They don't necessarily have the same standards applied to everybody, and we don't seem to have anybody who can bring that together."*

Technology Use: Reflections on the Use of E-Mail

Scott has nearly the same technology options as Kent: outside of face-to-face conversation, Scott can communicate with coworkers via e-mail or voice mail. For Scott, a computer network provides a unifying force for a department physically scattered throughout the building, although the network is rarely used as a site for the exchange of important ideas: "I use e-mail to get messages... primarily about department business, notices about both personal things -going away lunches — and business stuff — there's a new virus, check your PC. Sometimes [his manager] puts a message out there that he wants you to respond to.... It's useful from a business point of view, and also a social point of view, too. It helps to have something unifying."

However, Scott noted that there were "no real conversations" over e-mail. The network, like most others at NetCon, has limited connection to those in other departments. However, according to Scott what really prevents electronic communication between departments may be rooted in social factors rather than technical ones:

One of the things that [a previous senior manager] wanted to implement was [a special e-mail system], which is very much a conversational thing, attaching notes and comments to this data base of ideas. It pretty much just sat there. People used it to send mail, but I don't think anybody used it in the way it was intended for a kind of development way of collecting data.

Someone would have an idea, and then you could attach everyone's comments to that idea.... I'm sure it could work, but not sure it would work here. It would take a certain culture — it would probably work great at Lotus or someplace else that's more open.

Scott attributed the lack of success for this system to several factors. First, it was implemented among a large group of engineers whose project was in jeopardy. With the uncertainty of possible reassignment or even job loss in the air, people did not want to express opinions or complain in so public a forum. Second, Scott said that he and others noticed that management did not use the system.

Finally, although presented in a positive light by management, employees felt the system might be used to monitor them. Indeed, Scott, unlike the other participants, did not favour a division-wide e-mail capability. But like the other participants, Scott thought highly of voice mail. He noted that it can be used to prompt people to attend meetings, by using the broadcast list feature: "It's a good, thorough thing to do." Further, Scott stated: "Voice mail is good for, well, it prevents information from getting lost. You can leave a message and the message will be there.... From that standpoint, it's pretty useful.

You can call someone and be pretty much assured that they'll pick up the phone at some point. I think it's just primarily more certain." The voice mail system at NetCon really is not that permanent; unless a user takes special actions, the system erases stored messages at regular time intervals. However, as Kent noted, the voice mail system does provide convenient asynchronous communications, one of the major benefits reported for e-mail by researchers such as Sproull and Kiesler.

When asked to comment on composing for voice mail in comparison to composing text, Scott, in contrast to Kent, does not see voice mail as a medium to convey substantive messages: "I would never leave a voice mail message that is too complex to express verbally.... I'll say 'Call back.' If I were trying to convince somebody of something, I wouldn't do that on the phone."

Analysis

Scott, a technical communicator, enjoys writing. He feels more comfortable submitting more complex ideas or requests in written text. Kent finds writing "tedious" and definitely uses voice mail more extensively than Scott. Part of this may be owing to differences in job responsibilities and time constraints, but part, I think, is due to their quite different perceptions of their strengths as communicators.

While many other factors may affect technology use, Scott's and Kent's choices among similar media options may be due in part to their differences as individuals. However, corporate culture enters into Scott's technology use at another level. Scott perceives the various levels of corporate culture in somewhat more negative terms than Kent, particularly upper management. Whereas he sees e-mail as a unifying force for his department and views a sense of cohesiveness within the department as desirable, he is suspicious both of broader e-mail connectivity and of use of e-mail for substantive exchange of ideas.

It could be that a certain level of distrust for corporate management has coloured his view of technologies that could link employees across departments — that this kind of network, despite its stated purpose, might be a tool for management control.

Use of Technology: Hierarchical Networks and Fax

Cara's job is very different from those of the other participants. Their jobs, in one way or another, concern the development of new products for NetCon. Cara supports NetCon's existing products; that is, she identifies solutions to errors (programme or human) in NetCon's software products. A brief description of this support process is necessary here. When customers experience a problem, they first contact a local support representative. If the local person cannot solve the problem, that support person, or the customer, calls NetCon Division directly for a higher level of technical support.

Cara provides this kind of support for international customers. As problems arrive, they are logged into a problem tracking database implemented on a mainframe-based, hierarchical network. It is 15- or 20-year-old technology. Cara's department does have e-mail capability that is accessible even to customers, but it is not heavily used.

She noted: "I know we have e-mail. Every time I turn on my PC in the morning it says 'you have no e-mail.' It definitely is not used much internally." However, although there are no real conversations over e-mail, support engineers have learned to use the problem tracking database as a kind of forum where people can reference each other's work and exchange ideas more actively than on any of the e-mail systems I observed at NetCon. This is not an easy system to use for this purpose: They have adopted a single response area for this, an assigned field for providing problem descriptions that permits the entry of free-form text. They refer to this internally as the status text. The system does not allow status text entries to be specifically addressed to individuals; however, individual support engineers locate status texts that interest them by referencing problem numbers.

They can then enter additional comments to the status text if they wish. Some exchanges I reviewed in status text fields went on for several days with a variety of support and development engineers involved. In these written conversations, they reference past solutions, documentation, and common experiences.

It can become an even larger conversation. Some local support engineers and large customers have access to the problem tracking system but do not have the system security clearance to add to the status text. They read the status text and join the discussion through phone calls, memos, or faxes; often, summaries of their comments are included by engineers who have the required level of clearance.

Fax is another important technology of communication to Cara and the other support engineers -- much more important, it appeared, than to the other research participants. In dealing with international customers, Cara must deal with language barriers and significant time differences: Some people seem to use the phone [to communicate with customers]. It's hard enough just to hear someone long distance on the phone, with the accent on top of that.

In talking to places in Africa, you have to be careful taking turns. When I talk, he can't; and when he talks, we have to wait. We have a tendency to interrupt. I had to curb that, and to laugh! I'd lose half a sentence because I laughed. I'm just not polite. So I just send a fax, especially with the time differences. You can fax anytime.

Fax permits virtually instantaneous communication, but minimizes, among other things, the possible pitfalls of different cultural styles of conversation. Voice mail could overcome the time differences, but the need of both engineer and customer in this setting is for highly detailed technical information. Cara noted that fax communication allows the support engineers to specify exactly what kind of information they need from customers.

Analysis

Cara's case is particularly illuminating for two reasons. First, in a department where she feels marginalized in everyday interaction, Cara contributed regularly to the "status text" conversations, where her technical insight was valued in group problem solving. Cultural norms shifted in this context: instead of gender, common background, or a shared "us against them attitude" that characterized the support department, technical expertise is what counted in the problem tracking system.

This is not so much a case of a communications technology masking cues to culture, ethnicity, or gender, as a case of a shift in the value system within the world of the computer system. Also, the use of the system itself is interesting. It was so dated, had such a complex user interface, and seemed so inflexible that, in my original research plan, I almost ignored it. However, the support engineers felt a strong need to collaborate, an important need to share technical information. The problem tracking system provided a means to accomplish this — between adjacent offices as well as geographically dispersed sites.

It provided a site for communication that was all their own as employees in other departments had no interest in using the system, and it was unlikely that management outside of the department, who are viewed with some distrust, would go to the trouble of reviewing status text entries. In contrast to the e-mail system, where electronic communication was possible between

NetCon and Computer Corporation but nobody really wanted to communicate, the users here adapted a very difficult computer system to become a vehicle for the vital exchange of ideas. In short, what the problem tracking system emphasizes is that:

- A real need must exist to use the technology,

- The system has to connect the people necessary to carry on the conversation, and
- A technology can reinforce a sense of community insofar as it is not likely to be monitored. This use of the problem tracking system was not part of overall corporate communication planning, not an anticipated use of technology; yet, it emphasizes how important contextual factors become in choice of technology.

Another reason Cara's case is interesting centres on the use of fax technology. Here the contextual factors are not based in perceptions of corporate culture but in the realities of international business.

Extensive use of fax with international customers allows Cara and her coworkers to simplify potential language problems, accurately transfer technical information, avoid the time zone difficulties of phone conversation — and still, when required, have virtually instantaneous communication. Fax combines the familiarity of paper with the speed of synchronous phone lines.

2

Communications and Line Manager

A public communicator and business executive. He draws from this rich background in discussing two kinds of business communication. First, he examines communication within a moderate-sized business organization. He looks at demands on management and employees and discusses the need for a two-way flow of information.

He then turns to communication between the company and a variety of special audiences outside the company. Lacy argues for communication approaches that begin with concerns of the receiver. As a practitioner of public affairs both in and out of government for some years, I came to the world of corporate line management very much aware of the role of effective communications in attaining organizational and personal goals.

There was nothing very mysterious about the ideas of source and receiver, channel and message selection, or audience analysis. I had a pretty good idea of how to assess—and manage—public perceptions of the organization. But I was not prepared for communicating in an environment that had the profit motive as the driving force for all organizational activities.

What I found as a line manager of a manufacturing/service facility for a mid-sized manufacturing corporation was a bit of a revelation for me. Our company, although not one of the nation's industrial giants, had substantial assets in about thirty locations, employed almost three thousand persons, and possessed a reputation in its chosen markets as a solid, quality-directed, and reliable supplier of services and products. And no one, except our employees, customers, and a few thousand stockholders, really cared. General public perceptions of our firm were, to put it kindly, ill defined. Never, to my knowledge, had we overcharged the government on a defence contract, endangered the public safety by polluting the environment, been the object of a hostile takeover, or been involved in any event that might have caused the media to focus its unblinking gaze on our firm.

In any case I was hired as a facility manager—not a public relations flak—and it did not take long for me to adjust to the idea that our customers were our audience and that all they expected was to receive fair value for the dollars they spent on our services. What I also discovered was that organizational survival in the marketplace depends solely on making money. Profit is the reason for being for all corporations.

Naturally, there are other goals, like providing jobs, expanding technology, providing money-saving products for the consumer, and a variety of additional worthwhile motivations. But every activity in every corporation has the need for profitability hanging over it. Profit is the canopy that gets the organization safely to the ground. Lack of profits will invariably lead to a rapid fall and a sharp, sudden stop, followed by prompt disappearance of the firm from the marketplace.

The essential concern for keeping the bottom line in the black creates needs within the organization. The organization must recruit and train competent people, establish a network of reliable suppliers of materials and services, and organize internally to ensure that all activities are properly managed.

It must create financial conditions that will ensure a viable cash flow and plan for growth by acquisition and market expansion. Perhaps most importantly, it must create an effective communications structure that will tie all of the diverse functional activities of the organization together and permit them to work in harness while traveling the rocky path to profitability.

OBJECTIVE-DRIVEN COMMUNICATIONS

The way an organization communicates, both within the organization and outside of it, is conditioned and limited by the objectives it sets for its operating units. Many companies, including my own, have adopted the socalled "management by objective" system.

Management by objective involves the establishment of individual objectives by individual managers—and approved in turn by their bosses—which must be attained within some agreedupon time frame. The idea is that if each manager develops and attains objectives that contribute to the fulfillment of the corporate objectives, the aggregate effort will lead to attainment of corporate goals and the employee will be rewarded accordingly. Not a bad idea!

It is also not without its perils. The principal danger in such an arrangement is that although most of us are conscientious and hard working and share the interests of our employers, we are also eager to do well. Permitted to set our own objectives, therefore, we are likely to select those that are more or less readily attainable. Unfortunately (or fortunately for the company), our bosses are not likely to give us much of a chance to select only those objectives that are, in the vernacular, a piece of cake. Objectives, we are told, should exceed our grasp by a little bit so that we are driven by them. In other words, good objectives are moderately impossible.

But having selected some moderately impossible objectives, we are faced with the task of criteria that prove our success at bonus time. Usually we try to quantify the objectives in terms of numbers of dollars, or man-hours, or sales calls, or project completion dates. In so doing, we create information needs. The need for information in turn creates the need for communication methods that permit us to acquire it. Therein lies the problem.

Managers of functionally specific activities quite naturally develop objectives that are functionally specific. And even though the chosen objectives may be consistent with the goals of the organization, they are often not consistent with one another. For example, the sales manager who has as his principal short-term objective the broadening of the customer base convinces his boss of the importance of making a greater number of sales calls. They agree on an objective, and the message then goes out to the sales force that aggressive coverage of new prospects is the order of the day. The need is therefore created to enable the sales manager to guide and direct, manage, and measure the effectiveness of the activity. In addition, the sales manager also needs documentation for all the new sales contacts to show his boss during the next quarterly performance review that the moderately impossible has been accomplished.

To acquire the needed documentation, the sales manager is likely to establish an accountability reporting system that will provide a continuous flow of detailed information about the day-to-day activities of the sales force. Such accountability systems usually take the form of elaborate written or verbal reports. Because the sales manager cannot spend most of each day talking to salespersons and the sales force cannot spend half its time preparing written reports, the sales manager may use a telephone answering/recording system or a similar one-way communication device that will promote more efficient reporting.

Meanwhile, the hardworking salespersons have set their own objectives. The sales objective is almost always measured in dollars of sales rather than in numbers of calls. If the product or service requires long periods of customer service testing or evaluation or substantial follow-up sales activity, the level of sales by individual salespersons is likely to diminish as most of the time and effort is devoted to calling on new prospects. Moreover, the salesperson may find that the reporting requirement eats up a lot of time that could be more effectively used in other more productive activities.

Tension between the sales manager and members of the sales force develops as the divergence of their objectives becomes more pronounced. Salespersons become less conscientious in their reporting, and the sales manager's objective is threatened as sales calls go unreported. Because the communication channels established by the sales manager provided for only a one-way flow of information and because his objectives diverged from those of his salespersons, conflict results. A top salesperson gets fed up and leaves the company for a job with the competition—taking her customer list with her. The sales manager misses his objective and begins updating his own resume.

Similarly, the production manager whose objective is to increase productivity in the work force needs information relative to that objective to measure his progress, effect the needed changes, and, of course, demonstrate to his employer that the moderately impossible is being accomplished. The production manager, with a specific objective, needs specific information and, to no one's surprise, establishes specific communication channels designed to provide functionally specific information on input, throughput, and output.

Although the manager's communication device, perhaps a daily time sheet or job history record, may have been designed primarily for acquiring information that could disclose areas of potential productivity improvement, uncover quality problems, improve work flow, or help contain costs, it might easily be perceived by the members of the work force as a management surveillance tool.

In this instance the consequence of the production manager's inability or unwillingness to make the work force aware of his objective and of the means he has elected to achieve it could result in problems with unions, loss of highly trained people, and reduced productivity.

The essential points here are

- The objectives of individual managers must align with those of the managed,
- The information needs created by the manager's desire to attain his objective must be accommodated by the use of communication methods and channels that permit employees to perceive accurately true motivations of the manager, and
- One-way communication devices characterized by personal accountability reporting requirements are of marginal utility if their main purpose is to collect

information that can be used to demonstrate to a manager's boss that the moderately impossible is being accomplished.

UNDERSTANDING AUDIENCE OBJECTIVES

The problem of conflicting objectives within an organization is perhaps even more troubling in the effect it can have on an organization's ability to communicate with its external audiences. Central to dealing with the problem is an understanding of who the audiences are, what their objectives may be, and how they can be reached.

To communicate effectively with our audiences requires that we understand their goals and how they set objectives to attain them. That understanding is absolutely necessary to the development of effective communication channels and messages that will not only reach our audiences but also have the desired effect on their behaviour. But it is not enough to take a seat-of-thepants, intuitive approach to achieving the needed understanding. Effective audience assessment dictates effective planning.

Identifying the Audiences

Each organization differs; but in a line-operating unit such as the one I manage, there are essentially three external audiences: our customers and potential customers, our immediate community, and those agencies that regulate and oversee our activities. Clearly, each is likely to have its own goals that in turn create the need for objectives to attain them. Their goals and their chosen objectives will differ substantially from one another.

Existing customers, already convinced that your product or service will help them make or save money, most probably have as their main objective the meeting of their own production schedules or the maintenance of their own quality standards. Potential customers are likely to have a need for pricing information that will aid them in assessing the cost effectiveness of your product or service. The community in which you operate probably has as its main goals economic growth and the maintenance of a safe environment. Regulatory and oversight agencies have the goals of protecting the worker, the consumer, the taxpayer, or the customer from workplace abuses, shoddy workmanship, price gouging, pollution, unsafe conditions, or unfair trading practices.

Evaluating Audience Objectives

The potential conflict between your own production objectives and those of your customers, for example, should be apparent. As a service activity, your production scheduling must conform to the scheduling and quality objectives of the customer. The most effective means of communicating with a good customer is to deliver a quality product or service on time.

But to do so requires a high level of understanding of mutual constraints, capabilities, and limitations. That understanding must be reached up front. In a world where Murphy's Law ("If something can go wrong, it will!") is operative, prudent managers will set up customer communication channels that will permit them to forewarn their customers of glitches.

Conversely, if managers expect customer understanding of their internal problems, they should be sensitive to those of their customers and be prepared to bend a little when customers get themselves in a bind. But to establish communications based on an understanding of mutual objectives requires managers to recognize that their customer is not a disembodied name on a letterhead or purchase order. The customer purchasing agent, its salesperson, its expediter, its quality control inspector, its general manager, and its vice-president all have specific objectives that they are working to attain.

If your objectives or those of your employees collide with those of the individuals within the customer organization with whom you must communicate, the divergence will soon become apparent and your customer will begin looking elsewhere for another source of the product or service. When we view the community in which we do business as our audience, it becomes apparent that the close interpersonal channels of communication that characterize our communications with customers may not be appropriate. The community may be large or small; urban, suburban, or rural; affluent or disadvantaged; residential, industrial, or commercial.

Community needs may be centered on economic considerations such as the desire for more jobs or growth of commerce and industry, or they may centre on population limitation, neighbourhood preservation, or environmental purity. The community's governmental units may be small and characterized by heavy citizen involvement or large and anonymous. There may be sharp differences between citizens' groups as to the desired direction of the community. In short, most communities comprise diverse and often divergent interests.

How, then, do we align the objectives of our company with those of a community comprising individuals and groups having widely varying objectives of their own? First, it is useful to understand something about the organization of the community. Is the principal governmental unit the city, the county, or some other instrumentality? How and to what extent does the community government interact with state and federal government agencies?

What role do service organizations play in molding and expressing opinion in the public arena? Are there advocacy organizations such as community action and environmental groups operating in the community? Are trade and labour unions in the community influential or weak? What general position does the local media take on key community issues? Armed with answers to these sorts of questions, a line manager should be able to assess the general direction of public perceptions towards business activities.

Moreover, the manager who understands the community organizations will be better able to gain access to those individuals and groups in order to assess the intensity of their perceptions on issues that impinge on his or her company's activities. Second, with a good understanding of the direction and intensity of opinions held among the various community groups, the manager can assess potential audience reactions to the operations and activities of the company. More importantly, the manager should be able to anticipate probable community reaction to his or her own plans for change or growth and develop objectives for implementing these plans that conform to those of the community.

Finally, as a practical matter, the manager must decide whether to become actively involved in the community by joining service organizations, openly supporting the positions of certain groups, participating in charitable activities, or pursuing a continuing programme of public relations through the media, a speaker's bureau, or other similar public affairs channels. The choices are, of course, dependent on the character of the activity. If the company is a principal supplier of jobs in the community, if it happens to be a generator or treater of hazardous waste, or if it engages in any activity that might prompt public or community attention, prudence dictates that advance planning accommodate the public affairs implications of the most likely contingencies.

Our third principal audience, regulatory and oversight agencies, is a special case. Every company, particularly those engaged in manufacturing, comes under the scrutiny of a variety of governmental and industry associations while carrying out its day-to-day activities. In my own unit, we enjoy frequent contact with the Federal Aviation Administration, the Occupational Safety and Health Administration, the Defence Contracting Agency, and the Environmental Protection Agency (EPA).

In addition, we have compliance requirements for standards developed by the American Petroleum Institute, the American Society for Test and Measurement, the Society of Automotive Engineers, and the American Society for Non-destructive Testing, among others.

Each regulatory agency has as its specific objective ensuring compliance with procedures and standards it sets for regulated activities. Compliance with the established procedures and standards is a prerequisite to doing business in regulated areas. Moreover, compliance is not free. In fact, it is quite expensive and time consuming. For that reason, effective managers should understand that their own objectives must conform to those of the regulating agencies and industry associations. But it is not enough merely to conform. It is also necessary to communicate with regulatory agencies in a way that will permit sustained operations on a cost-effective basis.

Too often, when a guy in a white shirt and Hushpuppies knocks on your door and says, "I'm from the federal government and I'm here to help," managers experience a state of dread that progresses to anger, through defiance, then almost inevitably to abject defeat. It has been my experience that planning to communicate with regulatory agencies can ease the pain somewhat.

The first step of the process is to determine which among the company's activities comes under regulation and by whom. The second is to determine the nature and extent of the regulatory provisions.

The third is to take the agency at its word and ask for help. By enlisting the assistance of the regulatory agency, it becomes a participant, if not a partner, in developing procedures for compliance that will meet agency objectives for conforming to the established standards. Representatives of regulatory agencies ordinarily are like the rest of us (except they have better benefits packages), and if we demonstrate a willingness to make their jobs easier, their response to our own objectives and concerns is likely to be more positive.

In summary, accurate prediction of audience response to an organization's activities involves not only identifying the audiences and determining the direction and intensity of their positions but also understanding that effective communication requires alignment of the objectives of the participants in the communication process.

SELECTING A MESSAGE

Communicating with potential customers tends to be more message oriented than channel oriented. That is, the goals of the potential customer are usually to find a product or service that better serves its own needs for improved productivity, performance, or cost reduction. Those individuals within the customer organization trying to acquire information to meet their established objectives may have a need for specific cost and performance information, or they may be seeking generalized information that will merely heighten the level of comprehension and knowledgeability about the class of products or services available.

The content and style of the message should conform to the specific needs of the potential customer. The manager and his sales staff should be aware that message content and style ought to be selected to elicit a particular audience response. Usually, audience responses progress from attention to comprehension to compliance to action. Thus, for example, a project engineer comes across an ad in a trade journal (a mass communication channel) that gets his attention because it promises cost savings in an area in which he has a functionally specific objective.

He fills out the bingo card, circles the appropriate ad number, and sends out the postage-paid, self-addressed postcard. Some time later he receives a packet of literature in the mail. He reviews the literature, and with heightened interest calls the company and arranges for a salesperson to make a presentation (an interpersonal communication channel).

The salesperson arrives and makes a bang-up presentation. Audience comprehension is nearly complete. The salesperson then asks that her product or service be tried and evaluated. The project engineer weighs the recommendation against his own needs and decides to comply with the salesperson's recommendation.

The project engineer agrees to service testing and, because the product performs beyond expectations, recommends to the management that the product be specified for a particular application. The project engineer's manager says okay, if the price is right. A request for quotation is prepared and forwarded to the salesperson. The salesperson responds and the quotation is reviewed by the project engineer's management to ensure that the product or service will prove cost effective. The salesperson is summoned to write the order and the final audience response action is complete. One of the principal dangers when communicating in the selling process-and certainly one of the most frequent—is for the salesperson to misperceive the intentions of the prospect when selecting message content and style.

If the prospect's objective is to gather data about the product or service for the purpose of assessing cost effectiveness, the message content should focus not on the technical merits of the product but rather on those features that impact positively on cost. How expensive is the product or service relative to that of the competition? What sort of economies may be expected if the volume or scale is increased? Can delivery times be shortened? And so on.

The style of the message should likewise fit the audience, accounting for known predispositions and objectives. If the audience objective is to acquire hard technical information to be used in making qualitative assessments of the potential effectiveness of the product or service, it would not be appropriate to adopt a light breezy narrative style.

Rather, the message should be straightforward, business-like, and comprising concise data summaries relating to the technical attributes of the product or service. A final and important consideration about message selection: The message must be relevant. The road to the unemployment office is paved with the remains of managers who delivered their well-conceived messages to the wrong audiences.

The marketing manager who insists that salespersons use a canned presentation runs the risk of squandering his or her resources unless the product or service possesses more or less universal utility for the general population. Such products as vacuum cleaners or encyclopedias sold door to door lend themselves to canned messages, but the marketing of industrial products or services requires considerably more forethought and planning to ensure that the right message is transmitted on the right channel to the right audience.

SELECTING THE COMMUNICATION CHANNEL

The manager of an operating unit within a larger corporation will likely have some influence on the determination of the type, character, and extent of media advertising used by the company, but generally the line manager's role in channel selection is limited.

A company doing business in a limited geographic or functional area will probably have assigned salespersons who have inside or outside sales responsibilities that require frequent interpersonal contact with customers and potential customers. That means reliance on telephone or face-to-face communications.

The manager also may have some resources for conducting direct mail or telemarketing campaigns and perhaps some capability for developing audiovisual materials. Whatever the available resources, the principles of effective channel selection are relevant to their use. The channel of communication, like the message, will vary with the audience. Audience size, composition, and predisposition must be considered when selecting a channel.

If the audience comprises a small number of engineers located in an office for the prearranged purpose of discussing a specific application of the product or service, the interpersonal channel most certainly will not call for use of the sort of audiovisual aids that would be appropriate for a larger, more heterogeneous audience. However, even though small group communications rely heavily on interpersonal channels, it is possible to achieve impact of the mass media channels through audiovisual devices.

With the development and availability of video recording equipment, for example, it is economically feasible to offer audiovisual presentations. Rather than merely presenting the small audience of engineers with a written test report declaiming the merits of a product, it is possible to present a pictorial record of the actual testing using the most powerful of today's persuasive media channels, television. Use of video recordings has several advantages. The content can be edited to remove extraneous material and pared to a specific time length. Audience attention is likely to be focused more closely on the message. And, perhaps most importantly, message credibility supported by actual images is likely to be enhanced. But there are also disadvantages. Taped presentations that overlook technical standards may appear fumbling and amateurish. Before attempting to use video recordings, it would be wise to become familiar with the technical features of taping.

Similarly, slides, films, and audio recordings can prove useful in small group business communications. But the advantages of their use should be weighed carefully against the disadvantages. Many a sales presentation has been derailed because the audiovisual medium was not appropriate for the audience, the setting, or the message. Direct mail campaigns may be used effectively by managers to get their message to larger audiences. For the manager of a company, direct mail has the principal advantages of reducing the cost per contact and broadening the level of audience exposure to the product or service.

Direct mail has the main function of gaining audience attention. The design of the message, though, should also increase audience comprehension, elicit compliance, and move the audience to some specifically limited action response. The principal disadvantage of direct mail is that your letter, flyer, questionnaire, or literature will have to compete for the audience's attention with an avalanche of similar communications.

Direct mail communications are probably best utilized as a device for responding to a previously expressed audience interest in your product or service. In the course of participating in trade shows, seminars, symposia, or other similar events, the manager should make a concerted effort to accumulate business cards and attendance lists for the purpose of later communicating with those individuals who have demonstrated an interest in learning more about the product or service. The manager should ask two key questions before embarking on a direct mail programme. Has the audience expressed an interest in the product or service, however ill defined? Will the message elicit the desired audience response? If the answer to either is negative, you might as well save your stamp. Many of the same considerations apply to the use of the telephone in the marketing function. If there has been a previously expressed audience interest, telemarketing can be an effective tool to further broaden the potential customer base. Also, it can be extremely useful in establishing interpersonal relationships with prospects since the telephone provides some opportunity for the immediate interchange of ideas on an interpersonal basis.

In my company we have many good customers we have never met in person but with whom we have extensive telephone contact. A word of caution is in order. Long-distance telephone calls, even with the lower rates available today, can become expensive and time-consuming activities. For a company offering a specialized product or service and having limited marketing resources, the telephone shotgun approach to marketing is likely to be less than cost effective. For that reason, target audiences should be carefully selected when using the telephone.

Another communication channel is the newsletter or house organ. These print media can be used internally within the organization, directed to external audiences, or both. Generally, newsletters or newspapers should convey messages that depict the positive aspects of the organization, such as accomplishments of employees, new production capabilities, or improved products. They may also cover changes in personnel assignments, advanced technological developments, and industry-wide news items.

Newsletters and house organs are generally perceived by employees as controlled by management and therefore have less credibility than public print media. For that reason, they should utilize a format and style that are informative rather than persuasive. Content should focus on the non-confidential business activities of the company from the perspective of the employees or customers rather than the management. For example, a story relating to a new product might centre on the reactions of the quality control manager to the product's role in reducing rework, with supporting quotes from a satisfied customer. Similarly, stories relating to customer activities supply opportunities for publicizing testimonials to the benefit of the company's products and services while providing a publicity channel for the customer. It should be noted, however, that newsletters should not be used for dissemination of directives from management or to discuss internal problems. The employee readership will be turned off and the customer readership could not care less.

Finally, the manager of an operating unit may be able to make use of the public mass media for publicity purposes. If the character of the business is such that its activities have relevance and importance for the community or some significant segment of the public, it may be desirable to issue periodic press releases to local media or to trade journals, to use press conferences to announce favourable developments, or to seek to participate in local public service radio or television programmes.

There are several major benefits of using the mass media for publicity purposes. First, the public media are not perceived as controlled and the message is likely to be credible. Second, publicity is far less expensive than paid advertising. But on the downside, the manager should be aware that once the press release has been issued, the information it contains and any follow-up media interest are out of his or her control. In summary, every organization has its own set of goals, arranged in a hierarchy determined by the general culture of the organization. To reach these goals, individual objectives are established that create needs for communications both within the organization and outside of it.

The type, extent, and character of the communication modes and methods are determined by the information needs of the individual. Too often, these needs are satisfied by the establishment of functionally specific, unidirectional, and close-ended communication devices that do not account for the objectives of the audience. The result can be conflict and failure to attain established objectives. Dealing with the problem requires an understanding of the communication process, with particular emphasis on how audience characteristics and objectives must be observed in effective formulation of messages and selection of channels. Communications should be a prominent part of planning for objective fulfillment.

In a perfect world, all communication methods, messages, and media would be perfectly adapted to both organizational goals and audience objectives and there would be little chance of failure. However, in the less than perfect world of free enterprise, without effective communication there is little chance of success.

3

Targeted Communication

The business and political mainstream today, it is that nothing can be accomplished without effective communication. No products can be bought or sold, no services dispensed, no candidates elected. Communication is the lifeblood of this society, serving to keep alive our system of commerce and government. A failure to communicate successfully can be devastating to an organization. Companies and candidates live or die by the skill with which they manipulate the communication process.

Moreover, as we pass deeper into this information age, the need for institutions to master the techniques of communication increases even as these techniques become more sophisticated and complex in this information-rich environment. For the business community today, the capacity to instruct, to persuade, to market a product, or just to become known among desired audiences is not a means to an end, but an end in itself.

It has been said that communication, like gravity, is recognized by everyone yet fully understood by no one. We all have an innate sense of how to communicate, at least at an interpersonal level. Language, a major tool of communication, is natural for us, and long before there was any formal investigation of the communication process, people were getting across their points of view and interacting with each other with few apparent problems. Since development of the printing press, which introduced the notion of "mass communication," and more recent advancements in telecommunications and computer sciences, the process of communication has taken on a new, complex dimension. Indeed, our capacity to understand the communication process lags behind our ability to manipulate it. We know that certain techniques work to bring about desired ends, even though the reasons for the success of these techniques often may evade us. Although formal study of communication dates back over two thousand years, modern incarnations of the field involve a hearty blend of journalism, rhetoric, and the social sciences, including social psychology, sociology, and political science.

Using techniques acquired from these fields, researchers have identified features of communication processes that can help find answers to difficult communications problems. We have been able to develop models that identify relationships among key components of the communication process. We can provide not only a descriptive scheme but also a plan to alter features of the process.

Thus, we can ensure greater success in achieving communication goals. As we proceed from what we already know about interpersonal communication to mass audience settings, the process becomes increasingly complex, both strategically and tactically. The public communicator deals not with one or two message recipients, a direct and relatively unencumbered communication process, but with a host of audiences and audience members.

Each member of the mass audience has peculiar interests and needs, different media exposure patterns, and unique interpersonal networks that ultimately influence the impact of mass media messages. In addition to these receiver differences, the public communicator must consider the various characteristics of the media that will carry the message. Media time and space are costly, so selecting appropriate media channels is essential to achieve the greatest possible effect with the least possible expense. Choosing the wrong media combinations wastes money and may diminish the success of a communication campaign.

People in business, politics, and other fields now recognize that they need to ensure the maximum possible effectiveness of their public communication programmes. So it becomes increasingly important to know about the considerable advances made in communication studies. Public communication is both a science and an art. Science, by prescribing the strategy and direction of a campaign, should provide a basis on which to apply the art.

Decisions for the approaches to and the selection of components in a public communication campaign are most logically predicated on tested principles that have demonstrated success under diverse conditions. These techniques can yield the greatest possible audience impact when the communicator's position is relatively weak (how we can make the best of a bad situation) or when one must deal with skeptical audiences, frightened audiences, or audiences whose members are hostile to the advocated position.

Inasmuch as recent technological advances have produced a generation of sophisticated communication media, the public communicator must rely on increasingly complex techniques to affect audiences and promote the success of a campaign. Costs, time, and the importance of issues at stake for businesses require such developed and resourceful designs.

MEDIA ENVIRONMENT

Media Structure and Availability

To appreciate the rich and complex communication environment in which the business communicator has to operate, it helps to understand the basic media consumption patterns of people today.

As suggested, consider the channels through which people receive information by describing two broad categories we call "general" and "narrow audience media."

Television

The mass media, which bear common messages designed for use by individuals with diverse personal characteristics, have saturated the information environments of industrialized nations. In the United States alone, there are 1,264 full-power broadcast television stations and an additional 408 low-power stations in operation. Moreover, the number of new stations has increased every year since the inception of the medium in the mid-1930s. This suggests we have not yet reached the saturation point at which the U.S. population cannot support additional stations.

Not only are the numbers of regular UHF and VHF stations continuing to grow, but new regulations permit more flexibility in programming and ownership. This has caused a surge in the number of regional low-power television stations designed to extend diverse programming to local audiences. In addition to the 409 stations currently in operation, construction permits have been issued for an additional fifteen hundred stations.

The FCC expects an additional two thousand licenses to be granted by 1990; some industry estimates are as high as four thousand additional licenses. The appetite for broadcast, cable, and taped audiovisual programming appears insatiable. Cable television, which got off the ground in the mid1970s, has seen remarkable growth. By mid-1986 some 46.8 per cent of American homes were connected to cable systems. At that time, 6,844 cable systems were in operation. It is projected that by 1990 over half of the nation's homes will be cable wired. The lure of cable lies in the picture quality it can deliver and in the diversity of programming it can provide viewers who demand a wide choice of material.

No longer satisfied with the standard programming offered by the three major television networks, viewers are eagerly seeking out and paying for additional sources of diversified entertainment. One of the most significant technological innovations of the media industry is the video cassette recorder (VCR). Preceded only briefly by the video disk player, which met with poor public reception because of its inability to record off the air, the VCR has been received enthusiastically by viewers.

Since 1975, when Sony introduced the first commercially available VCR, nearly 40 per cent of American homes have become VCR equipped. Furthermore, industry statistics reveal the rate of VCR adoption is accelerating every year. Without question, the VCR represents an important step in the evolution of mass communication technology. With VCRs, people enjoy two distinct advantages: First, they receive precisely the kinds of programming they want, when they want it. Videotape rental stores, clubs, mail-order houses, and other programming support industries offer viewers a range of material that could never be offered through broadcast or even cable facilities.

Literally tens of thousands of titles, many with subjects appealing only to small, esoteric audiences, can be purchased or rented. This allows the consumer to select programming actively rather than to wait passively for shows to be carried by broadcast or cable television stations. Time shifting, the second advantage of VCRs, allows people to prescribe their own viewing schedules.

With automatic timing devices, they can programme their VCRs to record shows for later playback. Such a feature allows one to watch a competing programme or to do something else without missing another desirable show. The A.C. Nielsen Organization reports that time shifting is such a critical feature of VCRs that as the composition of the work force changes, soap operas have become the single most taped category of television programming. Rapidly developing technology has during the last two decades introduced to the commercial market innovations that have been accepted avidly by the American consumer.

These new designs have not replaced existing media but have supplemented them. In other words, with the advent of cable television, people have not abandoned commercial television, they simply have become accommodated to the new media form.

Similarly, although VCR owners spend a good deal of time watching rented movies, they have not given up watching commercial television—they have just abandoned other activities to make room for the innovation. A. C. Nielsen reports that as people add cable and VCR equipment to a television set, they spend increasing amounts of time in front of that television.

Radio

As the popularity of television, in all its forms, has grown over the years, one might expect interest in the alternative media by the American people to have diminished proportionally. With few exceptions, this has not happened. Radio, for instance, the most obvious competitor of television, has not faded from the American media repertoire as some had predicted. In fact, since television has become commercially viable, the number of radio stations has increased by more than 280 per cent.

Initially, in an indirect way, television did have an adverse impact on FM radio when in 1945 the FCC froze this service in order to provide bandwidth space for expansion of television. It was not until 1961, and the authorization of stereophonic transmissions, that FM began to recover; it received another boost in 1964 when the FCC limited AM-FM simulcasting. Through this action, broadcasters were encouraged to provide separate AM and FM programming that had the effect of offering considerable format diversity. The number of radio stations increased dramatically over the years to their current high levels of 4,839 AM and 5,170 FM stations on the air.

Newspapers

Although the character of newspapers and magazines has changed since television came along, the viability of these print media remains strong. There has been a considerable consolidation of newspaper ownership during the last twenty years, but the number of dailies has remained relatively unchanged since the early 1960s. The number of weekly papers has dropped somewhat, however. There were 9,108 weeklies in 195.

- Despite this drop in weeklies, the newspaper industry has not been ravaged by television's competition, even though it has witnessed changes in readership patterns. In order to retain large audiences, however, newspapers have had to modify their content and approach to news presentation.

Magazines

Magazines, too, have changed in format, but their circulation today is more than double what it was twenty-five years ago. Single-copy sales have increased by 39 per cent and subscriptions have increased by 59 per cent. As magazines have grown more specialized in their appeal to narrow audience subgroups, room for new magazines on the market has increased.

It has been said that if more than ten people share a common interest in a subject, a magazine will be published to serve that group. Magazines serve a special role in the media mix of entertainment- and information-seeking Americans, and while titles may come and go, the industry remains well situated in today's media market. By delivering very specialized audiences, magazines have become a particularly useful medium for business communicators.

PUBLIC USE OF MEDIA

Media usage characteristics of American audiences reveal a population that is dependent on a heavy diet of information and entertainment. As the following statistics reveal, Americans spend more time engaged in media pastimes than they spend in any other activities except, perhaps, sleeping and working. Throughout their waking day, people in this culture are immersed in a crowded media environment.

Television

A television set in the average home was on for seven hours and ten minutes every day, representing the highest figure in this category ever recorded. With one exception in 1977 (when household viewing dropped eight minutes per day), daily set usage has increased every year—there never has been a recorded decrease.

Similarly, personal viewing statistics reveal a persistent racheting upward since commercial acceptance of the medium nearly four decades ago. Average daily viewing times in 1960 were estimated to be around two hours; twenty-five years later this figure increased to nearly four and onehalf hours.

Following a substantial amount of daily viewing as youngsters (just over four hours per day), teenagers lower their overall viewing time as they become involved in school and social activities (about three hours and twenty minutes per day).

At around eighteen years of age, however, people resume a heavier viewing schedule that they maintain and even increase throughout the rest of their lives. Older audiences (over fifty-five years) are the heaviest viewers, spending, on average, more than five and one-half hours watching television every day.

Age is not the only characteristic by which television viewing can be delineated. A. C. Nielsen (1986) reports that females typically watch more television than males (5.19 to 4.4 daily viewing hours), and those in lowerincome brackets (under $19,999) watch more than those with higher incomes (over $40,000) (household average of 7.0 to 7.8 hours daily). Those with cable or VCRs tend to spend more time watching television, perhaps because they have greater programming variety to stimulate their interest, perhaps they are inherently heavier viewers who have purchased auxiliary equipment to satisfy their greater appetites.

Whatever the reason, as programming variety increases, so, too, does television usage. Despite these differences evident within population subgroups, mainstream American audiences devote a considerable amount of time to television viewing. Although abundant evidence substantiates the importance of television, the time commitment alone shows that, for many, television viewing is not a casual activity to fill time, but the mainstay of their daily lives.

Radio. With such a large portion of the day committed to television viewing, one might expect there would be little time left to spend with alternative media. Generally, this is not so. The Radio Bureau of Advertising, the average American listens to more than three hours of radio every day. Although much listening may occur as a secondary activity, where radio serves as a background to higher-priority endeavors, radio programming stands as an important feature of the media diets of most people. Even though nearly all stations routinely offer some form of news summary (thirty-eight radio stations employ all-news formats), it is entertainment and music not news and information that attracts radio audiences. Among the radio stations operating in 1985, 28 per cent aired country-and-western music, 24 per cent offered adult contemporary, 10 per cent carried top forty or rock, 9 per cent played middle-of-the-road music, and 7 per cent provided easy listening formats. About 2 per cent were news/talk or all news. The remaining stations had a variety of formats including religious, classical music, and foreign language programming.

This once-mass audience medium has, during the last forty years, expanded into varied programming formats. Radio has evolved into a channel that enables communicators to reach narrow segments of the population with specific and directed messages. Different formats appeal to different groups, and it is this natural audience selection that serves the process of targeted communication.

While the audience composition of the three major television networks differs little, constituent audiences of radio stations vary greatly. Within the radio station audience, however, there is often considerable uniformity. Radio audiences are specialized. They have a measurable similarity of demographic traits that provide public communicators with a natural forum for targeted communication strategies. Radio audiences may be smaller than those of television, but to the public communicator, the nature of an audience is often more important than its numbers.

With the possible exception of all-news formats, which draw more acute audience attention, radio typically is used as a background medium that provides company in an automobile, sets an atmosphere, or just breaks the silence. Few people sit in front of a radio with the unbroken attention they usually give television, so usage figures must be interpreted with such characteristics in mind.

Advocates of the medium argue that this passive attention allows advertising messages to make a subliminal impact on listeners, to have subtle cognitive effects that may ultimately translate into attitudinal and behavioural modifications. Such effects remain to be demonstrated empirically. Nonetheless, despite arguments dealing with the potential impact of radio messages on listeners, exposure statistics remain: People spend more time listening to radio today than at any other time in the history of this medium. Radio continues to serve the communicator as an important point of contact with public audiences.

Newspapers

While radio and television have enjoyed considerable popularity in all demographic categories during the last four decades, for large segments of the population newspapers have lost considerable ground. Younger audiences, obviously the most important group for sustained newspaper vitality, have failed to adopt the readership patterns of older audiences. As recently as 1967, a readership survey found that among people aged fifty to fifty-nine, 78 per cent read a newspaper on a daily basis, while 64 per cent of those in the twenty- to twenty-nine-year-old group read papers every day.

By 1977, however, readership differences between the two groups had grown considerably. Although older respondents continued a strong pattern of newspaper readership (76 per cent) among the twenty- to twenty-nine-year-old group only 42 per cent reported reading a newspaper every day. These statistics and others recorded in recent years suggest newspaper usage is changing among younger audiences who, some in the industry fear, may carry such habits with them throughout their lives. If this is the case, newspapers face the considerable task of discovering ways to attract and retain young readers.

Reasons for the loss of young audiences are a matter of speculation. One immediate answer, not unanimously accepted by media researchers, is newspapers' competition with television. As people watch ever greater quantities of television, they have less time to spend reading a newspaper. This argument becomes even more focused in light of polls that have shown that for the last twenty years Americans have preferred to get their news from television rather than from newspapers. Without getting into a debate over the substance of television news, presentation style, and summary format, accessibility and ease of use have made television the news medium of choice for most Americans. Others contend it is not so much the competition from television as it is the hectic and erratic life-styles that conflict with newspaper home delivery.

Most newspapers rely on home delivery for the bulk of sales; therefore, when population employment patterns conflict with newspaper delivery schedules, overall readership is bound to decline. This argument holds that young people are most likely to engage in such employment patterns and life-styles, so young people are most likely to omit newspaper reading from their daily schedules. Publishers of *U.S.A. Today* gave such reasoning serious consideration.

As the second largest national newspaper, *U.S.A. Today* sells about one in five copies through newsstands and vending machines. Merits of this argument will be determined, in part, by statistics gathered over the next several years on whether better marketing and improved availability of newspapers through means other than home delivery increase newspaper readership among younger audiences.

Whether television or hectic life-styles account for diminished newspaper readership, particularly among younger audiences, it remains clear that uses of newspapers among American audiences involve a lot more than just news. Studies by numerous organizations, including the American Society of Newspaper Editors, have found that the largest number of readers turn to newspapers for advertisements, advice columns, comics, features, and entertainment. People read newspapers not to learn the news, about which they might have little interest and would rather get in a more enjoyable format on television, but to relax.

The role of newspapers in the American media diet is changing. It was once thought television would offer the headlines while newspapers would provide analysis and a more rigorous treatment of a story. Although this stratified approach to news presentation may appeal to certain segments of the population, it clearly is not appropriate for the largest. It assumes an active, news-seeking population that does not exist. In order to retain audiences today, many newspapers are not providing depth but short accounts, leaving details and thoughtful analyses to news magazines.

They are trimming news in favour of features, hard reporting for soft discussion. Newspapers have been able to retard the exodus of readers by following readership trends and providing material demanded by shifting audiences. Newspapers still continue to attract reasonably large audiences because of their willingness to provide what readers want, but readers are not much interested in the news.

Magazines

It would be incorrect to conclude from our discussion of newspapers that print media in general are suffering at the hands of broadcast media. There is little question that magazine formats have changed owing to the pressures of television, but the medium has not suffered. There are more than eleven thousand titles currently available in the United States, an increase of one thousand in the last five years alone. People read a variety of magazines and spend a good amount of time with the medium. Total circulation has increased steadily over the years. The MPA reports that 90 per cent of adults read a magazine during the average month, and they read an average of 7.82 different magazine copies during the month. Magazines appear to be alive and well.

As suggested, present a variety of statistics in this discussion, but first must offer one caveat. Our figures report general observations that summarize readership habits for the average reader for the average magazine. With more than eleven thousand titles, it is difficult to interpret such averages. There is incredible diversity among magazines and their audiences. In fact, it is this diversity that makes the medium so attractive to public communicators who recognize important differences among audiences and use magazines as a means of reaching individual groups. Readers of the *Columbia Journalism Review* will probably not be much like readers of

Dirt Rider; Harvard Business Review readers will not resemble readers of *Seventeen*. There are great differences among magazines, and so it follows there are great differences in the characteristics of their audiences. Statistics reported here may imply a more unified audience than actually exists. With this warning in mind, according to statistics gathered by the MPA, the average magazine reader has these traits: The person is married, is thirty-seven years old, and lives in a three-or-more-person household. He or she has graduated from high school, has a fulltime job, and earns 15 per cent above the national average income. The heaviest readers look somewhat different. They are about the same age, but they are college educated and earn considerably above the national average income. About 75 per cent retain their copies of magazines and refer to them at least one additional time before discarding them. The MPA reports that "magazine imperatives" (heavy magazine readers who are also light television viewers) are likely to be involved in public and social life, politics, and community activities. They are also likely to entertain more and attend spectator events outside the home.

These traits and others suggest magazine readers are prime targets for advertisers. As we have stated, such statistics may so generalize magazine audiences that they lose their meaning for any specific application. Audience details on individual magazines can be obtained from commercial sources and from publishers. The essential elements in this discussion of magazines and their audiences are these: Magazines remain popular with American audiences. Each magazine has a unique audience profile. People who read a particular magazine tend to be similar to others who read that magazine. Magazine formats are changing to accommodate the evolving needs of their audiences, and these needs have generally been towards specificity and narrowing of interest area.

DIRECT MAIL

Direct mail has become increasingly important as a means of audience contact. Will take a more detailed look, at how it can be used in a public communication campaign. It is easy to obtain usage statistics on the mass media since there are only a relatively few outlets. Over the years industry watchers have gathered reliable and detailed information on how people use radio and television and even the eleven thousand magazines currently in publication. Direct mail statistics are more difficult to assemble. Every business, agency, and organization serves as its own outlet. While there may be hundreds or thousands of media channels, there are millions of direct mail channels, making it impossible to compile specific usage information. Direct mail usage is therefore based on assumptions and extrapolations, and even compilers of these statistics caution that there is a reasonable margin of error in the data.

Nonetheless, the DMA has attempted to track the use of direct mail based in part on U.S. Postal Service reports. Over the years there has been a steady increase in the mailing technique. Between 1982 and 1985, there was a 40 per cent increase in the total number of direct mail pieces. In 1985 the DMA reports there were more than 55 billion direct mailings within the United States and 16 million from the United States to overseas destinations. It is evident that direct mail is becoming increasingly popular among U.S. companies and organizations. They are using direct mail to get their messages across to voters, consumers, and supporters.

They are sending letters, brochures, fliers, coupons, and dozens of other forms to convince, cajole, inform, and stir people about issues of all sorts. Direct mail picks up where the mass media leave off. Direct mail provides targeted and personal contact with audiences. Computers, sophisticated mailing lists, and other technological advancements have made direct mail a convenient and affordable way to reach specific audience members. It enables communicators to shape their messages to meet individual needs. An effective communication programme must account for all essential elements of the communication process. Occasionally, a seat-of-the-pants campaign brings about the intended education or persuasion of an audience, but such examples are few and far between. The mass communication process has become far too complex in recent times to allow campaigns based on a hunch to have much success. With the expanded array of available media options, exposure patterns of audiences have become more complicated and difficult to pinpoint by intuition. The vast array of messages competing for attention diminishes the probability that audiences will recognize any one of them and that, by even a smaller chance, the message will have an intended effect on individuals. One observer estimates the average American is exposed to some sixteen hundred commercial messages per day but notices only eighty of them. Only twelve of these messages, Parker says, elicit any response at all from the recipient. In order to be among the fortunate few to win the notice of an audience, communicators must draw from a variety of techniques to improve their chances in the competitive information marketplace.

The complexity of media exposure patterns and competition for audience attention present obstacles that some public communicators are willing to concede when they conduct a seat-of-the-pants campaign. Most acknowledge the inadequacy of such an approach, however, when faced with current message production and placement charges. Production and distribution of messages are expensive. Radio spots may cost several hundreds to several thousands of dollars to produce. A thirty-second radio spot aired during drive time in an average city may cost as much as four hundred dollars or more. Television spot production has run as high as several hundred thousand dollars for a thirty-second network-quality advertisement, although the average is a little under $100,000. Smaller television stations may charge several hundred to several thousand dollars to air a thirty-second spot during prime time, and for the same time slot, networks typically charge between $150,000 and $200,000. Of course, for special programmes, network rates can be even more shocking.

THE SMCR MODEL

The Competition for Audiences

In a poorly planned public communication programme, not only does the communicator stand to miss the audience entirely, either because of a poor selection of media or inadequate message preparation, but also, given the sizable charges for time and space, he or she may waste money in the process. Recognizing this waste compels business and political communicators to abandon seat-of-the-pants strategies. Over the years a good deal of practical experience, field research, and academic study have unfolded essential components of the communication process that serve to guide the business communicator in making intelligent decisions. They assist the communicator in asking appropriate questions about the audience, media, issues at hand, and goals for the communication programme.

Informed strategies enable the communicator to see important links among these components and the interrelationships that serve to explain how the manipulation of one component affects other components. A useful starting point for an examination of the communication process is with the Berlo model, which records four principal components inherent in nearly all communication scenarios: a Message, a Channel, and a Receiver (SMCR).

Certainly this is communi-cation in its most basic form. A source sends a message through some kind of channel to a receiver. Who says what, how, and to whom? Nearly every communication event, no matter how simple or complex, involves these four components. This elementary model is fundamentally simple yet beguilingly complex. It is accurate yet, it is not complete. Basic communication students study this model to gain an understanding of communication. As suggested, use it here as a paradigm for complex public communication strategies.

The Source

The source, which in a majority of cases will be the company, spokesperson, or political candidate, is that individual or group who is perceived by a receiver as the originator of the message. Who does the receiver think is the source of a message? For instance, when Bill Cosby performs E. F. Hutton's television commercials, there is a strong likelihood that Bill Cosby is considered by most television viewers to be the source of the message—not the investment firm. A senatorial candidate may hire a speech writer during a campaign, but when the candidate delivers that speech, he or she will be perceived by the audience to be the source of that message, not the speech writer.

Perceptions of the receiver, then, are critical in discussions of the source. Despite those who may be behind the scenes of a public communication, it is essential to consider audience perceptions of who the source may be. Audience notions about the source are no small matter in the public communication process. As a composite of physical appearance, voice, demeanor, and more, may be the most critical feature of the entire communication event. That determines the message acceptance by and the impact on an audience.

A source that comes across well to audience members will promote attention and enhance the persuasiveness of the message. A source that fails to appeal to the intended audience will yield poor results. Perhaps because the importance of the source has long been known to public communicators, a good deal of research in past years has focused on the characteristics associated with an effective source. Specifically, these studies have asked what makes a source believable to an audience and what enhances the capacity of that source to persuade an audience to accept the message. What is it that makes a source credible to an audience?

Although as suggested, provide an in-depth examination for the purposes of this introduction as suggested, note that in most studies three component parts constitute source credibility: trustworthiness, expertise, and charisma. Trust worthiness deals with the inherent faith and confidence audience members place in the source. First, the source that does not have a stake in an issue and so stands to gain little from an audience's acceptance of a message will be viewed as more trustworthy.

Additionally, if the source is known to audience members and has, over time, consistently provided good, honest, and accurate information, he or she will probably be perceived as trustworthy and the message viewed more positively. For years, CBS news anchor Walter Cronkite provided information that audiences perceived to be factual and believable, and so he was rated consistently as among the most trustworthy people in America. Expertise is often measured by college degrees, years of experience in a field, awards, and citations for excellence. A source who can demonstrate expertise reveals his or her capacity to deal authoritatively with a topic.

An aeronautical engineer will be perceived by audiences as having high expertise when discussing flight characteristics of a new aircraft. The president of a successful brokerage firm will be perceived as an expert on stock market matters. Note, however, that expertise is subject specific. Although the stockbroker may know Dow Jones, this investment expert is out of his or her element when discussing aeronautical designs. Audiences recognize these limitations and are quick to confine source expertise to subject areas.

Finally, charisma, or dynamism as it is sometimes called, is the peculiar quality possessed by some people that grants them special influence over others. Although this trait is ascribed to the source, it is really a matter of personality, appearance, and demeanor recognized by the receiver as compelling features of that source. Some audience members may sense strong charismatic qualities in a source, while others are unable to detect such presence. A teenager, for instance, may be driven to near hysteria by the magnetism of a rock star. The teen's parents, however, may not recognize anything remotely attractive in the same musician. Charisma, then, like trustworthiness and to a lesser extent expertise, is a trait perceived to reside in a source.

Two features of source credibility emerge from this brief discussion. First, each of the component parts of credibility is imputed to the source by the receiver. It could be argued that the source may possess certain qualities of trustworthiness, expertise, and dynamism that can be measured on an absolute scale. For example, the source may have no evident stake in the issue at hand and may have consistently provided accurate information. Furthermore, this source may have college degrees to demonstrate expertise and may be an attractive person who can speak well and move audiences. Unless the intended receivers recognize and value these features, they are meaningless. In sum, we can consider the credibility of a source only as a function of the receiver's perceptions. Therefore, public communicators should plan their strategy not only to get out the message but to get out the message about the messenger as well.

The second observation about source credibility also involves the receivers: Audience members vary considerably over what constitutes a credible source. Different receivers ascribe different levels of credibility to a source because of different value structures, exposure levels, interests, and a host of other factors that make one audience member unlike another. There is no such thing as a generic, highly credible source that can be effective with all audiences.

There are only some sources that are perceived as highly credible by some receivers. In order to maximize the benefits from selecting a highly credible source, the public communicator must carefully match source characteristics with concerns of the intended audience. Often this means the communicator must give up one audience in favour of another or develop a stratified campaign that presents different messages borne by different sources to different receiver groups.

"One source fits all" may not work in any given campaign. We may need to reach young audiences with a sports figure, religious audiences with a member of the clergy, professional audiences with a respected authority in the field. To make such a determination, we must examine the group and the nature of the topic. These features of source credibility suggest a noteworthy dimension of complexity in the public communication process.

The Message

The messages you deliver as a business communicator will join the thousands of messages available to your intended receivers every day. People in this society are inundated with messages clamoring for their attention and demanding action.

Everyone who has a product to sell, an idea to promote, or a candidate to elect wants desperately to get just a few moments of the receiver's attention. Public communicators must be aware, however, that public audiences are not without their defences. In order to cope with the glut of messages incoming from the media, direct mail, and other sources, people employ three psychological defences that save them from message overloads. Known as the "selectivity processes," these defences take place at three distinct stages of message processing.

First, selective exposure occurs when receivers simply choose not to pay attention to a message. They may either avoid the message entirely, for instance, by switching to another channel when the commercials come on or tossing a direct mail envelope, unopened, into the trash. They also may choose to avoid a message through a "gating" process that blocks from their awareness the information right in front of them. They simply choose not to notice it. We have all sat in front of a television set and ignored commercials. We may talk with others in the room, pick up something to read, or just think about something else while the advertisement is underway. Indeed, the selective exposure process saves audiences from having to deal with more information than they are willing to consider.

If a receiver chooses to pay attention to a message, he or she still can defend against its effects with a selective perception strategy. Selective perception recognizes that audience members each come to a communication event with a different set of experiences, interests, and needs. Their interpretation of the message, tends to match their preconceptions. A speech by a GOP candidate may be viewed more positively by a Republican than a Democratic receiver because the Republican is predisposed to see good in candidates from his or her own party.

Almost nothing the GOP candidate says, though, may be viewed positively by the Democrat. Each perceives the message differently because of general dissimilarities in outlook and group identification. Finally, different receivers come away from a communication event with different recollections through a process of selective retention. We all remember what we wish to remember about a message. If the message has no particular appeal, we may choose to forget everything about it. Alternatively, we may remember only those portions of the message that hold some utility or attraction. Farmers may remember every detail of a weather forecast, while an office worker recalls only vaguely whether or not to carry an umbrella to the office. Children often remember minute details from television toy commercials long after such information has faded from adult memories.

Despite the best intentions of public communicators to get a message across, audience members have the final word on how that message is likely to affect them. Out of this discussion of messages comes this important observation: Public communication audiences are not undifferentiated masses that react in unison. Individual characteristics result in a wide array of responses. In order to have the greatest impact on the largest possible number of people in an audience, the business communicator must recognize how people process messages, anticipate their reception of and response to these messages, and develop a strategy that brings about a desired outcome within the audience.

Experience and field research have disclosed a number of techniques that can assist the business communicator to develop messages that achieve desired results. Effective ways of presenting a message can help prevent receivers from blocking out the information. Techniques that take advantage of what is known about the way people process information can ensure the maximum impact of a message. Fundamental to all of these procedures is this recognition: The receiver lies at the heart of the communication process. Any attempt to impose a strategy that ignores this fact will probably fail.

The Channel

The channel is the means by which the message gets from the source to the receiver. For public communicators, this nearly always involves either the mass media or direct mail. We have already seen the extent to which American audiences are exposed to these channels where, on an average, we spend nearly ten hours every day watching, reading, or listening to some medium. Thus, public communicators do not have to encourage people to increase their media exposure. Instead, they must locate by medium the audiences they wish to reach, then use these channels as vehicles for their message.

It is helpful to recognize that people turn to the popular media for two general and basic reasons: to seek information and to seek entertainment. Of the two, entertainment seeking is for most audiences the dominant motive for media usage. Many experts believe even informational functions of the media must contain a good measure of entertainment in order to attract and retain large audiences.

The network evening newscasts, the most information oriented of television programming, are heavily adorned with entertainment features. Stories are selected for camera opportunities, and correspondents often are chosen more for their physical appearance and voice than for their journalistic prowess. Sets are bright and majestic; the new computer-generated graphics are far more elaborate than required simply to convey information. Human interest features now command large portions of the twenty two-minute newscasts. Among the accounts of hard news stories that ever make the air, most are compressed into thirty-second clips. Relatively unadorned, in-depth news programmes such as the "McNeil-Lehrer Report" have been relegated to public television stations, drawing no more than 2 per cent of American audiences.

Even news magazines, considered the highbrows of informational channels, blend into their news features a heavy measure of summaries, short analyses, quick reviews, as well as slick graphics, artwork, colour photography. In spite of or, more likely, because of the ornamentation of informational material, audiences continue to seek out media for information about people and events. Their motivations range from idle curiosity to a genuine need for information. In the first case, they may want to learn about events in another part of the world, not because they could possibly be affected directly, but because they find some satisfaction in knowing about things occurring beyond their immediate scope. People also seek information because they have a direct and personal need. The media provide an ongoing catalog of information about various products and services, the weather, local government decisions, sales at neighbourhood shops, and a host of other items that have day-to-day utility.

Such information seeking by audience members is deliberate and often a matter of routine in daily media usage schedules. Businesses wishing to disseminate information will find details about customer information-seeking habits of considerable benefit in planning which media (or channels) to use in disseminating facts about their product or service. Of particular help will be details about the specific media usage patterns of different audience subgroups. Expect success only when there is a careful match between the selected medium and the desired audience.

Business communicators could solve many of their problems if audiences came to them for information. They could then become information brokers dispensing facts and figures, descriptions, and promotional material to those interested in their product or service. In such cases they would work only with those who expressed a need for information and would avoid those who did not. Such a system would be efficient and relatively inexpensive—it would also be unlikely. In today's market, business communicators must actively promote among audience members a desire for information. They must use every known technique to deliver their messages in an interesting, compelling form. Their goal is to stimulate receivers to learn about and develop an interest in their product or service, with the ultimate objective of selling goods or ideas.

Much information, then, comes to unwitting receivers. Information acquired in a forum where that information was not sought and learning was not intentional is referred to as "incidental" learning. Television viewing provides a good example. People, of course, watch television to be entertained, not to be educated (or persuaded) by commercial messages. In the process of being entertained, however, they are exposed to advertisements that attempt to persuade, inform, or in some way affect them. An entire industry of television (and most other media) advertising is predicated on the expectation that even though audiences may have selected a medium by which to be entertained, they are nonetheless likely to learn from or be persuaded by commercial messages that accompany that entertainment. From this view, entertainment serves to lure, to attract, and to hold viewers long enough to subject them to commercial advertisements.

Information transfer from the communicator to the audience, then, may occur as a result of information seeking when receivers search actively for information or as a result of incidental learning when information acquisition is a by-product of the entertainment. Channel selection in each case may be quite different. Audiences seek certain media as a source of information. They use others primarily for entertainment. The nature of the channel, the audience, and the message must factor into decisions by public communicators if they are to select the best media mix for the information/persuasion task.

The Receiver

Although the receiver appears last in the Berlo model, we view public communication as a receiver-centric process. Recognizing the receiver is central to all aspects of a communication. It is not only a healthy philosophy that demonstrates concern for audience needs, it is a necessary component in a strategy that guarantees the greatest audience impact. To underscore points made, we argue that source characteristics of trustworthiness, expertise, and charisma cannot be viewed by some absolute set of criteria but from the perceptions of receiver groups.

It is more useful to regard credibility as a source characteristic inferred by the receiver than as possessed by the source. Similarly, the efficacy of a message is not absolute. Some messages work with some audiences and some work with others. There are no guidelines one can follow to craft a message that will have an equal and effective impact on all audiences because messages are audience specific. Public communicators need to examine the specific requirements of individual audience groups and shape messages that specifically attract their attention and make an appeal to their interests and sensitivities. Finally, for purposes of public communication, the media (or channels of communication) can be defined only in terms of their audiences.

A message delivered over a channel that is not attended by desired audiences misses any hope of having an impact. Costs of poor channel selection can be high in terms of programme success and budget. Not only does the receiver have a bearing on these other components of the communication process, but also a variety of receiver characteristics, in and of themselves, are important. It is necessary to understand receiver groups along several dimensions, the most fundamental of which are demographic categories.

What are their ages, income levels, and educational traits? Depending on the issues under consideration, it may be important to identify audience members' religious backgrounds and political party affiliations, their marital status, and number of children. Other demographic features may be appropriate depending on specific subject material. Demographic traits that place audience members in distinct population classes, it is often essential to develop a more complete understanding of audiences with specific reference to the issues at hand. What are the general political attitudes among those who plan to vote Democratic or to support a county referendum? What do we know about those people who plan to buy a new car or take a vacation this summer or who eat at fast food restaurants at least twice a week? Answers to these sorts of questions can be important in the development of a marketing and communication campaign strategy.

THE COMMUNICATION PROCESS

Reasons for Communicating

If we were to ask a small group of businesspeople to list reasons for needing to communicate with their customers, we might anticipate responses such as these: to sell a product or idea, to inform about some feature of a product or of the business itself, to build better customer relations, to stimulate interest in a product or issue. As diverse as these reasons may appear, communication specialists recognize two broad categories in which people engage in communications: to inform and to persuade.

Even though as suggested, attempt to deal with these as two separate categories, the distinction between them often will become cloudy and ill defined. Nonetheless, in order to provide a convenient point to begin this discussion, as suggested, assume this two-point classification. To understand the distinction between communications that inform and those that persuade, recognize that we become familiar with a novel issue in two stages: knowledge acquisition and attitude formation.

Knowledge

In the first step, a receiver obtains knowledge about a topic. This knowledge may be complete, in which case all information about the subject is successfully acquired by the receiver. It is more likely, however, that information the receiver obtains will be incomplete in some details. This may be a result of insufficient information supplied to the receiver (the message is not complete), inadequate attention of the receiver to the message (the receiver selectively disregards information), or a combination of both.

Apart from incomplete information, a more troublesome condition exists from the communicator's viewpoint: A receiver's knowledge base may contain incorrect information or information that is, in some way, distorted. Here, the trouble may lie in the message or the receiver. Each can affect the accuracy of knowledge in one of two ways. First, information in the knowledge base may omit relevant details from story accounts, presenting only one side of an issue.

For example, in a congressional newsletter, we may learn that our representative voted to reduce federal taxes, suggesting we have great reason to celebrate. But we are not told this action will require an increase in state and local taxes.

Compensation for reductions in federal revenue sharing (necessitated by the tax cut) will force tax hikes in other areas. We have learned only the good news—none of the bad—and so have not been given the entire story.

A second form of information distortion may simply be an inaccuracy of some sort—a lie, a factual error, or a faulty representation or interpretation. In addition, inaccurate information may be a product of distortion or exaggeration or a characterization of details that are out of their correct proportion. For instance, the old "fish story" often has an accurate foundation—someone really did net a fish—only in the telling of the story, the fish may have acquired new and impressive dimensions.

The public communicator struggles to modify such distortions because they contain an element of truth particularly resistant to correction. Fundamentally they are correct; factually they are distorted and inaccurate. In these cases, messages bear information that may be distorted or wrong. The message source may err or intentionally deceive the audience and so present faulty information.

If receivers are naive and have no basis on which to refute the inaccuracy, they may accept it as fact, thus contaminating their knowledge base. But the source of inaccurate knowledge often may be the receiver him- or herself, who, through processes of selective perception outlined earlier, may deliberately or unwittingly distort information that becomes part of this knowledge base. We like to believe that what we know is accurate and true, and often, in order to maintain that conviction, modify incoming information to conform to our preconceptions.

If we strongly support one team in a football game, we may "see" many fouls by the other team that go unrecognized by referees. We may recognize bad manners only by the other candidate in a political debate. We may hear nothing but sweet music in our own children's recitals. Our knowledge base, what we understand to be true, is constructed not only by input from outside messages, which may or may not be accurate, but from our own perceptions born of what we already hold to be true. It takes a skillful public communicator to change the knowledge base of receivers who are committed to a position and believe that what they know is accurate.

Attitudes

Knowledge is the precondition for attitude formation, a second feature of receiver response to an issue or event. Once we know about something, we tend to form attitudes about it. They may be subtle, ill-formed, and weak attitudes, but nonetheless they represent our inclinations, dispositions, and evaluative feelings towards a subject. Understand several features of attitude formation: First, attitudes need not be articulated to exist.

We do not need to state or even to recognize consciously our attitudes about a product or person before we performance on them. We often buy one product instead of another not because we have explicated our feelings about the relative advantages of each, but because of some faint likes or dislikes that subtly bring us to make a selection. We may vote for a candidate because of some vague, ill-formed impression rather than for well developed and rational reasons.

Second, attitudes often are formed with incomplete information. Most of us have neither the need nor the desire to construct our attitudes from complete information that guarantees objectivity and rigor. Occasionally, for important decisions that have serious implications, we may become more analytical and thorough. But even in these instances, we terminate our investigation once we are comfortable with an evolving attitude.

From this point forth, through the processes of selective exposure and selective perception, we seek out and interpret information that confirms the attitude. In this sense, we often deprive ourselves of valid and significant information that would otherwise contribute to an objective and rational process of attitude formation. Few of us are so temperate as to keep a completely open mind, particularly on matters about which we hold strong convictions. The third feature of attitude formation derives : Attitude formation is not often a conscious process that we approach in a logical, orderly manner. At times we may prepare to make a major decision by consciously seeking and evaluating information from many sources that contribute to a sound, well-reasoned judgment.

But most of our attitudes, particularly those about less-pressing issues, are shaped over time through slow, ongoing processes that often take place beyond our recognition. While we may develop an uncontrollable enthusiasm for our product, we can rarely expect public audiences to share our excitement—either about the product or about the messages dealing with our product. Attitude formation often occurs subliminally and incrementally.

People do not always seek information on which to base an attitude. Often such information must be imposed on them. A casual exposure to a message, a glimpse at the product on a store shelf, a passing conversation—all contribute to developing attitudes. While we have argued that attitude formation is often a slow, passive activity, at times people approach matters with surprising enthusiasm.

When people perceive something to be important or to have some recognizable utility, they become more active in the information-seeking process and develop more acute sensitivities to messages dealing with the issue. People in the market for a new automobile or appliance, or who are planning a vacation, often develop an interest in the array of possibilities and seek out information that will enable them to make an informed choice.

This characteristic response to issues of perceived significance suggests a technique through which the public communicator may make an impact on listless audiences. First, elevate the perceived importance of an issue. Show the audience how this matter relates directly to them. Cultivate within the audience a perception of personal relevance and concern for the topic.

Then, proceed to deal with the substantive issues. For example, the large federal deficit has long escaped the concern of average Americans. In order to generate support for budgetary reform, a political candidate first must demonstrate how the deficit impacts, or will impact, on the average voter. Only then can the candidate get on with the job of convincing people about what should be done about the problem.

This characteristic response to issues of perceived significance opens a wide range of opportunities through which the public communicator may make a substantial impact on intended audiences. The initial strategies of many communication campaigns may be to elevate the perceived importance of an issue and thus cultivate among audience members a need to become more active in the information-seeking process.

Elevating the Salience of an Issue

A recurring fantasy of many business communicators is to have customer audiences aggressively seek information about their products. Expectations, of course, are that with skillful management of the communication programme, enthusiasm for information will translate into demand for the product or service. Many businesses, however, face the formidable task of stimulating among potential audiences an initial interest in the product and in messages that advance that product.

Agenda Setting

Our daily schedules are a mosaic of issues and events that demand our attention. Many of these are personal: a dreaded visit to the dentist, ways to occupy a houseful of visiting relatives, balancing our checkbooks. A large number of issues, though, come from beyond our immediate personal domains. What is the Soviet policy towards arms control? How can we manage the acid rain problem? What teams will make it to the Super Bowl this year?

Generally, for those matters beyond our personal experiences, the media serve as the primary sources of information. What we read and hear through the mass media factor into the array of items on our daily agenda. Agenda setting is really about the competition for our attention. At times a personal concern may become so compelling that we find little time or energy to deal with anything else. A single world event of major proportion may diminish the significance of all other events, intruding even on our personal lives. The assassination of a president, explosion of a space shuttle, and core meltdown at a nuclear power station are so important and so preoccupy the agendas of population members that by comparison all other matters shrink.

Except for circumstances where one or two events may dominate the agenda, we typically establish, among all the issues with which we must deal, an informal ordering according to their perceived importance. Then we apportion our energies in dealing with them. Increasingly, the media are playing an important role in this process, not only by revealing topics that may be included in agendas, but by suggesting a weighting for the topics.

Thus, they propose a rank order of importance. Considerable evidence substantiates that the media agenda serves as a model for individual agendas and, by extension, public agendas. Front page, top of the news, lead item stories become leads on the public agenda. Personal items factor prominently into the overall agendas of an individual, and a history of personal tastes and interests is important in how one perceives the relevance and importance of ongoing events. There is not, however, a one-to-one correspondence between the media and personal agendas.

The media serve rather as cuing agents. They suggest the relative importance of issues and events occurring outside the individual's scope of observation. Depending on individual characteristics and personal concerns, a person's agenda will usually reflect priorities suggested by the media. For public communicators to influence desired audience members, therefore, they must compete for placement on personal agendas by establishing the importance of a product or service. The ultimate goal is to get on the agenda and therefore be worthy of the individual's consideration. Towards this end, one strategy is to demonstrate the importance of a product, candidate, or issue at the personal level, thus exhibiting its significance among the things with which the individual must deal in his or her personal life. For instance, a communication campaign for microcomputers may attempt to demonstrate that such equipment will help a businessperson to do more work in less time, thus freeing him or her to spend more time with friends and family. The campaign implies that consideration of the microcomputer belongs on the personal agenda.

Depending on the nature of the product or service, the communicator may find it useful to link information in the campaign with issues beyond those of immediate personal utility. Demonstrating that a political candidate will help build the image of a community may have no direct usefulness to an individual, but it may be important in a larger sense of community pride. People do have concerns and interests that exceed their personal worlds. Getting on their agendas may be accomplished by demonstrating the importance of an issue among all issues competing for their attention, even those without direct personal implications.

The notion of agenda setting helps us to conceptualize how people view issues worthy of their concern and, moreover, how they establish a priority among those items. From the public communicator's viewpoint, it provides a usable description of a process instrumental in developing strategies to inform or persuade. People enter on their agendas things they feel are important or useful. In order to be considered by an audience, then, a product or service must be portrayed as having some significance.

Specific Techniques

A variety of techniques, applied under appropriate circumstances, may enhance the perceived importance of an issue. First, we may portray an issue to be important to others and, through inference or direct claims, assert a logic that will compel target audience members to acknowledge personal importance. People evaluate themselves by observing others. Recognition that an individual's comparison group has adopted a prescribed attitude or has engaged in some recommended behaviour will probably suggest importance.

Simply that other people are paying attention to an issue implies an inherent significance. If those with whom we identify find value in something, then we, too, may wish to examine it further. Advertisers have used this technique with considerable success.

Among the best examples are television political advertisements in which a candidate is shown speaking before throngs of adoring onlookers. Political conventions capitalize on this technique with camera shots of clamoring thousands enthusiastically supporting positions aired from the podium. The message in these cases is clear: Here are casts of thousands—made up of people just like you—who see great merit in these issues and in this candidate. If they recognize something important here, shouldn't you? Perhaps, upon inspection, these issues will hold some significance for the audience member, but at this point that cease is unimportant. This is only an initial step in the strategy to establish the legitimacy of the issue and to create the perception that something here is important enough to merit further attention. Remember at this point we are employing a tactic that will enable us to enhance the importance of a topic, to place it on personal agendas.

Characterizing a topic as important to comparison groups is only one of several approaches to establishing the significance of an issue. Another widely used tactic involves the linkage between something we wish to promote and something already important to audience members. We then equate our issue with one already installed on individual agendas. Successful use of this technique can establish the prominence of an issue within a short time. Consider a recent example in which medical research confirmed the role of calcium in preventing osteoporosis.

News of this discovery spread quickly. Because of its importance to public health, it has achieved a prominent place on personal agendas. Little was required to "promote" the significance of this information, given its inherent value to this health-conscious society. However, is found during the months that followed the revelation. Advertisers sought to demonstrate a linkage between the calcium content of their products and the now-recognized dietary importance of calcium. Vitamin companies, milk and cheese producers, and manufacturers of prepared foods that use high-calcium ingredients made bold claims in their advertisements.

They touted the health benefits of their products. In print and broadcast media, advertisements stated the virtues of calcium, then tied a specific product to the issue. Implications of such strategies are evident. While audiences may not have thought much about grated cheese before, if they think calcium intake is important—and we now all know it certainly must be-then they must also think cheese is important. The association between the product and the larger issue is evident.

A third design often used to establish a sense of the importance of an issue is a two-stage process involving first the creation of the perception of a need (where none already exists) and then identification of the product or service that can gratify this need. One might argue that audience members will see the logic of paying attention to something once they have been impressed with the need it is designed to satisfy. Through this approach, one creates a need where it had not existed before. People who, for their entire lives, have gotten along without a product or service must be convinced that they cannot now live without it. Although such an approach is often difficult, time consuming, and subject to problems, it does have a reasonable history of success.

An example is found in the burgeoning microcomputer industry that discovered an important first step in its marketing strategy: to convince small business owners they needed a microcomputer to maintain their competitive edge. Since the beginning of time, though, businesses have been run, many of them very successfully, without computers.

The industry, consequently, had to create the perception of a need for computers before it could mass market its innovation. Because of successful development of this perception, acceptance by a few early adopters, affordable prices, and other support marketing schemes, computers have in a short time—fewer than six or seven years—become as commonplace in offices as typewriters. With such a revolutionary innovation, one that had so few precursors that could have prepared an audience, it was essential that potential adopters become stimulated to recognize a need. There are, of course, a wide range of needs that may serve the purposes stated in this discussion. The computer example describes a professional need to improve efficiency and remain competitive.

But there are personal needs, too, that may be examined. For instance, consider the need to be informed about a topic (which perhaps may serve even deeper needs, such as the needs for self-esteem and the respect of others). Promoters of news magazines, adult education courses, and self-instruction computer software often suggest the need for a person to be knowledgeable about a given issue. Audience members may never have considered purchasing such a product until they were convinced of their need to be informed about issues or events.

Successful use of this technique stimulates audiences to recognize their need for information, then proposes a specific product as an answer to that need. Professional and personal needs are among many that have been used in recent campaigns. Scores of others include those based on stimulation of social, physical, and psychological categories of needs. Need stimulation generally includes the early phases of product promotion, but alone cannot sustain public attention in a product or service.

Assuming audiences recognize a genuine need for a product or service (and do not ultimately conclude there is no real need where one was suggested), other communication and promotional activities must be employed to continue audience interest and attention. Although need stimulation techniques may continue as part of an ongoing strategy, they are most effective in the early stages of a campaign to elevate on public agendas the merits of an issue. That critical portion of the communication process where perceptions are elevated sufficiently to render an issue worthy of audience consideration—in other words, to enter the issue onto the audience agenda. Paraphrasing previous writings on agenda setting, this phase of the communication process is designed to suggest not what audiences should think, but what they should think about. Messages in this phase do not attempt to inform or to motivate as much as they attempt to suggest the issue is worthy of a person's attention. Only after the relative importance of an issue has been recognized by audiences and has drawn their attention can the communicator begin to instruct and to persuade.

THE PERSONAL NATURE OF PUBLIC MESSAGES

Differences between an interpersonal and a mass communication event involve more than just the number of people participating. Although the size of the audience is worth considering, such a recognition neither has heuristic value to the public communicator nor does it suggest several other significant distinctions.

In order to serve the purposes of communication planners, as suggested, propose several important differences that not only distinguish interpersonal from mass communication, but also that ultimately will suggest various communication strategies. The nature of feedback or the flow of information from the receiver to the source is one of the major differences between interpersonal and mass communication events.

The principle of feedback was recognized in biological and physical sciences long before it was applied to the study of human communication. Biological homeostasis is maintained through a complex network of feedback mechanisms that report temperature, chemical balance, and other information about the status of the body. The brain receives and coordinates this information and, in a normally functioning system, if conditions depart much from a narrow margin, responds to bring them back to normal.

For instance, in the human body, when biological "gauges" detect an overheating condition, they transmit a signal to the brain that responds with appropriate directions to the sweat glands, blood vessels, and skin pores to "air condition" the system. As these measures take effect, feedback signals again go to the brain and the cooling system is turned down. This process is in constant operation, allowing the body to send continuing messages to those organs that keep the body operating properly. Examples of cybernetics or the study of automatic feedback control systems are plentiful in the physical sciences as well. Home-heating and -cooling units utilize feedback signals from thermostats to regulate burners and refrigeration coils.

Turboprop aircraft engines maintain precise speed through delicate sensors that regulate the flow of fuel and pitch of the propeller. Complex systems such as spacecrafts, submarines, and even new model automobiles rely on feedback control systems.The quality of feedback is important in determining its value to the system. Quick, accurate feedback provides the information necessary for an appropriate and effective response to conditions. Delayed or incorrect information contributes to a breakdown of the entire interactive process. False information from sensors in rocket motors has caused more than a few catastrophes in the space programme.

The common element among them is feedback, or the transmission of information. Moreover, a unit of information (or the message) presented at one point is dependent in part on messages that precede it and will affect those that follow it. This is true for maintenance of temperature in the human body, for conditions aboard a space vehicle, and for the entire range of human communication activities. It may be evident that the exchange of information within a physical system helps regulate functioning of that system, but how such information factors into the human communication process may not be as obvious.

Imagine having a conversation over a telephone that has a broken earpiece. Under such conditions, you can talk to someone but cannot hear the response. Furthermore, you obviously have no visual cues on which to base a cease about the success or failure of your attempts to communicate with your "silent" partner. In other words, you are unable to obtain any information from the other party—you cannot receive any feedback. Such a one-sided conversation would soon deteriorate and the process end. While this interpersonal communication example describes an obvious outcome of feedback deprivation, such a problem, commonplace in public or mass communication, often goes unrecognized. Public communicators—business communicators—routinely send messages to intended audiences without ever receiving or examining information from receivers, who, after all, are the other participants in the communication event.

Such a unidirectional flow of information is as illogical in these mass communication settings as a conversation over a telephone with a broken earpiece. In each case the communicator has no sense about the reception of the message. There is no way of knowing if the receiver understands what is being said, is being persuaded by the arguments, or, in fact, is listening at all. In both instances messages may be ineffective or may be falling on deaf ears. No one may be listening. Feedback lies at the heart of any communication event—mass or interpersonal. We must have some information about the reception of our messages in order to know whether or not we are successfully affecting our intended audiences. Conversations proceed incrementally. Each portion takes into account and reflects previous messages that set a tone and provide context for the interaction.

The next sentence in our conversation will be predicated largely on the previous sentence offered by the other person. Feedback from others in the conversation—or our audience—keeps us from talking to ourselves. No less is true of a mass communication event, which shares a common structure with these interpersonal settings. Both involve a message, a source, a channel, and a receiver. Both require the source to have some information about the receiver in order to initiate the communication process (even if it is just knowing a receiver is listening), and both are certain to fail if there is not ongoing feedback providing information about how well the message is being received. It is often easier to recognize the more visible problems of inadequate feedback in interpersonal than in mass communication. First, in the interpersonal setting, results generally are more immediate. We know quickly if another person in the conversation is listening or not. We know quickly whether or not we are being understood and often get a prompt indication about the success of our attempts at persuasion. Also, in the interpersonal context, we are able to sort out better the effects of our specific messages from the effects of other messages. Often in the mass communication setting, an assortment of messages go to our audiences, making it difficult to determine the impact of our particular message. Finally, in the interpersonal setting, we usually have available a much wider selection of cues from which to conclude reactions to our messages.

In face-to-face encounters, we can read body language, observe facial expressions, and learn a good deal of information from vocal intonations that may reveal true feelings or provide more accurate detail about a person's reactions. As mass communicators though, we may discover the quality of feedback available is not as rapid, specific, or rich with detail. So because of difficulty in obtaining feedback or interpreting it, we may ignore the need for it. Business communicators are notorious for conceiving a communication strategy based on hunches and guesswork rather than on solid information about audience needs and interests, media usage patterns, and reactions to earlier messages. In these times when people are confronted with more information every day than they can possibly take in, there is great competition for public attention. Moreover, media charges for time and space are extremely costly, contributing to a compound problem.

The business communicator may be spending a great deal of money to develop and send messages that either cannot compete with other messages and so are not heard at all, or are not particularly effective in persuading or informing an audience even if they are heard. The inherent problem with such an approach is that it ignores the audience ways:

- The communicator decides what he or she wants to tell the audience (without considering what people already know or wish to know or how they feel about the topic).

- The communicator decides where the message will be disseminated (without first confirming that the audience is attending the selected medium).
- The communicator then does nothing to listen for an audience response.

Feedback information (used here in the loose sense to mean any information from receivers) before, during, and after the communication campaign has been ignored. Predictable results are, as in the one-way phone conversation, that this communication scenario will not succeed. The communicator has wasted company time and money.

For business communication this is absolutely crucial—not in any academic sense, but in a pragmatic sense. With acceptance of this premise, the entire process of business communication shifts emphasis. Business communication goals and objectives must not begin with hunches, but with feedback data from desired audiences. The communication process must begin where the messages end; or, to take this one step farther, communications end where they begin. If they originate in the imagination of a communicator and fail to involve feedback information, they will have little impact on intended audiences.

THE NATURE OF AUDIENCES

Audiences today are a complex aggregate of people, varied in their lifestyles, needs, and capacity to process information. Popular currents stream through these large populations, but on most matters there exist subgroups that hold individual views and express unique responses. Consequently, the notion of mass communication, which we, should be dispelled and replaced with the concept of targeted, directed, tailored communication.

A single message cannot convey the essence of a theme to an entire population. It takes a variety of messages, each developed with a different pitch, to blanket that population. There can be no single mass message because there is no single mass audience. There are only clusters of smaller audiences, and even these are ephemeral groups, ad hoc, coalesced around only a single issue at a single time. Business communicators must focus on these subgroups. The communicator, by obtaining feedback information, must discover these groups, learn about them, know their needs and their habits, learn what appeals to them and what repels them. The communicator must learn about the character of these groups, discover how they react and how they interact. Businesses must learn about these transitory collections of audiences, and they must move with them when they disband and re-form in new clusters around other issues.

A snapshot is not sufficient. The world these days is too dynamic. There are too many events. There is too much information competing for people's time and attention. The camera must always be kept running. The business communicator must constantly monitor the changing mood of audiences as events impact on them and they proceed through rapid evolution, day by day, event by event.

The central problem faced by public communicators concerns the means they use to gain an understanding of—obtain feedback information from-their audiences. Few, if any, of us have an intuition capable of sorting among large audience populations and arriving at a formula that holds the calculus of their needs, interests, and potential responses. The complexity of this task far exceeds the capacity of any individual. Given the current state of technology, though, both hardware in the form of computer technology and social science procedures for audience measurement, the public communicator has available a wide range of techniques that can provide accurate, thorough, and timely information about potential audiences.

Information gathered through well-recognized methods can provide the feedback so necessary to begin and to sustain a communication programme. With this knowledge about desired audiences, communicators can cultivate an appropriate image of the business as a message source, shape a meaningful and effective message, and select suitable channels to reach that audience. Audience assessment techniques are notably successful at identifying, defining, and characterizing subgroups in larger audience populations. In other words, these methods of audience measurement provide the specifications necessary for audience targeting. Targeting, involves the recognition that many smaller, unique, and identifiable groups comprise the general population. Targeting seeks to reach them individually with messages designed to have specific appeal. Theoretically, targeting renders public communication more like interper-sonal communication. Its considerable advantages include addressing individual needs specifically, not just general concerns with a generic, one-size-fits-all message. As competition for audience attention grows, communicators must find it increasingly important to focus their messages and fashion them to deal with individual concerns.

As suggested, examine techniques of accessing specialized, targeted audiences, not as a supplement to reaching large, public audiences, but as an alternative to it. Some businesses, because of the nature of their product or service, may need to single out a narrow portion of the population. Targeting in such instances is an obvious strategy. Others may wish to reach broader audience parts but may choose to do so by subdividing those larger audiences for more specific handling, using the targeting techniques advocated here. Both instances involve similar procedures.

MASS VERSUS TARGETED AUDIENCES

From a theoretical point of view as well as for practical application, think about mass and targeted audiences as lying along a continuum of audience characteristics. Such a scheme places at one end audiences with a homogeneous set of traits and at the other audiences with heterogeneous traits. In the first case, audience members are all alike with regard to a particular feature.

For instance, they may all be Republican or all owners of sporting goods stores or all have similar attitudes towards tax reform. In this portion of the continuum, audiences can be identified as sharing some identifiable, common characteristic that links them and provides a common bond. Audiences at the other end of the continuum represent a great blending of characteristics that hold contrasts and evident distinctions. People in these heterogeneous audiences may come from all political parties, work at different jobs in different industries, and share no common philosophies. In their issues of concern, such eclectic audiences display no apparent similarities. They are identified by their diversity and are alike only in the consistency of their differences.

For purposes of discussion and planning, as suggested, identify homogeneous groups as targeted or narrow audiences and heterogeneous groups as mass or general audiences. In dealing with these two categories, we employ communication strategies that differ in several dimensions. First, our choice and presentation of the message source will vary. For the targeted group, as suggested, select a source that has particular appeal to and credibility among audience members we wish to pinpoint. In source selection for the mass audience, as suggested, attempt to appeal to the greatest portion of the group by choosing and displaying a source with the greatest general acceptance.

The topics we select and the messages we develop also vary considerably between these two audience categories. For targeted audiences we can become focused and specific and provide arguments that meet the particular needs and expectations of audience members. The best we can do with mass audiences is to develop a generic message that attempts to embrace the largest possible number of people. Such messages are often measured by their success at having the greatest meaning and the least offense to the largest audience (which often means aiming at the lowest common denominator). Finally, the channels we employ for these audiences differ considerably.

With targeted audiences we use a prudent approach. We disseminate information through channels that appeal specifically to people of concern to us. Trade and association publications reach people in specific professions. Radio stations reach people with particular tastes in music who can often be narrowly defined by demographic features. Direct mail enables the communicator to provide specific information on a one-to-one basis. For mass audiences we usually turn to television or newspapers that best deliver audiences that are heterogeneous or have a blending of traits. During prime time, for instance, television audiences represent a cross section of the population with people from all demographic, professional, and ideological quarters—in other words, audiences that meet the definition of heterogeneity.

Two observations underscore the approach to specialized communication adopted: First, targeted communication is nearly always more efficient and successful than mass communication; second, even large, heterogeneous mass audiences can be, and nearly always should be, subdivided into component target audiences. Targeted communication enables the public communi-cator to engage in a communication scenario like interpersonal communication. Armed with thorough and accurate audience research data (feedback information), communicators can shape their messages to meet the particular needs of homoge-neous audience blocks.

The communicator can employ precisely the arguments, techniques, and approaches that best respond to the receiver through the iterative process of two people in a conversation. Targeted communication is incisive, effective, and more streamlined than the alternative mass communication approaches, which often have enormous waste. Mass communication has some use for products and services that, like water and air, are resources used by everyone. As long as one can argue that products have differential appeal among audience members, though, one must consider dividing these general audiences into component units.

Consider, for example, a political candidate running for congressional office. First, the candidate obviously wants the largest number of votes possible and needs support from people of all ages, races, income brackets, and political parties. Second, the candidate (or the "product," from the marketing perspective) embodies a collection of traits that may appeal differently to individual quarters of the voting population. In other words, some features of this candidate will interest some voters and other features will appeal to other voters. Although a successful candidate must attract a wide range of audiences, the best strategy to win greatest support is not by treating this audience as a single, undifferentiated unit but by dividing it into blocks for individual treatment.

Audience feedback data, for instance, may suggest that the candidate's position on social security is particularly strong with the elderly, or the position on development tax appealing to the business community, or the stand on foreign policy pleasing to conservatives. Dividing voter audiences into specific target groups for individual handling will be far more successful than running a generic campaign that treats the entire population as a single blended mass.

At the heart of targeted communication lies a recognition that receivers are the foremost factor in the equation. We must first identify receiver needs and interests before we can determine what our message should concern or how it should be presented. We must know what our particular receivers look for in a source and what kind of source they will trust and consider credible. Only with this information can we select and portray our source in a way that maximizes audience impact.

We also need to learn about specific media usage habits of target audience groups in order to determine which channels we should use. We may find a half-dozen or more target groups in the mass audience and so prepare a communication strategy that provides separate tracks for each. From this orientation arises the view of audience-based communication presented. It is essential that the business communicator recognize the logic and practical utility of beginning the process by considering the receiver. This book focuses on the techniques of obtaining audience information and provides a thorough discussion of ways to interpret and use this information to develop successful, efficient, audience-based communication programmes.

4

Media Usage in Targeted Communication

Media usage is obviously integral to communication programmes of any reasonable dimension. We examine each of the primary mass media—television, radio, newspapers, and magazines. We also devote a part to direct mail. Our purpose is to highlight the features of each medium that contribute to its value as a tool of specialized communication. The media are not empty vessels that carry messages.

They impart a character to the messages they transmit. Their capacities to carry information are different, as are their effects on audience members. It is essential for the development of a successful specialized communication campaign that communicators recognize the strengths and weaknesses of each medium.

CHANGES IN MEDIA USE

A population deeply involved with the mass media. The statistics demonstrate that media are not just pleasant additions to our lives. They are integral components of our existence. Hardly a moment goes by that we are not in contact with one of the broadcast or print media. Large numbers of homes, known as "constant television households," have the television on from the moment the first person awakes in the morning until the last person retires at night.

Most homes have magazines, newspapers, and books lying around, always available to absorb an idle moment. And now that portable radios have become truly portable through miniaturization and lightweight headphones that deliver sound of superb quality, we can take our music wherever we go. We are truly people of the media age. As technological innovations provide ever greater varieties of media and more flexibility in the ways we use these media, the complexity of usage patterns has also grown. We are moving away from times when the media joined people into common exposure tracks.

For instance, in the mid- 1950s when the three major television networks provided the primary source of programming, those watching prime-time television had to be viewing one of these three networks. Everyone watched essentially the same thing. This is not so today. In a recent study by one of the authors, interviewers investigated the television-viewing habits of two hundred fifty teenagers in a medium-sized city and found that during any half-hour prime-time segment, they had been watching as many as twenty-five different programmes.

They selected from network and cable channels as well as from movie, concert, and special interest tapes played on their VCRs. The medium that once brought us together as a population with shared experiences now divides us by the vast programme diversity it offers. Apart from the sociological implications of this phenomenon, there are important practical considerations for business communicators who need to reach people wherever they are. In the "old days," it seemed easy. There was one-stop shopping.

You could go to one newspaper or one television or radio station and cover the market; you could reach large portions of the population with a single communication. Diversification of media usage patterns has made media selection procedures considerably more complex; and if current trends continue as expected, these procedures will probably become yet more involved.

While such trends appear to create a good deal of trouble, they may actually provide a number of advantages. As audiences sort out and attend specific media, they become smaller and more homogeneous. This homogenization can serve the needs of business communicators who so often wish to focus their efforts on strong, prospective customers rather than waste resources on larger audiences, only a portion of which are of interest. With the character of media changing so quickly, it is becoming increasingly more difficult to provide a convenient typology of the media based on audience characteristics.

Traditionally, television has been considered a broad appeal, large-audience medium whose content and style interest massive audiences. Certainly, this remains the case today, although audience statistics suggest that with some exceptions the vast popularity of large programme blocks has been eroding.

Nonetheless, for special programmes, television can still command immense audiences with an unmatched potential of reaching millions of people at a single moment. One television network reported in the mid-1970s that a greater number of people viewed its presentation of "Hamlet" in a single evening than all the combined audiences of the play since Shakespeare wrote it more than four hundred years ago. What power! What potential!

In times of great crises or of great ceremony, people en masse turn from a variety of media to one of the three networks. These great audiences again joined in a common experience. On such occasions the strength of this medium and the power of truly mass communication become evident. In the last half of the 1980s, however, television in transition from its days as a large mass medium, offering broad appeal programming exclusively, to its next stage in this evolutionary process. Television, like magazines and radio, inevitably will become a targeted, narrow audience medium.

Targeted Media

As we examine techniques of communicating with specialized audiences, we are intrigued by the potential offered through targeted media. Certainly, under limited conditions, when business communicators wish to reach broad customer groups and have little concern for the makeup of those groups, they should consider using the medium that can deliver the largest possible numbers, even if that audience is a demographic grab bag. But when they need to reach a population subgroup or several subgroups with individually tailored messages, they should seek such audiences through targeted media.

Targeting is the key to specialized campaigns. Targeting is the essence of audience-based communication. The receiver lies at the heart of the communication process. Throughout this book we demonstrate that each step begins with consideration of the intended recipients of a message. We have reworked the Berlo SMCR model to include the receiver not just as an endpoint of the process, but as an integral component in each step constituting the communication event. Portrayal of the source should be developed in light of receiver concerns and impressions.

The message content and delivery require close analysis of receiver needs and interests. In our discussion of channel manipulation, we rely heavily on identifying characteristics of the receiver to design effective approaches. As we turn to an examination of the media channels through which messages are disseminated, the receiver continues to play a key role. From the business communicator's viewpoint, the worth of the media lies almost entirely in the kinds of audiences they can deliver. Either they provide the kinds of receivers we are interested in reaching, or they do not. If they fail to supply desired audiences, we should not consider them. If they do offer desired audiences, several additional considerations must enter the decision process.

First, do they reach the entire intended audience or only a portion of it? If they reach only a portion, in what medium do we capture the missing segment? Do they reach not only our intended audience, but also large numbers of receivers of no concern to us? In this case we must decide if the additional audience members impose added cost. If we should decide the audience composition is acceptable, we must then ask if that medium provides the physical characteristics to distribute the message. For instance, if we need to show a picture or diagram, we must consider print or television. If we need to provide statistics and details, we may be restricted to print. If we wish a good deal of repetition, then radio should be examined. These and a variety of other considerations about physical properties come into play when we decide which medium or combination of media should be selected in a public communication campaign.

The Media Effect the Message

Remember that the media are not like those hollow pneumatic tubes that carry checks back and forth at a bank drive-up window. The media have characteristics of their own that are imparted to the message. They effect the message and alter the way audiences receive it. The media engender or reinforce certain perceptions of legitimacy and truth in a message. They contribute directly to the perceived importance of a message, thus elevating among audience members the salience of a topic.

Legitimacy and Truth

"I know it's true; I read it in the newspaper." "I saw it on the evening news; it must be so." Through years of exposure, people have grown to recognize that mass media in this country routinely present accurate and dependable information.

Owing largely to such consistency, they expect the truth, and they trust information carried by the media. Commercial advertisers exploit this notion of truth. One late-night television advertiser, after making some remarkable claims about a product, proclaimed that "what we have told you must be true; they wouldn't let me lie on television." We are not suggesting that audiences naively accept any line tossed out by the mass media.

We are proposing, however, that the effect of honest, accurate, and well-documented information is augmented by its presentation in the media. Some researchers speculate that audiences perceive that the media have a purging effect. They believe that a source might mislead one person but would not risk discovery of a flawed message presented to large public groups. Others hypothesize that messages are accepted as true because audiences assume federal and state laws prohibit inaccurate advertising.

Whatever the explanation, there is good reason to believe that the truth and legitimacy elements exist and can work in favour of the communicator, particularly in the presentation of new and relatively unfamiliar subjects. When audiences have no prior information about a subject, a communicator can expect to enjoy some legitimacy by virtue of the media vehicle alone.

Salience

In addition to the legitimacy and truth factors, each of the media contributes, in varying degrees, to the salience (perceived relative prominence or importance) of a subject. People accept that of all world events, the mass media report only those most noteworthy.

Newspapers discuss the important events in a city council meeting, not the routine matters. They provide playby-play coverage for the most important sports teams in a league or local area. Evening network news programmes report only stories of the greatest national importance.

With years of media experience, people expect the media to sort among the universe of information, to identify and disseminate only the most significant messages. The name of someone they know in print for the first time—that person must be important to be mentioned in the paper. Part of the acculturation process in this society includes an awareness that the mass media recognize the importance of certain people or issues. Our discussion of agenda setting examined the dynamics of this process.

Even media practitioners operate on this principle in seeking and identifying stories for their own news operations. Interviews beget interviews. Could an item discussed on the six o'clock news go unnoticed by a city editor who may have missed it for the newspaper or initially chose not to cover it? News directors and editors are voracious consumers of competing media to see which stories their competition thought important. A noteworthy review of the impact of media on this society came from the seminal work by Paul Lazarsfeld and Robert Merton. These Columbia University sociologists recognized the media convey information not only in the words and pictures they carry, but in a more subtle way simply by carrying information about a topic at all.

The mass media bestow prestige and enhance the authority of individuals and groups by legitimizing their status. Recognition by the press or radio or television testifies that one has arrived, that one is important enough to have been singled out from the large and anonymous masses, that one's behaviour and opinions are significant enough to require public notice. Message salience is not confined to news items. Well-developed commercial and educational messages enjoy the same benefit. One study conducted in Michigan sought to measure the effects of a coordinated media campaign on public perceptions of a complex set of international trade issues. As expected, pretesting revealed that local audiences were initially unfamiliar with the topic, and among those who had some familiarity, most thought the international trade issue was unimportant. For six weeks following the pretest this research provided for a carefully programmed use of major media (radio, television, and newspapers) that reached more than 1 million people.

This campaign disseminated general mass media information along with targeted messages to specific population subgroups. Messages employed the same formats that might be used by any business communicator (thirty-second radio and television spots, partial-page newspaper ads) and did not involve more lengthy promotional techniques (talk shows, features, special news stories, etc.).

Essentially, researchers designed the campaign to increase the public's knowledge about international trade features and policies and to elevate public perceptions of trade importance (salience).Postexposure studies confirmed the success of the communication campaign: First, when compared either with pretest results or with findings from a control group, scores on items measuring public understanding of international trade issues increased significantly. Of particular relevance here, the data indicated a marked increase in reviewers' perceptions of trade as an important national issue.

The media campaign increased salience of the topic and elevated it on the public agenda. When asked specifically in the posttest why international trade was important to the United States, many respondents suggested it was chiefly because of the media attention. They simply assumed it must be important or it would not have been discussed in the media.Various features of this research apply to business communication practices:

- Although the topic—international trade—did not concern a specific product or service, it did provide an acid test. It measured the media's capacity to relay information and increase the perceived importance of a not inherently interesting issue.
- With proper use of targeting techniques and by using the media alone, even an obscure, dull, and complex issue can be promoted on the public's agenda.
- If such an issue can be packaged for a general audience, then the media can accommodate similarly almost any concern. Any topic, no matter how esoteric or complex, can fit into the targeted, audience-based approach to public communication.

This study is important for our purposes because it relied on the same media tools available to the business communicator: spot radio and television messages and periodic newspaper ads. Based on pretest studies, it targeted various subgroups with specially designed messages sent through popular media.

Researchers knew the individual concerns of these target audiences and knew the medium through which it could best reach them. The media are all important in executing the strategy of targeted communication. Some media blanket the entire population; others deliver specific audiences for special treatment. For efficiency and effectiveness, communication strategies should focus on narrower groups through carefully selected media.

INDIVIDUAL MEDIA CHARACTERISTICS

The four major mass media and direct mail have unique qualities, strengths, and weaknesses. As suggested, examine them here and discuss research findings about each.

Television

Of all the media available to the business communicator to reach large, undifferentiated audiences, none is so potentially powerful as television. With its capacity for instant transmission from any point on the globe and its combination of sight and sound that engage two senses simultaneously, television dominates American media diets.Journalism professor and television critic David Littlejohn suggests that television may be the most potent of all the media, playing a dominant role in the media repertoire.

Television is the most thoroughly attended to, most pervasive, and probably most influential means of propagating ideas in the country today. It can be instantaneous in its reach, intimate generally in its reception. It can exercise the most extraordinary sensory and emotional appeal. You can find authorities who believe that it molds minds, fixes modes of perception, and determines what is thought of as desirable and even real for hundreds of millions of people.

The large amounts of exposure time given the medium have prompted concern over how society may be affected. Dr. George Gerbner and his staff at the University of Pennsylvania have demonstrated, in their Cultural Indicators Project, that viewers often form their impressions about society based on life as portrayed on television.

In his work, Gerbner attempts to plot a profile of social events as depicted on television against viewers' perceptions of these events as reality. For instance, in his research involving television's portrayal of violence, Gerbner has attempted to learn if those who spend more time watching television (which contains a good measure of violence) are more likely than others to perceive the real world as a violent place. Essentially, his findings conclude that such a relationship does exist. Gerbner and others have found that television

- Displays common patterns repeated in endless episodes, which provide a paradigm for learning
- Teaches, even though people attend the medium for entertainment, to pass time, and other reasons unrelated to educational fuctions

Cultivates within audiences a sense of reality commensurate with the way it depicts life. This conception of television's power has been well studied in the communication literature. Some have called television the "window to the world" because many people look there to learn about life and the world.

They believe what they see—not only in news programmes but in scripted programmes as well—that television accuratcly portrays characteristics of the real world. In 1982 the National Institute of Mental Health (NIMH) released an exhaustive study that examined thousands of reports, papers, and books assessing the effects of television. Observations of the NIMH advisory board summarized more than ten years of research. Among their ceases were the following:

The research findings of the past decade have reaffirmed the powerful influence of television on the viewers. Almost all the evidence testifies to television's role as a formidable educator whose effects are both pervasive and cumulative. Television can no longer be considered as a casual part of daily life, as an electronic toy. Research findings have long since destroyed the illusion that television is merely innocuous entertainment. While the learning it provides is mainly incidental rather than direct and formal, it is a significant part of the total acculturation process.... Television viewing is so entrenched in American daily life that it can only be regarded as a major socializing influence almost comparable to the family, the schools, the church, and other socializing institutions.

No doubt television is influential, in part because of its great popularity. For Americans, television has become a friend, an educator, an entertainer, and more. Eric Sevareid has called television the "national hearth." A concise account of several important features of television is taken from ceases of the U.S. government international trade project discussed earlier: Television is immensely popular and among the variety of reasons for its popularity, people watch television because other people watch television, and to keep in social tempo, people listen to the beat of television.

There is solid evidence that television can foster credibility of a source and establish importance in a subject. Television can create awareness of an issue and impart information to the viewing audience. Furthermore, television serves an agenda setting function which works to elevate the salience of an issue in the public eye. It has been proposed that viewers expect all important issues to be displayed on television and if an issue is not found on television it cannot be very important. People have come to accept that any issue worth public attention will be found on television.

The strengths of television have important implications for business communicators, not only for information transmission but for persuasion and company image building. As suggested, discuss several essential functions of television that contribute to a communication campaign. First, let us restate the basic design of targeted communication. That targeting is the selection of elements in a communication programme that meet the specific needs of narrow, homogeneous subgroups within a popula-tion. During the last few years, as advances in technology (namely, cable, satellite signal reception, VCRs) have provided a greater variety of viewing options, television has become more adaptable for reaching specialized audiences.

Even with conventional network-affiliated stations, one can narrow audiences by selecting particular time periods. For example, consider weekday afternoons when there are large female audiences, or particular programmes such as "Golden Girls" that attract older audiences. With the new television outlets, however, one can identify demographic groups not only by time and specific programmes but by station. Teenagers are attracted to music television channels, sports enthusiasts to all-sports networks, and people interested in current events to twenty-four-hour news formats. Television audiences are breaking away from the large audience blocks that once clustered around generalviewing programming and are re-forming in narrower groups around specific interest material. As these expanded outlets diffuse further into the population, the targeting capacity of televison will become increasingly more valuable to the public communicator.

Whether we are considering television as a traditional mass audience medium or as a focused targeted medium, its characteristic communication power remains unaltered. Receivers will continue to increase their patronage of the medium. They will continue to be affected by what they see. And they will continue to ascribe the elements of trustworthiness and salience to what they observe on the screen. Differences, of course, will be found in the size of audiences, which we expect will become smaller, and in the composition of audiences, which are bound to become more differentiated but more alike within themselves.

So, despite these inevitable changes, the business communicator can use television as a powerful tool to reach a variety of audiences. The mass media, as we have said, impart a sense of trust in a message. Communicators who use the media can expect to enjoy an elevation of trust in their messages because of the media vehicle. Television is particularly well qualified to build not just trust in a message but also credibility for the company behind the message. We have described how three essential components constitute credibility, or the quality of perceived confidence and believability: trustworthiness, expertise, and charisma. The communicator can use these components to influence an audience. How customers view a company along these three dimensions may determine whether or not they wish to do business with that company.

If they view a company as honest and caring for customers, as experienced and knowledgeable in its field, and as exciting and dynamic in its business practices, they will be more likely to have confidence in that company. While development of such an image involves many factors, not the least of which is actually possessing such characteristics, the business must be able to project these qualities to customers. Television, with its parallel bandwidths of sight and sound, can be particularly helpful in such a task.

Trustworthiness

People identify with people they see on television. They come to believe that they know these people. Television newscasters are better known and rated as more trustworthy than newspaper writers and editors. This may be so because people associate a face and a voice with the name of television personalities but cannot with newspaper professionals. People are more likely to trust someone they think they know than someone they view as an abstraction—a disembodied name. Perhaps they believe someone looking directly at the audience (into the camera) is more likely to be honest than someone who records his or her thoughts out of view. We like to meet people face to face, and television makes this possible.

Political candidates have been instructed to use television for this purpose. They are told: Talk into the camera, contact voters directly, let them see your face, hear your voice, feel your concern as you express your interest in them and seek their interest in you. A large number of political television commercials today are designed to fortify the trustworthiness of a candidate. They show the candidate and even the candidate's spouse and children to make viewers feel they know this person. Almost all political consultants agree that television is the principal medium for developing a sense of familiarity and trust among voters.

Examples of trust building through television are not limited to politics. Many businesses rely on the medium for the same purpose. Consider the Tylenol scare of 198

- Following the serious erosion of trust in its product after several deaths attributed to tainted Tylenol capsules Johnson and Johnson faced the formidable task of recovering its reputation. Specifically, the company had to rebuild public trust in its capacity to deliver safe, effective pharmaceutical products. As a major part of its public communication campaign, the company developed a series of television commercials stressing the trustworthiness of Tylenol. It used the word "trust" throughout its scripts and linked use of the product with physicians, nurses, and hospitals in which the public places great trust. Although the company used other media in the campaign, it credits television with playing a major role in restoring public trust.

Television may not deserve its reputation for trust, however, because it can mislead viewers and it may at times be used by people with less than noble intentions. Nonetheless, it has the capacity to instill a sense of reliability in the images it projects. Businesses with image problems or undesirable trustworthiness ratings should consider using television in a mass or targeted audience format to bring about a change.

Expertise

While television is by no means uniquely capable of conveying the expertise of a business, the dramatic nature of its presentation and illustrative powers enables this medium to be most effective in getting across this quality. The demonstration of a product or service in action may convey better than writing how well it works, how much the company knows about its field, and how capable that company is of delivering the goods. Seeing is believing. A company may tell someone about its expertise in the print media or on radio, but on television it can show the audience evidence of its claims.

Take, for example, the overnight delivery services that wish to demonstrate their ability to move a package across the country in a matter of hours. Television provides evidence of expertise by showing their elaborate procedures, equipment, and trained personnel. Viewers see a package leave New York and arrive hours later in Los Angeles. These commercials are effective because they show scenes that cannot be described as dramatically in print media or radio. From such commercials, audiences learn about a company's expertise by seeing it in action. Several years ago, American automotive companies discovered that large numbers of U.S. consumers believed foreign automobile manufacturers had a higher level of engineering and production expertise than did domestic companies. As a result, many people felt foreign cars were better and, despite higher costs, were buying them over American cars. As part of an elaborate marketing scheme to draw back American customers, Detroit manufacturers stressed in many of their television commercials the expertise of their engineering and production staffs.

They showed complex computer designs developed by their expert engineers. They brought cameras into the production line and showed trained workers checking the quality of cars about to leave the factory. Television did more than describe the expertise of these companies; it showed how this expertise was applied to the product. In this case where expertise had such an obvious visual component, television was a wise and natural choice. American automotive companies have made some gains with U.S. markets.

For many products and services, television may not be the best medium in which to cultivate perceptions of the company's expertise. Its general audiences may be inappropriate for a product with limited appeal. Furthermore, in instances where this expertise is not easily demonstrated visually or where such credentials are cumbersome to handle in a thirty-second commercial, other media may be more appropriate. But in circumstances where these restrictions are not applicable and where the product has sufficiently wide appeal to merit this medium, television can be most effective.

Charisma

The projection of charisma or dynamism, the final component in our consideration of source credibility, may be important to many companies. Perceptions of dynamism suggest a strength and resourcefulness of a company willing to do what is necessary to develop a product worthy of purchase. Never ignore consumer perceptions on such matters. A flat, colourless image does not build confidence and does not inspire interest in a company or its products.

When research reveals low charisma ratings, a company may wish to bolster its image among target audiences. It may enhance its image as powerful, up and coming, exciting, and at the cutting edge in order to demonstrate power in the marketplace. Television excels at showing activity and movement. It also can demonstrate a rich voice, show off a lively personality, and convey emotion. Television has been a natural platform for contemporary religious leaders, not just by projecting their charisma, but often by amplifying it beyond real life proportions.

The current microcomputer market offers an excellent example of an environment in which companies are eager to be seen as exciting and dynamic. They want to be recognized as big, powerful, innovative, and at the forefront of technological development. Among the most successful are those using television. An IBM personal computer advertisement may offer the best example of television use. The spot involves the now-familiar Charlie Chaplin character who bungles his operation of a roller skate factory by using old accounting, inventory, and production techniques. In his factory, people crash into each other, run out of necessary parts, and never can reach manufacturing quotas.

The business is on the brink of collapse. Determined to make a change, Charlie installs an IBM computer and quickly learns how he can reduce his problems, increase production, and run a more efficient operation. This fast-paced spot demonstrates that the computer can correct problems and bring success. It shows the chaos of the precomputer days and the calm of the postcomputer days. It is difficult to imagine how IBM could have achieved the same effect so concisely with any other medium.

Cost

Expenses for communicating through any medium are derived from production of the message and buying the time or space in which that message is disseminated. There is great variance in television costs for both of these features according to market size, station popularity, and sophistication of media usage. Larger markets, and so larger audiences, are more costly. Airing of a thirty-second commercial in a small market may cost no more than one hundred dollars, whereas that same commercial in a major urban area may cost many thousands of dollars. Clearly, all cost considerations must take into account population considerations of the market.

When we buy media time, we buy access to audiences. The larger the audiences, the higher the costs of air time. Market size is one determining factor of audience size. Station popularity is another. Some stations draw larger audiences than others because of programming popularity, promotional efforts, and signal strength. Nearly all stations subscribe to ratings services and know the size of their audiences since these statistics serve as a principal factor in determination of rate schedules.

Salespeople for television stations are eager to share and "interpret" these data with prospective clients. Be careful about claims and descriptions of audience size. We have seen cases where each of three stations "proves" it is leading in a single market. Be sure you understand the parameters stations are using to assert their leadership position. If you are interested in reaching the largest possible general composition audience, look at the total audience percentage for comparable time slots across stations.

If you are interested in audiences with specific demographic traits, be sure each of the stations provides statistics on these audiences for comparable time periods. Production costs for television commercials vary widely. At the low-cost end, a television station can send out a camera crew with a minicam to tape a thirty-second message delivered by a spokesperson for the company.

The station will then add music and graphics and put the final product on cassette. The advertiser can also provide the station with a finished commercial that has been developed by a professional production company. Production costs for such spots are nearly always more expensive, ranging from a few thousand to tens of thousands of dollars or more for each spot. Cost factors include talent, location and setting, graphic features, format (film or tape), research, and other equipment and staff for the production. While most businesses would not need network-quality commercials, it is interesting to note that production of some national commercials has cost several hundred thousand dollars each. If a business plans to use a professional production company, it is best to work through an advertising agency.

Television advertising costs are also determined by the time of day during which a commercial is aired. As we have said, the size of an audience is a major determinant of costs, and clearly audience size varies throughout the day. There are larger audiences during prime time than there are at 2 a.m. Consequently, commercials aired during these periods are priced accordingly; prime-time rates, obviously, are more costly than night-owl rates.

We should also consider audience composition. Prime-time audiences are bigger, but they may not necessarily be better than those in another portion of the day when people with specific characteristics make up the audience. Nielsen statistics reveal soap operas attract female audiences and Sunday afternoon sporting events draw males. Children watch television on Saturday mornings and older people watch Saturday evenings.

If we are selling soap powder, beer, breakfast cereal, or retirement communities, we may get more for our money by selecting times other than prime time. For businesses selling products that have broad public appeal, prime time may be attractive, even though it may cost more than other times of day. When considering the use of television for a public campaign, shop carefully.

Buy into markets, stations, and time slots that deliver only the audiences you need. Television is a costly medium, and audience overkill can waste money and quickly erode a media budget. Also, pay for production that delivers only the quality you need to get your message and image across to your audience. Production costs can devour a budget. A high-cost, slick spot is of little value if there are no remaining funds with which to air it.

Television Summary

Television is a vastly popular medium with an influence on its viewers that is now becoming even more apparent. Television not only reaches nearly every household in America (97 per cent saturation), but also occupies more than four hours of people's lives every day.

It commands the viewer's respect and imparts credibility to those who appear on the medium. Television increases the perception of truthfulness and sincerity of its subjects, and it raises in the public mind a belief that subjects discussed on it are important. Television is particularly successful at inspiring trust because it can show the faces and air the voices of those who appear there.

It instills in its audiences a sense of familiarity with the communicator in a way not possible with any other medium. This medium comes as close as any to the human interactions people have every day. With its graphic presentations, television can show expertise in action. In other media a business must describe how the skill and knowledge of its employees bring about a better product or service. On television, proof of the expertise can be shown in the service or product. People believe what they see, and television shows them the evidence.

As a dynamic medium, using rapid shifts and changes in pictures and sound, television offers a natural forum for the portrayal of a company's charisma. If a company needs to project an image of excitement and dynamism, television is an obvious choice.

The current climate of change, however, makes television use a tricky venture. The increasing numbers of available channel options have been accompanied by a reduction in strength of the network-affiliated stations. With the added targeting possibilities offered by segmented audiences comes a complexity heretofore unseen in use of the medium. Despite these added dimensions that must be considered, television, properly used in conjunction with other media, can make a powerful and decisive impact on a business communication campaign.

Radio

Radio stands as a versatile, targeted mass medium because of its production flexibility and audience focus. Despite considerable changes in the basic structure of the medium during the last forty years, it remains extremely popular for business communicators. For our purposes, several features of radio stand out. First, the number of radio stations continues to grow every year, providing a greater number of audience outlets and ever more refined and narrow audiences.

Radio accommodates the targeting needs of communicators. In addition, costs of using radio stand at a considerable advantage. Compared to television, radio production costs are low, and so are the costs of airing a commercial. These features allow flexibility in the creation of a wide variety of ads and in frequent repetition—the number of times a commercial may be aired. Unlike the development of television commercials, which often require a good deal of production time, radio advertisements can be produced quickly, allowing the business communicator to announce timely messages with little delay.

Before we examine these advantages further, let us review the development of radio. Its history reveals that it has become a targeting medium through which the communicator may reach specialized audiences. As our recount of this history will demonstrate, this once-mass audience medium has adopted a targeted audience format not as a preference, but as a matter of survival.

As the first broadcast medium, radio was without a precedent to suggest its utility for owners or audiences. The earliest public use of radio was to broadcast music, if only to a limited number of listeners. Newspapers were among the early owners of radio, and they used the medium as a public relations tool to sell more papers, not as a communications medium with its own special utility.

Even early business communicators such as General Electric and AT&T, which purchased radio stations in order to advertise their products, failed to recognize the broader commercial uses of the medium. They devoted their air time to the promotion of their own products and did not recognize that money could be made selling portions of this time to other businesses. In 1922, however, the AT&T-owned New York radio station WEAF found that radio, like newspapers, could be a profit-making enterprise.

The word was out, and entrepreneurs around the country began buying radio stations, audiences began buying receivers, and commercial radio began its rapid diffusion into the American media repertoire. In the years that followed, radio provided mass appeal programming formats that attracted large, heterogeneous audiences. Elaborate big-band performances were broadcast live to national audiences. Live drama and comedy shows such as "The Green Hornet," "The Lone Ranger," "Fibber McGee and Molly," "The Shadow," and "Inner Sanctum Mysteries" delighted large, faithful audiences from all demographic backgrounds. Families gathered around the radio to hear the next installment of serials that captured people's attention and imaginations.

Advertisers, too, enjoyed this new medium through which they could reach large customer audiences. Radio provided a wide demographic and geographic mix of people to businesses wishing to promote their products or services to undifferentiated audience groups. Unlike today, when advertisers buy thirty- and sixty-second spots on a radio programme, in the early days national advertisers would underwrite and become identified with entire programmes. Lipton Tea was known as the sponsor of the "Arthur Godfrey's Talent Scouts" and Chase and Sanborn Coffee was well recognized as the sponsor of "The Edgar Bergen and Charlie McCarthy Show." Early radio had big productions, big sponsors, and big audiences. The late 1920s to the late 1940s was truly the Golden Age of Radio.

Then, about as abruptly as it had begun, the dominance of radio came to an end. Televison arrived and quickly became the favourite of American audiences. At the time, some analysts believed television was a gimmick of which audiences would soon tire. They predicted people would return to radio when the novelty of television wore off. Of course, this has never happened. Popular radio personalities shifted with their audiences to television, where they soon stole the limelight from radio. If talent and audiences went to radio, could advertisers be far behind? A final blow to the old radio formats came when the financial base eroded, leaving little opportunity to stage the great shows that once sustained the medium. Although radio never regained the prominence it once had enjoyed as the prevailing national medium, it did not fade away, but, adapted instead to a new role and gathered audiences around its new format.

Paradoxically, even as radio stations reeled from the arrival of television, the number of radio stations increased and the number of radio-equipped households continued to grow. With television as the principal broad appeal medium, radio was compelled to carve for itself special interest audiences. Recognizing that large homogeneous audiences could never be recovered, radio stations selected formats to attract portions of those audiences. Audiences were divided naturally and sorted according to their interests in rock and roll, country and western, classical, and other music formats that appeal to particular listener groups.

Compared with television expenses, costs for such operations were reasonable, involving minimal outlays for equipment, and talent and a small business staff. The music, which served then and serves now as the mainstay of radio entertainment, was generally provided free by record companies seeking promotion for their latest hits. Income for these streamlined operations usually came from local small businesses seeking access to limited portions of the population. Since costs were low, so, too, were charges for air time, and this enabled even small companies, heretofore unable to afford radio advertising, to buy time.

What initially appeared to be an untenable position for radio turned out to be a positive stage in media evolution for station owners, audiences, and advertisers as well. Commercial development of efficient transistors enabled manufacturers to build radio sets that were rugged and energy efficient. These portable, or transistor, radios, as they were once called, allowed people to take receivers wherever they went. This meant greater audience patronage, and radio grew still further. Now, nearly forty years later, this dynamic medium is still changing to fit audience needs as it continues to add new stations and new formats. Largely because radio audiences are well defined and grouped into convenient interest and demographic groups, this medium offers a valuable channel for business communicators.

With demographic information on audiences readily available from a variety of sources, the communicator can select which stations will reach specific audiences within the general population. Messages can be developed with direct appeal to those audiences. They have potentially greater impact and generate more pronounced effects. Many businesses, for instance, use several approaches to promote the same product to different audiences, highlighting features of greatest appeal to each group.

A convenience store, for example, may promote its line of ice cream, soda, and chips to youth audiences on rock-and-roll stations, its beer and tobacco products on a country-and-western format station, and its fast food and convenient hours on easy-listening music stations often played in offices and shops. In addition, radio may vary the format and delivery of the spots to match the format of each station, thereby creating a special appeal through content and form to each audience. While audience targeting stands as a major consideration for business communicators, radio offers a variety of other valuable features.

For similar markets, radio is less expensive than television. It requires less lead time for message production and so allows messages to be more spontaneous. Because it offers only sound, it makes available a wide variety of creative possibilities. As suggested, examine each of these features in more depth.

Cost

For both production and the purchase of air time, radio can be a bargain. Radio production operations are simple, involving only a few components. In order to produce a radio spot, one must have a studio with a microphone, a mixing board, and a tape recorder or two. Also required are a script, an announcer, and a sound engineer who records the voice and blends it with any sound effects.

Not much more is needed. Because radio production is simpler than television production, it is also less expensive. Costs can be trimmed further by limiting sophisticated production requirements (such as complicated sound effects) and by arranging to purchase spots in quantity—they are cheaper by the dozen. In fact, many radio stations allow clients to avoid production costs entirely by providing only a script to the announcer or disk jockey who "performs" the commercial live.

The second expense of radio is the purchase of air time. Here, too, in comparable markets the costs of radio are considerably lower than those of television. We know of one station—admittedly in a small market—that will sell you thirty seconds during peak hours for just two dollars! As we saw with television stations, in larger markets, radio charges more. Nonetheless, radio time is relatively inexpensive. Several elements apply to the purchase of radio time.

First, like the telephone company that charges different rates at different hours, radio stations charge different rates throughout the broadcasting day, depending on the size of an audience. The largest audiences for most radio stations are in the morning, known as "morning drives," and the "evening drives". Usually, the midnight to 6 a.m. slot is the least expensive, and midday hours are priced between the drive hours and the night-owl hours.

Depending on the desired audience and budget considerations, the business communicator may select either the blocks of time acceptable for airing of the message or the specific times when the message is to run. In most cases the more specific you become, the more it will cost. There is one remaining option: the least specific of all purchase schemes, known as "run of station." Here the client arranges to have a specified number of spots run during the course of a week or a month, but does not stipulate the times when they are to b carried. Placement of the ads is left up to the radio statior This is the least expensive of all arrangements because th radio station can place the spots during the night-owl perio or insert them where other advertisers have canceled. In mos cases, though, to make this option more attractive, radi stations will agree to include some of the more popular tim slots in the total mix. In order to see exactly when the spot were aired, the communicator can, upon request, inspect copy of the air log.

Whatever approach is used, the low costs of radio usuall allow for repetition of a message. That is why radio is ofte called a "high-frequency medium." It is unrealistic to expe that exposure to a single message in any medium will influen an intended audience. In most cases, communicators rely o repeated exposure.

Owing to its low costs, radio is a particularly attractiv medium. While cost alone should not dictate the way medium is used in a communication campaign, it certainl must be taken into account for even well-funded operation Given that radio offers reasonable rates for production (whic permits development of a variety of messages) and tim (allowing message repetition), this medium always meri consideration in a communication programme.

Response Time

Although any of the media can react quickly to allow th communicator to get out a message in short order, radio particularly well adapted to this purpose. Businesse occasionally need to reach people without advanced notic For instance, they may need to announce a change in hour solicit sales help, promote sale of an overstocked perishab item, or announce the end of a strike and the beginning of shi work.

In such cases with short turnaround times in productic (or simply script preparation), radio can air a message with an hour of receiving the information. One of the authors h worked at radio stations that had agreements with regul clients to run such "emergency" spots whenever necessary. The typical music formats of most stations allow such an approach without disrupting the usual format.

Creative Possibilities

An interesting radio commercial, developed for the Radio Bureau of Advertising by Stan Frieberg, demonstrates the remarkably creative possibilities of the medium. The spot describes a sundae being made in Lake Michigan. An announcer provides play-by-play comment, and a number of sound effects set the tone.

First, the listeners hear chocolate sauce filling the giant pit left behind after the draining of the lake. Next they hear a mountain of whipped cream sliding onto the chocolate; then the heavy engines of a Royal Canadian Air Force bomber dropping a ten-ton maraschino cherry onto the thick whipped cream. Finally they hear the roar of ten thousand screaming extras who, we are told, have witnessed this incredible scene. Frieberg concludes: Would anyone like to try the same thing on television?

Television, because it provides both sight and sound, is a compelling medium, but radio can be even more powerful. Radio provides the sound, and listeners create the visual features of the message. All hear the same announcer's voice but envision differing pictures of his or her appearance. Cues in vocal quality, delivery, perhaps laugh trigger thoughts about appearance—height, dress, age. Our imaginations are powerful, and radio stimulates the imagination.

A programme particularly good at this in the old days of radio was called "Inner Sanctum Mysteries." Each episode began with the sound of groaning hinges as a large, old door slowly opened. Regular listeners of the programme say it was a frightful sound. These same listeners, though, who watched "Inner Sanctum" when it was televised found the door not nearly as frightening as they had imagined. With radio, listeners projected all their personal fears into their image of the door. On television the image was a door that frightened someone else. It was no longer the listener's private fantasy; it was a public sight. We agree with many advocates of radio that, by enlisting the listener's imagination, the business communicator can tap a particularly powerful persuasive tool. The sound of a product may be more compelling than its picture.

A description of an event may create a stronger and more lasting image than features shown. Radio offers creative possibilities beyond cost considerations. It makes available effects that either cannot be accomplished through other media or cannot be accomplished as well. These features of radio, along with its targeting potentials, relatively low production and time costs, and flexibility, make it a business communication staple.

NEWSPAPERS

The rapid rise to prominence of broadcast media during the last two decades has concerned many communicators about the viability of newspapers as an advertising medium. These fears are not entirely ill founded. Considerable evidence suggests that television and radio have stolen the thunder from newspapers. For fast-breaking news accounts, print can do little to compete with the immediacy of the airwaves—the broadcast media can cover live stories instantly from almost any location.

Even the old newspaper extra editions, once the popular way of announcing breaking stories, have faded from American journalism. Today, people learn first about major news stories from broadcast media, and most continue to follow the story largely through television. Roper polls reveal that since the mid-1960s the majority reports they receive most of their news information from television not newspapers. Compounding this observation, Roper has found that television is generally viewed to be more believable than newspapers for the majority of Americans.

On the surface the prognosis for newspapers does not appear good; however, a strange paradox in the statistics of newspaper subscription and usage patterns reveals this medium remains vastly popular. American audiences continue to buy 60 million copies every day. Moreover, newspapers outstrip the combined revenues of radio and television, receiving approximately 30 per cent of total advertising expenditures. Although before television newspapers received forty-five cents of every advertising dollar, the present percentage has stabilized in recent years.

Despite broadcast competition for advertising dollars, talent, and public attention, newspapers have filled a communication need for vast audiences. Journalism professor and former manager of the Louisiana Press Association Ronald Hicks, who has worked with and studied newspapers for many years, finds value in the newspaper as an important contemporary information medium.

Hicks highlights some of the reasons for newspapers' continued success: One of the most significant characteristics of newspapers is their flexibility. Their messages can be given varied typographic treatment and displayed in colour and in illustration; pages can be added as necessary; there is flexibility in terms of page size and format. Newspaper content "holds still": it has a degree of permanence which permits readers to absorb information at their own time and convenience. Complex issues can be developed to any necessary degree, yet there is a timeliness to newspapers because of the speed with which they can be put together and distributed. Their portability and low cost make for ease of reaching mass audiences.

For millions of American adults, the day begins and ends with a newspaper and a cup of coffee. Newspapers have become an accepted part of daily life. Leo Bogart, executive vice president and general manager of the Newspaper Advertising Bureau, considerable changes are afoot in the appearance and content of American newspapers. These changes, he argues, are largely a result of new technology, a growing concern for reader interests, and serious competitive pressures prevailing in the media business. First, Bogart's research has shown an increase in the ratio of feature material to hard news stories. Newspapers today are carrying more light, entertainment-oriented stories and fewer pure news stories than they have in the past. They also have increased the balance of local stories to world and national news, emphasizing neighbourhood and regional events more than global issues. Perhaps newspapers are conceding these larger stories to television and focusing their resources on matters that are not well adapted to the larger formats of television.

Finally, Bogart reports a reduction in the number of regular, special interest columns and features. He speculates that newspapers may be increasing the staff-written content or providing special interest parts that vary content from edition to edition rather than retaining identifiable, labeled features on a routine basis.

Several observations about newspapers may be made. Most clearly, newspapers have been affected by the popularity of television. This is reflected in the Roper statistics demonstrating a rebuff of newspapers for certain kinds of news and a greater credence by the audience in the veracity of television over newspaper versions of a story. Despite all this, newspapers remain popular, although audience uses of newspapers are changing as is newspaper content, in part to reflect readers' needs.

Perhaps gradual remolding of newspapers over the years has enabled them to find a comfortable place in American media diets. Newspapers do not attempt to compete with television; they serve yet another information function. They provide entertainment in the form of features, advice columns, comics, and games such as crossword puzzles. They provide news about local government, people, and events that are not adequately covered by television, and they offer local angles on larger stories.

Finally, they provide an important service for consumers by carrying information about available products and services. Nearly 65 per cent of the typical newspaper is devoted to advertising. When polled, the majority of newspaper readers claimed to pay attention to this material. This is good news for business communicators because it implies that while newspapers may be viewed less as a principal news source, they remain important as an advertising medium.

From our viewpoint, newspapers offer several features that make them particularly valuable: They have a relative permanence that renders them suitable for audience members whose schedules require flexibility. The physical and tangible characteristics of newspapers (which grant them permanence) extend the use of the medium to other than just information..

They are furthermore adapted to the presentation of complex information because they permit more studied exposure and they offer a wide assortment of formats to convey detailed and complicated information. Newspapers are both a general audience and a targeted audience medium. With careful selection and use, newspapers can be a real bargain for business communicators. As suggested, examine these points more closely.

Permanence

The permanence of newspapers permits readers to absorb the material presented at a time and pace convenient for them. In contrast to audiences of the broadcast media, newspaper audiences dictate when they will deal with the information and how much time they will spend on it. If they are attracted to an advertisement, they have the luxury of studying it and rereading it. This has obvious implications for communicators who deal with more complex or detailed matters.

This permanence, of course, is a result of the physical properties of the medium. Unlike ephemeral broadcast signals, newspapers can be touched and folded and cut with scissors. In fact, polls show the large majority of households routinely cuts coupons from newspapers or newspaper supplements for redemption in local stores and for mail-away rebates. Coupons are a successful marketing technique, drawing customers into an advertisement and into stores. Their use in newspapers has remained popular over the years.

Complex Treatment

The permanence of newspapers allows readers to move through a story or an advertisement at their own pace, spending more time to understand the information fully. Even though the broadcast media have been shown to convey complex information successfully, print can do a more thorough job with many audiences. Not only by providing readers the opportunity to study detailed information, but also by expanding the communication formats to convey this information, newspapers are an excellent medium for difficult and detailed subjects.

They can present more complex artwork such as charts and graphs, a task for which television is ill suited. They can present lists, schedules, road maps, flowcharts to help explain processes, and tables of numbers, prices, times, and scores. They can make lengthy descriptions more manageable and compress a great deal of information into a small space. Readers can clip, store, and share much information that cannot be adapted readily to the broadcast media.

Audience Appeal

As members of a newspaper audience, you are identified by the parts you read. Some portions of the paper—the general news parts—attract a large heterogeneous mix of readers. These audiences rep. resent a blend of demographic and interest groups that match the broad profile of the general population. Special interest parts of the paper draw smaller but more homogeneous audiences.

The sports part, for instance, draws larger male than female audiences. Business parts draw people in higher income brackets, investors, local entrepreneurs, and others interested in such matters. Food and home parts still attract large female audiences. The newspaper is both a general audience and a targeted audience medium. The targeting possibilities of newspapers are of particular interest for specialized communication.

In the sports part, most newspapers run ads for automobile products, home building supplies, outdoor equipment, and other products that often interest men. Even though women may also purchase these items, businesses base their placement decisions on market research information that shows men are the most likely consumers of such products. Efficient business communicators, of course, strive to focus on audiences that promise the greatest possible potential. It would be interesting to examine the possibilities of using newspapers to expand a market for home building supplies, to a nontraditional audience, say, women. Through research, a building supplies retailer identifies certain features of this business that are of particular concern to female consumers. For the purposes of this example, suppose it were discovered that many women were reluctant to shop at these male bastions because they were not familiar with the jargon and felt intimidated by sales personnel.

Instead, many shopped for such items in department stores or through mailorder catalogs where they felt less threatened. In such a case, a home building supplies outlet might hire female sales personnel to make the environment less threatening. They might train all their clerks to be more sensitive to people unfamiliar with industry terminology and in other ways attempt to improve the environment. With such changes in place, the retailer might then target female audiences with special information about these new services. Quarter-page ads in the food and home part aimed at women and based on the theme "We speak your language" could go a long way towards bringing in new business. The newspaper is ideally suited for such a targeted communication strategy.

Cost

For newspapers, as for any medium, when audience size increases, so, too, do advertising costs. For purposes of specialized communications, though, there is more to consider than just audience size—audience composition must also enter the decision. In towns with more than a single newspaper, examine the patronage of each to determine if there is a concentration of target audience members among subscribers of one paper.

Often, clear distinctions exist among audience characteristics of several papers. There are no savings in paying for an advertisement that misses the target group. Production fees also factor into newspaper advertising costs. A company can provide either a camera-ready advertisement or for an additional expense allow the newspaper graphics department to prepare the ad. Unless one has graphic arts skills and equipment, at some point there will be a charge for advertisement production. Generally, newspaper production departments charge the same as, or less than, freelance graphics companies. Elaborate art, photographs, colour, and a great deal of typesetting all contribute to higher production costs. Photographs and colour printing also elevate the cost. Finally, for cost consideration in newspapers as in other media, there are quantity advertising discounts. Salespeople can usually arrange considerable savings for advertisements run several times per week over a long term. Advertisers can also mix the size and placement of ads over time and retain lower unit costs.

Despite the attention given to a shift from newspapers to television among American audiences, recognize that while people may be obtaining much of their world and national news from television, their loyalty to newspapers remains strong for local items, entertainment features, and advertising. Sales are strong, the number of available newspapers is growing, and all signs suggest the medium will continue to be strong for the foreseeable future. For the business communicator, newspapers provide some permanence and tangibility and a forum to present more complex information than is possible with the broadcast media. Newspapers can work nicely in a targeting strategy and can fit into a modest advertising budget.

MAGAZINES

Just as television has revolutionized the communication roles of radio and newspapers during the last forty years, it has stimulated a major modification of magazines too. Such broad appeal magazines as Look and Life, which required large national audiences to support their production costs and attract a big advertising base, have given way to targeted format magazines whose audiences are bound by specific interests. More than ten thousand magazine titles are available across the country today, catering to even the smallest special interest group. One magazine publisher extends the challenge to "find me a list of names and I'll create a magazine for it!" This new role of magazines is explained here from a historical perspective: The rise of special-interest magazines and the related decline of general interest magazines has been the most significant development in publishing since the end of WWII. Television has hastened the growth of special-interest magazines by making people aware of all that there is to be aware of. The age of the Renaissance man is over. There is just too much to know for [someone] to be satisfied with claiming a little knowledge in many areas. The time is past when a magazine can succeed by only scraping lightly on every possible surface.

From the business communicator's viewpoint, magazines have three characteristics that set them apart from other media. First, the most attractive feature is the targetability of magazines. Of all the public media available, magazines permit the greatest degree of targeting. Next, remember that people choose the magazines they read, so magazine readers are interested in the subject they have chosen—there is even a good chance they will find the advertisements interesting! Research demonstrates that magazines usually are reviewed more than one time by a reader and that the pass-along audience extends the reach of each copy. Finally, as a print medium, magazines can accommodate complex information.

Because of their specialized printing methods, unlike newspapers, they also offer extremely high-quality reproductions. Such quality may be an important consideration for some communicators. Each of these advantages of magazines will be discussed in turn.

Targeting Potential

If you have ever examined the titles of magazines lined up at a newsstand (even an outstanding newsstand can stock only a fraction of the titles in publication), you may have begun to appreciate the level of audience specification available. For instance, there are dozens of computer magazines, each written with a different focus on computer issues. They are variously targeted to IBM users, Apple users, people who wish to apply computers to personal use, or those who use computers in a business setting. There are software and hardware magazines and magazines for used equipment. For sports fans there are general audience sports magazines and titles dealing specifically with football, wrestling, weightlifting, and even more specific titles covering pro or college football, Olympic or commercial wrestling; and the list goes on.

In addition to magazines sold at newsstands are those available only through subscription and thousands of others with restricted subscription lists, such as corporate house organs, association journals, technical magazines, and college journals. As the list of available magazines grows, the characteristics of attending audiences become more refined. The direction for magazines has been the continued focusing and narrowing of audiences, resulting in homogeneous groups represented by a specific set of identifying characteristics. By purchasing a magazine, people identify with others who share an interest in the same topic.

The proliferation of special interest magazines can be an extraordinary benefit to the business communicator wishing to seek out and contact special audiences. Not only have magazine readers already been identified with a particular area of interest, but they also have expressed a level of commitment to that interest. They have spent the time, energy, and money necessary to acquire the magazine. Through their purchase, they have affirmed an interest in the product or service the company wishes to promote. Magazine audiences are self-selected and become active participants in the communication event. Television audiences, by contrast, often view ads and spot announcements as extraneous events, and many become passive and some even hostile participants in the process.

Imagine yourself as a manufacturer of precision altimeters for small aircraft. Where would you turn to promote this esoteric product? You could use prime-time television because even owners of small aircraft watch evening television, but consider the enormous waste of such a decision. You would be paying large sums to reach a barely measurable portion of the audience. You could save a great deal of money and become more specific and no doubt more persuasive with your message if you were to advertise in a publication such as *Flying* magazine. Aircraft owners and pilots, people who read Flying, are already interested in new gadgets and equipment for airplanes.

It is also more likely they could afford such a purchase. Using this approach, you have an audience that is self-selected and already interested in the subject and that understands the technical features. They will require minimal tutoring. Overall, these readers are better customer prospects because of need, resources, and motivation. Consider another example, this time for an audio equipment retail chain whose products have wider appeal.

You must consider, therefore, a broader, more expansive audience. Throughout this book we have argued for the logic of subdividing larger audiences into separate groups for special treatment. The total effects of such an approach will exceed the alternative one-size-fits- all mass audience strategy. Customer research will probably reveal a natural division within such a clientele.

To emphasize, let us assume there are three major high-volume subgroups of audio equipment buyers: teenagers, unmarried young professionals, and upper-income, middle-aged men. Suppose, furthermore, our research indicates the following: The teenage group is interested in portable sound equipment capable of great volume if not greatquality reproduction.

Young professionals want not only high-quality sound, but equipment that has impressive appearance with digital read-out diplays, lights, and control switches. The middle-aged male buyers want high-quality equipment and are willing to invest a good deal of money for prestigious, upper-end items. With this information and no doubt a good deal more revealed by our research, we may find magazines an excellent vehicle for reaching the three audiences. We may use magazines such as

Teenage and *Rock Star* to promote the lower-end, high-volume equipment to teen audiences. Cosmopolitan, Playboy, and *GQ: Gentlemen's Quarterly* may provide a natural channel to the young professional buyers (again depending on our research findings). *Newsweek, Audio Magazine,* and *Stereo Review* may give access to the middle-aged male audio aficionados.

Throughout this targeting process, we rely heavily on research for direction. Research provides the basis on which to make decisions about how to subdivide the general audience, how to reach each audience group with persuasive messages, and how to select the media that will yield the greatest audience impact. Because magazines are so well adapted to targeted communication strategies, they provide an excellent example for the use of research.

Without detailed information on client audiences, there would be little basis, other than hunch, for making decisions about audience clusters. Specifically, how does one break the audience into subgroups? On age? Income? Education? Previous purchases? Ideological commitment? Or on some combination of these or other variables not immediately apparent? To use magazines to their fullest potential, the communicator must pinpoint target audience groups and identify their preferred magazine channels.

Research can further be used to identify the appeal with the greatest potential to inform or persuade group members. Magazines offer an efficient means of targeting audience subgroups, but decisions about their use (or, for that matter, the use of any targeted media) are best made with the guidance of thorough audience research.

Inherent Interest

Except perhaps at the dentist's office where we thumb nervously through any magazine available, we choose our magazines because they interest us. We find some appeal in the subject matter of a magazine, or we would not have spent money on it. This feature of magazine audiences, known as "receptivity," makes them particularly attractive to advertisers. Here potential customers have a natural interest in a product genre, and rather than viewing the message as an irritating interruption, which is often the case with broadcast media, studies have shown many magazines readers buy the publication specifically to read the advertisements. What an accommodating arrangement!

Although we may wish to use various design and other techniques to maximize readership of our ads, we do not face a major hurdle of resistance encountered in some of the other media. Take, for instance, *Organic Gardening*, a national magazine sold mainly by subscription, which focuses on techniques of home fruit and vegetable production without the use of chemical fertilizers or pesticides. Subscribers to this magazine have an interest in gardening in general and more particularly in a special form of gardening.

Most of these readers probably have their own gardens, see value in the organic approach, and are interested in the equipment and other facilities necessary for the hobby. Consequently, companies who deal in compost bins, tillers, mail order nursery products, irrigation systems, and other such products and services find a receptive audience through this specialized magazine. People view the advertisements not as an interruption but as a service and a desirable feature of the publication.

Audience Exposure

Several other attractive magazine features have appeal for the business communicator. The MPA, readers go through a magazine an average of 1.7 times, thus providing multiple exposure to advertisements and a greater opportunity for message effects. Work cited by the MPA (1985) finds a second exposure to a magazine advertisement boosts brand familiarity and belief in ad claims.

It also increases willingness to buy the brand and to maintain a level of recall. Clearly, the second reading is beneficial for message impact, and MPA statistics, magazines get that second chance with the majority of readers. Not only is a magazine read more than one time by a reader, but it is read by 3.6 people, effectively expanding the overall reach of each copy. Moreover, since each of these readers uses the magazine alone, advertisers are able to communicate information more effectively without the distractions inherent to group settings. Each copy of a magazine reaches a number of people, one at a time.

REPRODUCTION QUALITY

Although in practice there is a wide variation of reproduction quality among commercial magazines, technology available to the industry allows superior-quality printing. If the appearance of a product is important (such as in our example of flashy stereophonic equipment of interest to young professional buyers), magazines may provide the most effective means of showing off colours, details, and artful lines.

Manufacturers of automobiles, computers, major appliances, and even television sets, where product appearance is an important sales feature, make extensive use of magazines. Camera and film companies also use magazines frequently to demonstrate the kinds of photographs their equipment can deliver. Where product appearance is important, magazine advertising can become a persuasive medium.

In addition to allowing reproduction of high-quality photographs, magazine printing techniques enable the communicator to develop attractive charts and graphs that convey a good deal of information in a condensed space. Magazine quality permits intricate details to be presented in an attractive and pleasing format. Readers are first drawn to an advertisement, then introduced to details that may not be presented as effectively in other media.

Cost

The cost of magazine ad space is determined by several obvious factors. First, characteristics of the magazine itself include circulation, production quality, and, to a lesser degree, subscription rates, size of the magazine, characteristics of subscribers, and prestige of the publication. Generally, a wider circulation and higher production quality translate into higher advertising costs. Costs related to the other magazine features may be determined by what the market will bear. Most publishers naturally are in business to make a profit and charge the maximum rates advertisers are willing to pay to reach the audience delivered by the magazine.

Characteristics of any particular advertisement affect the cost depending on the frequency with which the ad is run, size, use of colour, and placement in the magazine. Rates tend to lower for more frequent placement, smaller ads, black-and-white ads, ads without photographs, and those placed in less conspicuous portions of the magazine. Before buying magazine space, consider several points.

First, how important is a particular publication? For instance, is *Stereo Review* the only magazine that reaches the desired audience, or will another, perhaps less costly journal deliver the same group? Often, some of the less-well-established magazines that nonetheless are reaching respectable audiences afford considerable savings. How much is the prestige worth?

Companies should avoid magazines that deliver a greater audience than is necessary. Remember one of the major advantages of this medium is its targetability—its capacity to reach precise audiences. If you buy more audience than you really need, that is, buy space in a publication with an audience that exceeds your target group, you forfeit the medium's targeting advantages. Finally, pay only for those features you really need. If colour and large photographs are not necessary to convey your message, why pay for such expensive features? Some think these elements draw in additional readership and therefore merit the expense.

While this may be so, one has to ask if audience attention can be attracted through less expensive means. Similarly, a quarter-page ad may be as effective for your purposes as a half- or fullpage production. Consider the added expense for the added dimensions. Review these questions and others with advertising consultants. In the long run, they may save costs by identifying features of magazine advertising that increase effectiveness.

MAGAZINE SUMMARY

Of the media that pinpoint receivers and deliver specific, targeted audiences to business communicators, none is so precise at its task as magazines. In specialized communication campaigns where targeting will play a major role, the logic of using magazines is compelling.

Magazine audiences are specific and they are dedicated. People buy magazines as an expression of their special interests, which extend beyond the editorial material to advertising content. Magazine ads are considered not as bothers but as bonuses and often are viewed as attentively. People often go through their magazines more than once and so are exposed more than once to the advertisements. This double exposure helps drive home a point.

Magazine readers share with others and so add a pass-along audience that increases the reach of the medium. With high-quality printing capabilities, magazines can provide sophisticated reproductions that go beyond other media in demonstrating the physical appearance of a product. Moods and images can be stimulated through the art of magazines. With their capacity to handle visual details and their permanence for readers, magazines can carry complex information in an acceptable, digestible format and, when necessary, do so in different ways with different audience groups.

DIRECT MAIL

Even magazines, with their impressive targeting capacity, cannot achieve the degree of audience specification possible through direct mail. Given the necessary information base and sufficient computer equipment, every member of an audience could receive a unique message targeted specifically to meet his or her particular needs.

While direct mail campaigns are rarely, if ever, so precise, they have grown increasingly more intimate in their contact with small audience blocks, dividing customer or constituent groups into very narrow units. Such a technique, applied to specialized communications, may offer many businesses a means of reaching certain audiences that cannot be contacted successfully through conventional mass media. Our meaning of "direct mail" for this discussion does not include just any communication sent through the mail from companies to customers.

We do not include in this category general delivery "occupant" mailings of sale fliers or handbills that everyone within a specified geographic area receives. Although this is a popular and often successful technique used by many local businesses and provides some measure of targeting (at the geographic level), it fails to meet the basic criteria for our meaning of direct mail.

Using our description, the practice of communicating through direct mail must meet the following criteria: First, audience members must be selected because of some particular trait or set of traits. For instance, everyone selected for the mailing list may be a college graduate, or a Republican, or someone who has bought a Chevrolet within the last three years.

More sophisticated audience selection procedures combine characteristics yielding, for example, a list of people who are college educated, Republican, Chevrolet buyers. Members of a direct mail audience may be selected for reasons including their demographic group identification (age, sex, and education), some ideological commitment (for example, their beliefs about ecology, nuclear proliferation, and First Amendment principles), or some particular identifying behaviour (for example, they purchased a product, signed a petition, or recently took a world cruise).

They may also be identified by group affiliation (such as membership in the chamber of commerce, the Democratic party, or the National Geographic Society), some special skill (for example, carpentry, mechanics, or public speaking), or special interest (stamp collecting, Zen study, or raising racing pigeons). Any characteristic that sets aside a person from the general population and identifies him or her with those of similar traits may be used as a basis on which to conduct a direct mail campaign. For our second characteristic of direct mail, the communicator must have some way to identify eligible audience members and use their names in the communication. He or she may accomplish this in a number of ways. Some who use direct mail techniques identify recipients by means of self-disclosure.

For example, many television evangelists (who incidentally are among the heaviest users of direct mail) often contact general audiences through television and radio and ask listeners to phone or write if they wish additional information or want to be on a mailing list. Those who respond are recognized by special computer codes and later contacted through letters that usually reference their previous contact. There are many other ways to identify special audiences. Mailing lists for just about any conceivable audience category can be purchased from commercial vendors.

Dunhill Business Mailing List Company, Inc., a large outfit in New York, has for sale as many as ten thousand separate lists. These lists are maintained on computer files and are constantly updated to ensure an accurate, complete collection. Dunhill and other similar companies sell computer-generated labels or computer files that may be integrated into popular business software for easy access. Considering the potential value to businesses and the significant cost of developing and maintaining such lists, the costs are reasonable (at around forty dollars per thousand names).

Many mail-order companies, associations, magazine publishers, and institutions also sell their mailing lists to businesses that want to reach certain categories of people. Most of us at some time have joined an organization or sent off for a catalog and soon after were deluged with mail from unfamiliar sources. More than likely someone made money by selling our names and addresses to these organizations. Political and special interest organizations such as the Democratic and Republican National Committees, the Sierra Club, and Common Cause make available their lists for cost to like-minded groups. This helps extend the influence and reach of such associations into populations that might be receptive to their positions. Finally, techniques of direct mail, as we describe them, must include a message specifically targeted to the receiver. In this characteristic lie the strength and purpose of the process. Direct mail is successful because it is directed. There is little purpose in sending material through the mail that could be disseminated more inexpensively through the mass media to all members of the general population.

We invest a good deal of effort and money in obtaining these specific lists, and it would be senseless not to benefit from the great advantages afforded by such targeted methods. Therefore, in our scheme, direct mailing procedures must have an evident component of targeting, not only in the selection of audience members but in the specification of messages as well. It follows that separate audience segments can be treated to separate messages designed to have a particular appeal. In a political campaign, for example, people in upper income brackets might be more interested in the candidate's position on tax policy than on many other matters.

So successful use of direct mail would include sending a letter and perhaps other information that would focus on tax issues. Working people with children might be interested more in the candidate's position on subsidies for day care; outdoor recreation enthusiasts might be drawn to a candidate's positions on the environment and forest land use. As people fall simultaneously into different groups, direct mail campaigns might combine these several interests into a single letter. As we noted earlier, audience research is necessary to identify the principal concerns within a general population. For targeted communication practices, however, and particularly direct mail, research is essential.

How else would a communicator know how to divide the audience and identify component subgroups? How else would one know the specific concerns of individuals within each of these smaller audience units? Research provides the insight necessary to discover a logic for targeting through direct mail. No matter how familiar a communicator is with a population, there is little likelihood that intuition can reveal accurately the information necessary to sort out a general audience and serve up the information that will prove most convincing to each member. Direct mail, like all methods of communication, is too costly to trust to hunches. Furthermore, if the issues at stake are sufficiently important to merit a direct mail campaign, it makes sense to employ research procedures most likely to ensure success. Through audience research, a communicator acquires specific information about who the receivers are and how they can best be approached through direct mail.

In each of the three criteria, then, the general audience mailer we discussed at the beginning of this part does not qualify for our specific meaning of direct mail procedures: It does not sort out audiences by any specific trait (except perhaps, in the broadest sense, geographic audience distinctions), it does not identify by name any specific audience member, nor does it make a distinction among recipients by targeting the message.

ADVANTAGES/DISADVANTAGES

Use of direct mail must be considered along with other communication possibilities offered by the mass media. As we have already discussed, radio and magazines stand as reasonable means of reaching targeted groups with specific messages. How does direct mail compare to these media? When might direct mail provide an advantage? Consider several features when deciding on the advisability of using direct mail in any particular application.

The most forceful feature of direct mail is its capacity to target an audience. With direct mail a communicator can send specific audiences specific information, custom designed to appeal to individual sensitivities. Letters are addressed directly to the individual, personalizing the message. Who among us in this day of anonymous communication does not take some pleasure in being treated with individual attention—even if we know a computer typed our name? From a theoretical perspective, such specific targeting made possible through direct mail techniques allows the mass communication process to come as close as it can to the rich, interpersonal communication environment. Interpersonal communication allows a one-on-one exchange, with messages designed to have specific appeal to one (or no more than a few) individual. Direct mail gives the communicator a means of getting in touch with a small number of similar people, using very particular appeals. Direct mail divides the audience and appeals to individuals, and by so doing provides an important tool for specialized communi-cation campaigns.

In addition to targeting, direct mail offers several other advantages worth noting. With this approach the communicator can send along coupons and special premiums such as pens, bookmarks, and other trinkets that may encourage a favourable attitude towards the sender. The gift also may foster in the recipient a sense of responsibility to read the enclosed letter or to scan the literature; after all, somcone has given the receiver something for free-the least he or she can do is see what that person has to say. Of course, this may have limited application for some groups; research can suggest those audiences for which including a premium would be profitable.

Coupons have been used with success in several campaigns to escalate the level of communication. It works this way. A company selects a list of prospects for a particular purpose and uses direct mail to contact each of these people. The material includes a form or coupon that the recipient is encouraged to send or bring back to the company. By returning the coupon, receivers show they wish additional information or to discuss matters further. With this technique the company trims its prospects' list to those especially interested in receiving more details.

It may even be used to set up a face-toface meeting with the prospect and company representatives. In both cases the coupon has worked to escalate the level of communication. In an exchange reminiscent of a conversation, the company sends information and the receiver responds with a request for additional contact. This establishes a productive dialogue with members of specialized audiences, increasing at each step the sophistication of the communication exchange. Targeting and the capacity to establish a basis on which to escalate the communication process with special audiences are two of the most attractive features of direct mail. The technique is not without its problems, however. First, in the minds of many people, direct mail and junk mail are synonymous. Some people never bother to open a "promotional" letter, and frequent senders of direct mail recognize this problem.

More than a few clever graphic artists have worked hard to combat this instant rejection of direct mail. They have developed a variety of techniques to invite readers into the envelope. Depending on the purpose of a mailing-the image a message source hopes to project and the tastes of the receivers-one or several of the following techniques may be appropriate. The first is the envelope "teaser," where a riddle or interesting question is emblazoned on the front or back.

One company provided instructions for building a curious-looking gadget but never said on the envelope what it was designed to do. The receiver had to open the envelope to discover the answer. There is no guarantee that people will look for anything but an answer to the riddle or question, but at least the technique might succeed at getting people inside the envelope. Some companies use bright, attractively coloured envelopes to draw the receiver's attention.

Companies who sell flowers, artists' supplies, and other products where colour is inherent have done well with this technique. It has also worked for companies whose product does not have a bright physical component but whose image is conveyed well by colour, for instance, travel agencies (who promise colourful tours and cruises) and businesses related to catering and parties. Certainly, colour may be effective in a variety of other applications, although one should be aware that such a display may be incompatible with the more sedate image some communicators wish to project.

While colour serves the needs of some, the "official look" has been adopted by others. Here, the envelope design resembles a bill or official mailing (for example, from the Internal Revenue Service). Usually a plastic window is used to display the receiver's name and address. The return address may have some official-sounding reference such as the "Office of the President" or the "Director of Finance." One would be unlikely to throw away this letter that might hold important information. Even if the receiver suspects that it is a promotional piece, does he or she dare take the chance?

Other designs have included letters that look as though they contain checks. Who would not open such a letter to see if, indeed, there is a check inside? Some include a good portion of the message right on the envelope, promising sweepstake winnings and chances for gifts and prizes—if only the receiver will open the envelope to look inside. Some audiences wise up to this trick, others fall for it every time.

For many direct mail campaigns designed to reach professional audiences, the best technique is to design a letter that looks like a letter. Use a standard, printed, business-size envelope with the person's name typed plainly across the front. We suggest the envelope bear the receiver's typewritten address rather than a gummed computer-generated address label. The gummed label is a last resort and should be used only if names and addresses cannot be typed directly onto the envelope. In a recent study, the authors sent five hundred surveys with typewritten addresses on the envelopes and five hundred surveys with gummed labels to a randomly selected list of public relations professionals.

Those who received envelopes with typewritten addresses were more likely to return the completed surveys. Although this study involved a great many variables, findings on this one feature suggest it does make a difference whether one provides that personalized look. With the easy availability of computer facilities, the typewritten look is within reason for many, even large-scale, applications.

Envelope feeders can be installed on printers connected to computers that automatically prepare each envelope. Software programmes minimize operator time. In order to complete the premium direct mailing, one must also personalize the contents of the letter and other material. Rather than using a generic salutation, it is more effective to use the recipient's name. It is also advisable to use the person's name in the text of the letter as well—for instance, "As you know,

George, it has become essential that..." Again, computer technology, already available to most businesses, makes possible such personalization. Inexpensive software allows one to insert the recipient's name in the text, wherever desired. The final appearance is indistinguishable from a hand-typed copy. In keeping with the strengths of direct mail, different letters can be developed for receivers with different backgrounds and interests. In this way, one of the disadvantages of direct mail—the junk mail appearance—can be converted into one of its greatest strengths. Envelopes and letters can look as though they were meant only for one person.

One additional feature of direct mail that may become a disadvantage is its cost. Large-scale mailings can be expensive. In such instances, one may wish to examine the logic of using direct mail rather than the mass media. Sometimes even such large-scale mailings are defendable because they allow targeting in ways not possible with the mass media. The anticipated results may be worth the extra expense. Even smaller mailings, however, can becostly.

By treating each audience member individually and providing customised, individually delivered messages, costs are bound to be a factor. On this issue of costs, we like to examine the purpose of a message, features of the intended recipients of a message, and the expected results of the campaign. If we are convinced direct mail can achieve results not possible through alternative means of message distribution, and our goals for a campaign are sufficiently compelling, as suggested, be willing to accept the higher associated costs. In special communications for business applications, direct mail is often a well-justified technique.

MEDIA MIX

The media as though their uses were mutually exclusive. Certainly, many of the media representatives would have us believe their medium was the only realistic way to proceed in a campaign. It has been our experience that several media often can be used in coordination to achieve a level of results not possible with just a single one. The media have different audiences and yield different effects. They can present information in different ways at different stages of a campaign. As different equipment serves different functions in a battle, the media serve different goals in a communication campaign; yet all converge on a single objective. Television, for instance, has been used successfully to call attention to messages carried in other media. Publisher's Clearing House runs many television commercials to alert people about direct mail pieces. Grocery stores often conclude a television spot by suggesting viewers see the local newspaper for sale prices.

The media also work well together to reinforce campaign messages. Magazines and television have been used by soap, toiletry, and prepared food companies who show the same actors and the same scenes and even use the same narratives in both media. The objective in these cases is to strengthen the message by displaying it in two formats. Seeing the message in each of two media may have a greater cumulative effect than seeing the message twice in a single medium.

Not only is the impact greater, but, when used properly, there can be considerable cost savings. Television commercials can be referenced by other media, thus extending the power of the medium without incurring its full costs. In direct mail, newspapers, magazines, and even billboards, advertisers may cite a slogan used in a television spot, or say something like "as seen on television." With this, the salience and legitimacy conveyed by television are evoked and used to reinforce these qualities in a product or service. The advertiser thus extends the impact of his or her television messages without having to pay for repeated airings. The commercial may run only a few dozen times, but enjoy an impact that is sustained through the other media.

Emerging from these few examples is the point that from the business communicator's perspective—the media are not in competition with each other. They can serve a complementary purpose. In a campaign that establishes a tone and provides cues that link together the family of messages disseminated over more than one medium, there is evidence of a synergy that yields greater results than might be expected from these media individually. The media can work together to magnify results of a campaign. We urge, therefore, that rather than a single medium, the communicator consider using a media blend.

Media selection must be based on several criteria: the purpose of a campaign, positions held by receivers, media usage traits of intended audiences, and financial considerations (costs of the media and resources of the communicator). In the context of other features involved in the general development of a campaign strategy, these factors serve as the basis on which to select appropriate media channels. We cannot provide here a formula to prescribe a precise means of identifying the proper media mix.

Many subjective considerations and unique local concerns make development of a generic scheme impossible. We can, however, discuss briefly the elements that factor into media selection decisions.

Purpose

The overall strategy of a communication campaign should be based in part on audience research and on the examination of each of the components of the communication process: source, message, channel, and receiver. The communicator then has a basis on which to manipulate features of the communication process to achieve the stated goals of a campaign.

The purpose of a campaign, then, will guide in selection of the media used to achieve these objectives. Consider an imaginary campaign for a small travel agency, using this strategy. The agency finds too much of its operation is going for low-yield activities such as brokering airline tickets and arranging for local tours, bringing small profit. To improve its earnings, the agency source decides to try attracting business for higher-profit luxury tours (the receiver) and a more elite clientele who travel more frequently and use first-class services (second receiver). Suppose further that investigation (research) reveals that those who use premium services have a poor image of the agency and do not think it capable of handling their travel needs. Such findings suggest a communication strategy that works not only on disseminating information about new tour packages (message) but on reshaping the agency image as well (second message). Considering the purpose of the campaign in determining media applications, then, selected media must (1) convey a new image and (2) disseminate information about new tour services.

Which of the media channels can best be used to achieve these purposes with the intended audience? We know the mass media can succeed at image building, and assuming research supports patronage by this audience, magazines may be an excellent way of conveying this appearance. Regional issues of prestigious magazines may provide the best vehicle with which to exhibit the new chic agency image. The second purpose of the campaign—to inform people about the agency's new tours (which may be delayed until the later portions of the campaign, when the new image has begun to take hold)—may best be announced in the travel part of the Sunday paper where changes can be made weekly. Radio, too, may be involved during this information stage.

An evaluation of the purpose of the campaign enables us to identify which of the available media may best bring about desired results from the intended audience. Elements that factor into this determination include:

- Availability of media
- Creative strategies (for example, if pictures are required)
- How much repetition is desired
- If a permanent print medium is necessary to list schedules and detailed information
- Time demands (how much advance time is required to prepare messages)

While these are important in relating the purpose of the campaign to media selection, three other criteria ultimately must contribute to final decisions on a media mix. Audience research reveals information about positions held by receivers and their media usage traits, the next two considerations in this process. The biggest mistake made by novice business communi-cators is to omit the research phase of a campaign. To save money or time, or perhaps because of some unyielding depen-dence on intuition, people sometimes embark on a costly communication programme without the benefits of research to guide strategic decisions. In this particular application, research would outline the attitudes and knowledge bases of the subgroups.

It would divide the audience into targetable groups (by demographics, predispositions, outlooks on the issue, etc.) and suggest ways each might be reached. For instance, we might learn that older potential clients of the travel agency prefer to take packaged cruises arranged through their groups or churches. They might not look closely at the agency's credentials or image, but rely on group organizers to examine such things before signing on with an agency.

This would suggest that we concentrate not on the end-users but on group and church leaders who broker such services for their constituents. This could save us a good deal of money and improve our chances of success. Research might discover that young, single travellers view premium cruises as a place to meet other people their ages. We also might learn that perceptions of our travel agency among this group are that we cannot fulfill their expectations. Perhaps they see us as stodgy or for some reason unable to provide the stylish service expected. All of this information about possible target groups is essential in identifying audiences and preparing unique strategies for each.

It is impossible to examine every contingency through examples, but the point is clear: Through research, we are able to describe and define individual audience groups and learn about the positions each holds towards the issues of concern and about us as a source. This information is essential in making decisions about media selection. Research also reveals where our audiences obtain their information. A good audience measurement study will identify media outlets patronized by audiences and suggest those that will deliver a concentration of our target group members. Obviously, such information is important in media selection and should be given serious consideration. The ideal media solutions are often not possible because of one final criterion—the financial consideration. More than any other factor, financial constraints establish the limits of our plans. Depending on the magnitude of difference between costs of the "ideal" media mix and the media programme we can afford, several solutions may be entertained.

First, we may consider using all of the media originally planned, but reducing the frequency of our messages. Rather than ten radio spots per week, we may run only five; two newspaper ads may have to serve the place of four. We may also cut production costs by reducing the number of ads produced. Instead of three different television spots, perhaps two will do. In this case, we may run the spots the same number of times, but rotate two rather than three of them. Another way to use all the desired media on a limited budget is to reduce the time or space of each ad.

Use quarter-page instead of halfpage ads, ten-second rather than thirty-second spots. Although we might anticipate the possibility of missing our target audience, we also might consider shifting our ads to less expensive time slots. Move prime-time ads to prime access hours, buy space in the back rather than the front of a magazine.

If, even with these measures, costs remain beyond our budget, consider these other changes: First, reduce message sophistication. Use a black-andwhite rather than colour magazine ad or line art rather than photos. Use voiceovers with stock footage rather than on-camera actors in television commercials. Although this may tamper seriously with our audience-targeting plans, fall back on secondary media within the general category.

For instance, use a less desirable television station or magazine because it is less costly. This would be acceptable only if our research indicated the fall-back medium retained a sufficient target audience block. Obviously, it would be unwise to select an alternative medium simply because it was cheaper, if it missed our primary target group. We would hope a combination of these economizing approaches would lower media expenses to an acceptable range. If even the pared-down programme exceeded budgetary limitations, there would be little choice but to begin eliminating the most costly media and allowing the remaining channels to get out the message. Problems here are evident.

By severing media outlets, one inevitably loses portions of the audience. We would also expect that any synergistic or compounding effects enjoyed in a multi-media campaign would be lost. Nonetheless, limiting a campaign to less than the ideal combination of media outlets is often necessary and with creative strategies can still be made to work.

One final point must be made about the relationship between campaign strategy and funding. Even though the budget may ultimately circumscribe the design of a communication programme, we feel strongly that it not be used initially to define the elements of that programme. In other words, we are opposed to the approach where one looks at the budget and determines from this how much radio time or newspaper space can be afforded. This method stands the entire planning process on its end. It allows financial concerns to override the thoughtful strategies of audience targeting.

It discounts individual audience subgroups, ignores the needs and concerns of these groups, and dismisses procedures that strive to match the audience with the media. Costs may limit but should not dictate a programme. It is hazardous for companies serious about reaching specialized audiences to skip over essential planning elements and allow costs to drive the design.

When using the plans we have endorsed, even though the ideal approach ultimately may be altered because of funding, a communicator makes informed changes in strategy, cutting here and there in a way that renders the best possible (although perhaps financially constrained) plan. Building strategy from a foundation of audience considerations is a proven success; building strategy from the budget down is a dangerous approach.

5

Interpersonal Communication

ONE-ON-ONE DESIGNS

In many business communication settings, interpersonal contacts will bring about the most tangible audience effects. Mass media messages can inform and, to a large extent, persuade audience members, but interpersonal communication will often serve to solidify attitudes and elicit behaviour. The use of interpersonal communication in specialized communication campaigns and explores reasons for its effectiveness.

We also examine how mass media and interpersonal portions of a campaign should be joined to achieve an effective communication package. Our love for the mass media has not dampened our passion for one-on-one, interpersonal communication. Distant third-party relationships, intrinsic to mass communication settings, have heightened our need to be treated as individuals. We appreciate the entertainment and information offered by the mass media, but we tire of being cast into large, anonymous audiences by programmers and advertisers who blend us into demographic blocks for generic treatment.

We prefer small shops to large department stores because the shopkeepers call us by name and cater to our personal needs; we know them and they know us. Letters addressed to us directly rather than to "occupant" usually attract our attention. A personal phone call or a visit from a political candidate has greater impact, not necessarily because of what the candidate says, but because he or she says it directly to us.

Throughout this book we argue strongly for the use of mass media in public communication programmes. Their success has been well documented; indeed, we cannot communicate on any reasonable scale today without extensive media use. We describe a form of communication that supplements the mass media. We present a background discussion and examine details of interpersonal communication techniques to expand the repertoire of options available for specialized communication campaigns. Some business communicators might find little application for such techniques. Other companies that have never considered such an approach to customer contact might find these methods an efficient and valuable means of reaching beyond mass media.

At the conceptual level, interpersonal techniques are no more than an extension of the targeting principles that have guided discussions of the mass media. The scheme that placed media on a continuum ranging from those that serve broad, heterogeneous audiences at one end to those appealing to narrow, homogeneous audiences at the other. For the large mass media, such as network television, audiences are characterized by the blending of personal traits.

These audiences represent a cross section of the general population. For narrow media, we see select audiences identified by their parochialism and uniformity. Among these audiences, for instance, we may find sports fishermen with a special interest in surf casting or gourmet cooks with a flair for pastries. In addition to special interest divisions, we may also identify narrow audiences by demographic features, ideological commitment, group membership, and a variety of other characteristics. We recognize such groups by their commonalities.

Such identifying features are important. They serve as a basis for audience targeting or focusing communication activities towards ever more specific, distinctive, homogeneous clusters. Taken to its extreme, targeting converges with interpersonal, one-on-one communication. Although definitions of interpersonal communication differ by author, most agree about what it involves. Wright describes interpersonal communication as "involving only a few people, often similar to one another in important respects, known to a communicator whose messages are addressed to them privately and are constructed and conveyed directly rather than through the complex formal organization of mass media". Rogers and Schoemaker see interpersonal communi-cation as involving a "faceto-face exchange between two or more individuals". Other writers offer similar descriptions that convey a relative intimacy between senders and receivers.

For our use of the term, people need not be face to face as Rogers and Schoemaker suggest, nor do they need to be similar, as Wright proposes. We hold that interpersonal communication, as applied to business communication, involves receiver-specific messages. The source tailors his or her communication for each receiver, progressively modifying messages in an interactive fashion based on feedback information. Interpersonal communication can be face to face or it can be interposed by a medium that permits a two-way flow of information (for instance, a telephone or two-way radio). Interactants need not know each other, although they must respond specifically to each other's messages.

INTERPERSONAL VERSUS MASS COMMUNICATION

Let us refine the notion of interpersonal communications for our particular application to specialized programmes by contrasting interpersonal with mass communication. We characterize these differences along several dimensions of utility for the programme designer.

These two forms of communication differ to the following features:

- Feedback characteristics,
- Audience selection features, and
- Channels of communication.

FEEDBACK CHARACTERISTICS

Information obtained by the source from the receiver. It may be information acquired before the communication programme begins. In this case it is used to formulate strategy by providing details about receiver perceptions of the source, positions on the issues, and media usage patterns. Furthermore, feedback information obtained during a campaign helps the communicator adjust and modify programmes to accommodate changing audiences.

At best, mass audience feedback information reflects the statistical average of the studied population. We can examine groups and clusters, but we cannot focus on narrow audiences without losing statistical validity or engaging in elaborate research designs. Moreover, the information we obtain in large audience settings usually is structured and constrained. It is derived typically from survey questionnaires that offer preplanned (and usually sender-developed) questions and answers. Extemporaneous responses unique to individuals are rarely manageable, given the nature of survey research that imposes a high degree of uniformity on the data.

Since our ability to generalize sample data to the overall population is dependent in part on consistent responses, survey research procedures strive to cluster and collapse responses into uniform arrays. Simply put, except for anecdotal purposes, individual responses have no statistical validity and therefore are of little use in understanding an audience. All of this suggests that feedback obtained from mass audiences has restricted application: It is structured, nonspecific, and limited in its capacity to describe small subgroups within the population.

These drawbacks, feedback obtained in mass audience settings is nearly always delayed. It takes time to develop, administer, analyse, and deliver data from a large audience survey, despite major efforts in recent times to speed up the system. One political consulting outfit in Washington, D.C. has attempted to expedite the process by providing an overnight polling service. These, of course, are limited surveys with a small number of questions delivered by telephone to a limited voter sample. Furthermore, there is little possibility for subgroup study, given the small sample involved. Strides are being made to deliver mass audience survey information faster than previously possible, but even these efforts fail to overcome the inherent delays in mass audience feedback. Several technological innovations are being examined to gather feedback quickly. Test units in Columbus, Ohio, and Rock Island, Illinois, have demonstrated the possibility for home television viewers to transmit their "votes" to a central computer for instant tabulation.

At least in this limited setting, we may be able to poll certain segments of the audience and obtain results quickly. Even here, though, it is difficult to conceive of feedback information in the mass audience setting approaching the speed and quality of interpersonal feedback. The short shelf life of data is one potentially serious problem with the delay of mass audience feedback information. During the time lapse between data collection and availability of information, conditions in the environment might change, rendering this information invalid. Take, for instance, a poll measuring public attitudes towards services provided by local governments. We know public attitudes on such issues shift daily according to headlines, public discussion, and other topics on the public agenda.

When we ask someone a question about government services may determine what that person's response will be. Our data gathered seven days earlier may not reflect public sentiment today. At most we can hope there have been no major events such as scandals in city hall or garbage workers' strikes that would affect large portions of the public, thus rendering useless any information gathered previously. Even without such major events impacting the population, we can anticipate some degree of change and therefore some inaccuracy as our data age. The older the data, the more skeptical we must become.

Feedback information available in an interpersonal exchange, however, is rich, specific, and rapid. Such characteristics enable the flow of interpersonal communication events to proceed with an ease and efficiency that cannot be replicated in a mass communication environment. Interpersonal feedback information is rich because it can contain a wealth of information on a number of levels. In a typical conversation, for example, we obtain information from the other person first by listening to what that person has to say. We need only ask if we want to clarify an ambiguous point or to get more details.

Typical conversations proceed through a series of repetitions that clarify, refine, and elaborate. Besides the words exchanged, interactants learn information from each other through nonverbal cues. Vocal intonation reveals intensity of feeling and emotion that may be missed by the words alone. When asked how they are doing today, two people may respond that they are "fine." The first may have an upbeat tone and a lively bounce to his "fine," showing a positive state of mind.

The second person's "fine," however, with its unhappy, listless timbre, reveals a sour, despondent mood. Both have said the same word, but because the response tone differed in each case, the information obtained is not the same. The first person seems to be fine; the second appears to be troubled. In this case and in many instances, according to some nonverbal communication specialists, the tone used reveals more of the truth than the words themselves.

Feedback cues in interpersonal settings go beyond the words and vocal tone. We come to understand other people in conversations by observing their gesticulations (arm movements and gestures), facial expressions, posture, dress, and other physical features. They exhibit more than their words convey. A fist shaken in anger reveals an intense feeling that words may not express adequately. To some, folded arms suggest a person is blocking or wishes to protect something. We interpret differently someone's laughter, depending on whether it is a chortle, a giggle, or a guffaw.

As with verbal tone, such cues communicate information that is often more complete and representative of a person's frame of mind than are his or her words. When these cues are joined with verbal and tonal information, the richness of feedback available in an interpersonal setting becomes evident. Compared to the mass communication environment, we have a greater variety of levels from which to draw, and at each of these levels we often find cues more complete and detailed.

Specific Information

Feedback information in an interpersonal setting is specific to one individual. We noted that mass audience feedback is a statistical average of data provided by a large number of respondents. From this we are able to understand general sentiments and trends within a population, but cannot pinpoint any specific individual. Even small target groups within the general population often elude us because they cannot adequately be represented in fact-finding research. In personal conversations, though, we can obtain specific information.

If the other person looks puzzled, or scratches his head, or expresses confusion or doubt, we know we must provide clarity or a new line of reasoning. The point is, we are able to provide a specific message because we have specific feedback information. Research and practical experience demonstrate that the success of our communications is directly related to the specificity of our messages.

Rapid Feedback

If, over a cup of coffee, you were to ask a friend whom she planned to vote for in an upcoming congressional election, you might have your answer within seconds. Assume you then asked why she intended to vote this way. Again, within seconds, you would have an answer. The feedback in such an interpersonal encounter is very fast. With such information at hand, you might then performance immediately to confirm your friend's choice of candidates or challenge her decision with the hope of bringing her around to your viewpoint.

By contrast, the same questions about candidate preference are the stock and trade of many political polling firms that attempt to learn how people in the general public plan to vote in upcoming elections. For these outfits, however, there is considerable lag time between survey administration and information availability. Days may pass before information about voter preferences is accessible to campaign staffs for forming strategy. As we have discussed, not only does this protract the communication process, but also conditions and voter sentiments can change, thus making the facts outdated. The rapid exchange of information common to interpersonal communications is one of its biggest advantages. The information can be used for an immediate response, thus sustaining the give-and-take features of interpersonal communication. It represents the individual's thinking at the moment; hence, it is fresh and uncontaminated by factors that occur over time.

In summary, despite the efforts of people in mass communication to improve the quality of feedback, it is doubtful that they can ever achieve the level of information we see in the interpersonal setting. The information in an interpersonal communication encounter is rich. There are a variety of cues that enhance and refine the communication's meaning. This information is specific to one individual and so allows individual treatment by communicators. Finally, the information (in most settings) is immediately available, allowing rapid assessment and response by others in the discussion.

Audience Selection

In mass communication settings, companies typically seek out the audience. In most of the recommended interpersonal designs, audiences seek out the companies. The distinction is significant for two reasons: (1) In the interpersonal context, audiences play an active role; and (2) they sort themselves into categories of interested information seekers. Businesses that employ interpersonal techniques find that in part because of these features, communication activities differ from those in the mass audience portions of their campaigns.

The receiver provides much of the energy getting information from the source to the receiver. In addition, largely because audiences are self-selected, a greater portion of the messages falls on receptive ears. A larger share of interested people exists in these audiences than in general mass audience groups. As suggested, examine these two features of audience selection in more detail.

The Active Audience Role

In the mass communication setting, the burden of audience identification is on our shoulders. We gather survey data; then, we sort through them to identify target audiences. We match up audience needs and interests with appropriate messages, and we locate the media best suited to deliver these messages to target audiences. During all of this, audience members are passive players, perhaps choosing to examine our message, perhaps not, depending on distractions, our skill at stimulating attention, and the whim of the moment.

In the interpersonal designs we propose, audiences come to us for information and thereby shift at least a portion of the burden to their own shoulders. They identify themselves as prospects for information and place themselves in the path of our targeted messages. By taking this role, they eliminate a portion of our responsibility.

Moreover, they commit themselves (however slight the commitment) to the communication transaction. They have expended an effort to call, write, or visit us, and accordingly have invested something of their own in the process. The time and energy involved in that phone call, or in filling out a postcard, or in driving to an exhibit represent a cost to the individuals that makes them more than passive onlookers. The most important clues to an individual's inner states are found in his behaviour. When we want to know how a person feels, we look to see how he acts.

The theory about the origins of an individual's self-knowledge predicts that he might also infer his own internal states by observing his own overt behaviour. We believe, since we are thinking, rational people, that if we engage in some behaviour, it must be because we have sufficient reason to do so. We find an uncomfortable inconsistency between incompatible attitudes and behaviours. We believe our behaviours are underwritten by a set of consonant attitudes. To expect otherwise would cause doubt about our own rationality. So it follows that if we can stimulate audience members to take an active role in the communication process by performing even some small behaviour, such as making a phone call or sending in a postcard, we may encourage formation of a positive attitude about the communication interaction. After all, they have invested something of themselves.

There must be something valuable in the communication, or, as rational people, they would not have bothered to spend the time and effort. We see, then, that by engaging an audience in the interpersonal features of a communication campaign, we have begun to change the general nature of the receiver. The simple step of involving people in an active way may encourage development of attitudes that render message recipients more receptive to our arguments. We should examine one additional feature of an active audience. As we describe recommended interpersonal programmes for business communication campaigns, the audience, through our promotion and encouragement, seeks us out for additional information. We then increase the level of information flow and ultimately establish a working interpersonal relationship.

At the point where receivers first request specific information and involve us in a one-on-one dialogue, they become the recipients of our offerings. They have requested something of us (even if it is only information designed to sell them something) and we have complied. To some, even limited degree, the recipients may feel a sense of obligation to us. After all, we have provided a booklet or letter, our time on the phone, or some premium based solely on their request.

The scales of fair play may be tipped in our favour, and the recipients may feel they owe us something—even if only a bit more time or further consideration of our position. We are not suggesting the recipients perceive a great debt for our small accommodation. We propose only that they have formed an attitude that establishes a more desirable relationship between the communicator and the audience. Note how this is different from, say, a direct mail campaign where the communicator sends out information and perhaps a premium.

Receivers may read the material for a variety of reasons; they may even sense an obligation because of the free gift. But since the material was unsolicited, they do not feel the same level of responsibility to the source. The company has not responded to their request and provided information at their bidding. They are not responsible for the sender's efforts in this case, and therefore have little sense of indebtedness.

In summary, when audiences assume an active role in the communication process, several advantages accrue to the business source. First, when audiences come to the source for information, they save that source a good deal of energy. Those who become involved in interpersonal programmes infer from their behaviours an attitude about their own commitment to the process. Finally, by taking an active role, audiences develop some sense of indebtedness to a company that has responded to their requests. Even at the outset, interpersonal programmes enjoy several advantages over mass appeal portions of a communication campaign.

Audience Sorting

One of the biggest challenges faced in targeted audience campaigns is the identification of groups that will have a special interest in the topic at hand. Success of the targeted communication process is based in part on the capacity of a company to be effective at this task.

Once the company has found its audience and established initial mass media contact, it is up to the receivers to recognize their interest in an issue and take the next step in the communication process. Interpersonal audiences are self-selected. Those who choose to engage in interpersonal portions of a campaign do so because they see something relevant for themselves. They recognize a personal interest or merit in the topic that appeals especially to them.

Two advantages result from audience sorting. First, we expect those who have joined the interpersonal audience to have a reasonable level of interest in the topic. They should therefore require less persuading, thus allowing the company to devote more energy to information matters. Interpersonal audiences also see that the issue relates to them personally. People who call hospital hot lines for help with particular medical or psychological difficulties do so because they are troubled by these problems. They not only take an interest in the response, but know the answer relates to their own condition. Consequently, people running these hot lines need spend no time convincing callers that the proposed solutions apply to their ailment. People call precisely because they recognize this relevance.

This sorting process yields an audience ideal for the business communicator. Of the entire population, these receivers are most likely receptive to persuasion. They are interested, so they will listen. They see relevance, so they need little urging.

Physical Setting

In most of the interpersonal communication designs proposed, we attempt to maximize the face-to-face (or voice-to-voice) contact between the source and receiver. Interpersonal programmes that work closest with people work best. An increase in the number of physical barriers placed between the source and receiver decreases the impact of the communication. Suppose we have fashioned our interpersonal communi-cation plan based on a correspondence course that uses the mail to carry messages between the source and receiver. This is an example of interpersonal communication. There is a one-on-one exchange of messages between the source and receiver, and each communication is tailored especially for the intended recipient.

There are considerable physical barriers, however, that hamper the rapid, efficient information flow we have come to expect in interpersonal scenarios. Even on a good day, the mail will be too slow to permit a smooth, unbroken flow of messages. We are also limited in the kinds of information that can be transmitted. We lose rich detail because elements such as nonverbal facial and body cues and vocal intonations cannot be transmitted. The only special feature of interpersonal communication retained is the specificity and focus enjoyed when communi-cating with one rather than many receivers. Here, physical barriers have become obstacles that weaken the communi-ation process.

Many companies recognize that the mail is inefficient as the mainstay of an interpersonal programme; consequently, they have turned to the telephone and primarily the tollfree 800 numbers to provide customers with a convenient alternative. They employ the phone to establish initial contact, then follow through with mailings or personal visits. In other cases the phone is primary for all phases of the interpersonal programme.

In several respects, telephone programmes are a vast improvement over a mail-only design. First, phones require little effort by audience members and are convenient. People who will not take time to fill out and mail a postcard may find a moment to place a free call. They can make a phone call on impulse. Writing requires more effort. Hence, we may expect marginal audience members to be drawn into an interpersonal communication programme simply because the phone is easier than the mail.

Phones also speed the exchange of information. No delay occurs between the delivery and receipt of a message, so one participant can react immediately to the comments of the other. Companies use phones to provide instant product information before and after a sale. Computer software companies maintain phone lines to explain new products and make immediate sales. Many also provide trouble lines to assist customers after the sale with technical information to get programmes up and running. Often, time and money are at stake for business software users; when customers need help, they need it right away.

Finally, the physical barriers imposed by telephones prohibit visual contact, but they do allow vocal cues. We hear not only what is said, but how it is said. We can often detect anger, excitement, anxiety, or pleasure by the way someone sounds. Sometimes in a telephone conversation, the most subtle cue—silence—can convey more information than words. For communications that require a visual component without special equipment, the physical barriers of the telephone obviously render it useless. For other applications, though, telephones do not seriously impede the communication flow.

Face-to-face communications are superior to all others. They permit the specific, directed message exchanges allowed by mail and telephone interactions, and, as in telephone conversations, they enable people to exchange information rapidly. However, they accommodate the full complement of nonverbal cues. Without any physical barriers to block, slow, or interfere with the exchange of information, face-to-face communications are superior. There may be other problems—logistics, cost, and resource commitment—but from the standpoint of persuasion, these interpersonal approaches offer the best communication environment.

CHANNELS

Mass media channels reach many receivers at one time, and interpersonal channels link the source to one receiver. It is easy to recognize the misappropriation of a channel. We would find it odd for Procter and Gamble to phone us (using a channel associated with interpersonal contact) with a thirtysecond discussion on the benefits of its floor wax. We expect to find such messages on television or radio. We also would find it strange if a senatorial candidate were to knock on the door of every home in the state to explain his or her position on pending legislation. Here, too, we expect to see such messages carried by one of the traditional mass media.

The use of public media for private messages also strikes us as strange. We laugh at the Romeo who asks his Juliet for her hand in marriage—in a newspaper classified ad. Many people feel awkward about televised discussions of sex by Dr. Ruth Westheimer. How can a topic so personal be aired in a medium so public? We feel acceptable channels exist for private communications, and these rarely include the public media.

Distinctions between public and private channels reside in the capacity of a medium to designate its audience. If a medium enables us to reach only one person, we consider it to be an interpersonal channel. If it cannot single out just one person, we call it a public or mass audience channel. Commercial radio stations, for instance, may reach targeted audiences, but they cannot pinpoint one and only one listener. So they are not considered interpersonal channels.

Ham radios and CBs, however, come very close to meeting the criteria of interpersonal media because people can use them to direct messages at individual operators. By the strictest definition, this is a hybrid category. Sometimes it can reach just one individual; at other times it may reach a large number of peripheral listeners. The telephone is the best telecommunication example of an interpersonal medium.

Feedback is one other characteristic that distinguishes public from private channels. In his early writings on comparisons between public and private communications, Deutschman noted that both could involve face-toface encounters. We can have a private (or interpersonal) face-to-face conversation over a cup of coffee or a public, face-to-face meeting at a political rally. Deutschman also observed that both could involve communications interposed by some medium.

Our private conversation may be interposed by a telephone, and our public communication may be interposed by television, radio, or newspapers. The difference between the channels is their capacity to carry a two-way flow of information; in other words, how well they carry feedback. Interpersonal channels provide for feedback. They allow the source to talk to the receiver, and they allow the receiver to talk back. The importance of feedback in distinguishing mass from interpersonal communication.

We provide better information when we know what the receivers want, and we may learn what they want if they can tell us. Faster, richer, more specific information is available in the interpersonal setting; mass audience feedback pales by comparison. In order to obtain such detail, we must have a channel that allows information to travel in both directions. In successful, interpersonal communication programmes, the communicator guarantees a two-way flow.

The trouble with mass communication is that movement of its feedback information is impeded. A channel that carries a sender's message cannot simultaneously carry a receiver's reply. This results in a unidirectional flow of information that is bound to be less responsive to audience needs than is a two-way system. When public communicators obtain feedback information, they must go outside their channel. They rely on public surveys, letters to the editor, phone calls, and other approaches.

Distinctions, then, between interpersonal and mass audience channels are twofold: Interpersonal channels can pinpoint specific receivers; mass channels cannot. Interpersonal channels allow a bidirectional information flow; mass audience channels work in only one direction.

RELATIONSHIPS BETWEEN INTERPERSONAL AND MASS COMMUNICATION PHASES

Traditional thinking holds that mass media channels inform, while interpersonal channels persuade. This scheme, the total impact of a communication campaign should be a product of shared responsibility between mass media that prepares the audience and interpersonal programmes that yield behavioural changes. Together these phases provide the combination necessary to achieve maximum impact on target audiences. We recognize merit in such a position and will adopt this basic paradigm in our proposals for the ideal targeted communication campaign.

However, we need to offer an important caveat about the suggested limitation of the mass media to play more than an informational role in the communication process. During the last decade, with increasingly sophisticated approaches to audience analysis and refined message development techniques, the mass media have demonstrated a greater capacity to serve as persuasive tools.

Much of the research that led to beliefs about the media's limited communication role was conducted more than thirty years ago when the media played a lesser part in our lives. Seminal investigations by Lazarsfeld revealed that people voted not in accordance with their exposure to mass media messages about a candidate, but in a manner consistent with their interpersonal communication patterns. In other words, Lazarsfeld concluded, the mass media did not persuade people to vote for a particular candidate. Instead, the media provided information to certain members of society, called "opinion leaders."

They in turn, through interpersonal encounters, persuaded others to vote in a certain way. Lazarsfeld called this process the "two-step" flow of communication. Information was disseminated through the mass media to opinion leaders; then, these opinion leaders persuaded the remaining members of society—the followers.

In a later study, Katz and Lazarsfeld examined the sources of influence on several behaviours including marketing, fashions, and movie going. Here, too, researchers found that decisions were made according to interpersonal contact and persuasion rather than mass media exposure. In other words, people looked to other people for their purchasing decisions. They sought the advice of others about products they purchased and movies they attended.

It was not the media but the recommendations of acquaintances that affected their final decisions. Note that Katz and Lazarsfeld found their respondents turned to different people for advice on different matters. For purchases of household products, for instance, people sought advice from older women, and particularly those with large families; young girls provided advice on movie going. Menzel and Katz looked at the product adoption phenomenon among physicians and discovered similar patterns.

Those who were the earliest adopters of new prescription drugs were most likely to be heavy readers of medical journals. They also maintained contact with professional groups by attending conferences and visiting medical institutions. Almost to a person, later adopters relied on the recommendation of other physicians before prescribing a new drug. Here, as in research on the general population, the interpersonal influence was most important in determining final adoption. Rogers and Schoemaker investigated these relationships between source influence and persuasion in other cultures. They examined innovation adoption patterns in India, Ecuador, and Colombia, among others, and found in these cultures, too, people used the mass media as a source of basic information.

They based their decisions to use a product, though, on interpersonal contact. These authors found evidence for this pattern in such diverse subject areas as boiling drinking water, adoption of birth control devices, and use of modern math. In these less developed cultures, as well as in more advanced societies, the mass media channels inform, the interpersonal channels persuade.

Findings from this body of research are clear; we have no objection to the general observations made about the roles of the mass media and interpersonal channels. We feel, however, the settings of these projects limit their general application to today's communication setting. In Lazarsfeld's work, people used the mass media differently than they do today. People see newspapers as suppliers of entertainment and local information rather than the primary, general news source it once was. They use radio as an important secondary activity, not as a primary medium to which they once devoted direct attention.

Television, the medium that today has become so powerful, changing the functions of all other media, was in its infancy during much of the early research. Moreover, media usage in U.S. cultures is vastly different from usage among third world cultures. We have a wider selection of broadcast and print media, and we take advantage of these options. Here is the issue: While early research pointed out an important relationship between mass media and interpersonal channels that no doubt remains in effect today, the strong distinction between them has become clouded.

The mass media are not as incapable of persuasion as they once might have been. Furthermore, in part because of the growing dominance of media in our daily lives, the nature of interpersonal relationships, too, has changed. Essentially, the media roles have shifted into the domains of interpersonal relationships. The media still inform, and interpersonal relationships still persuade; only the line between them is not as clear as it once might have been. Mass media certainly retain a strong track record for information dissemination, but advertisers also have found that the media can modify attitudes and influence behaviour. Persuasion through the media has become a more commonly recognized application.

POSITIVE FEATURES OF INTERPERSONAL CHANNELS

We examined three defence mechanisms that enable receivers to stave off the persuasive effects of a message. People can avoid or ignore a message and not have to deal with it at all (selective exposure). They can distort the meaning of a message so that it conforms to preexisting beliefs; in other words, we can hear what we want to hear in a message (selective perception). Finally, people may recall only portions of a message, retaining what pleases them, discarding what annoys them (selective retention).

Through any one or a combination of these processes, receivers become less vulnerable to persuasive messages. These mechanisms are in operation in both mass media and interpersonal communi-cation settings. Receivers are most likely to wield control, however, in a mass communication environment.

They can control, interpret, and recall without challenge. Broadcast media can be shut off or ignored. Turn the page of a newspaper or magazine, and a message is out of sight and out of mind. Despite the bells and whistles advertisers use to attract and hold audiences, in the final analysis, the receiver is in charge. Although a receiver continues to direct his or her own response to a message in the interpersonal communication setting, a variety of factors stands to weaken this control. As suggested, discuss each of these in turn:

- Receiver involvement,
- Custom message design,
- Social features.

Receiver Involvement

In most interpersonal portions of special communication campaigns, receivers are self-selected. They participate in one-onone encounters with company representatives because they wish to, and they typically wish to because they recognize some ultimate benefit to themselves. They have chosen to become involved. As a result the receiver usually becomes an active participant in the communication event. He or she has sought information and is then brought into the process, serving not just as a spectator (as in mass media settings) but also as a player in the interchange of information.

Receivers find it difficult, under such conditions, to ignore information provided by the source. People are conditioned to listen to someone talking directly to them. They listen to be polite, but they listen, too, because they have sought out this information. They became involved when they took a step from the mass media to the interpersonal environment. They are part of the interaction so they are more likely to fulfill their listening role in the give-and-take of a conversation.

Seasoned salespeople know how important it is to get prospective customers to verbalize support for a product. This support reinforces people's commitment and helps solidify their decision to make a purchase. They become advocates of the product through their own words. When a receiver becomes involved in an interpersonal programme, it is more likely that he or she can be coaxed into such a position. The source can urge and cajole the receiver using techniques not possible in mass communication settings.

Involvement also implies effort justification. Earlier we said that when a person expends energy on a task, he or she imparts a significance to it. We justify our efforts. Energies spent on a project suggest the project is valuable.

We often see this in operation among students who claim they deserve a higher grade on an exam than they were given. Surely twenty hours of hard study deserved more than a C. (What about performance?) We believe our efforts are worth a great deal; we see a value in them that is manifest in various ways. In the case of interpersonal programmes, we come to value our involvement more highly because it costs us something. Recognition of this belief can be used by the message source to improve the persuasive potential of an interpersonal programme.

Custom Message Design

In the interpersonal setting, a source has a chance to shape a different message for each receiver. Feedback cues on all available levels (depending on physical features of the setting, for instance, face to face or a telephone conversation) enable the source to read the needs and wants of a receiver and adapt a message accordingly. Through give-and-take, the source can progress through a line of reasoning using necessary tactics to make the point with each receiver.

Feedback issues have entered many discussions throughout this book. Indeed, how could one examine specialized communication campaigns without frequent reference to feedback information? Feedback enables the source of a message to better meet the needs of the receiver. For the present discussion, as suggested, investigate the role of feedback in the preparation of messages designed to overcome the receiver's selectivity processes.

Feedback in the interpersonal setting provides a running account of a receiver's reception of a message. Obvious cues such as direct questions show how well a receiver is processing the information. But subtle indicators also may provide information. For instance, a receiver's yawn, silence when comments are expected, or expressions of boredom suggest that selective exposure gates may be in operation. Rather than listening to the message, the receiver is mentally drifting and ignoring what you are saying. In a mass media setting, the communicator can do nothing about such gating.

In the interpersonal environment, though, a skillful communicator can employ a variety of tactics to bring the receiver back into the discussion. When the "drift" settles in, he or she can change the pitch and pace of the presentation, use humour to break the monotony, or restate the point using a different appeal. One of the strongest techniques to interrupt message blocking is to involve the receiver actively in the interaction. Ask questions and introduce rhetorical techniques that require an acknowledgment from the receiver. In face-to-face settings, the communicator can stimulate eye contact, use gestures, or show models and drawings to attract receivers into the discussion.

The use of such techniques depends on the reception of the message, and the communicator determines the level of reception by monitoring the ongoing flow of feedback information. A perceptive person can detect disengagement by the receiver and, through a variety of techniques, overcome the selective exposure gates. We know the selective perception process enables receivers to put their own meaning on a message and thereby distort the communicator's intent. Although receivers may get away with this in the mass communication environment, a communicator can do much to ensure a correct interpretation in the interpersonal context. Feedback, again, is the key.

In the give-andtake of a conversation, we often reveal our understanding of a message by asking questions, restating points to determine the accuracy of our impressions, and expressing related thoughts. Through such feedback the communicator can monitor a receiver's perception of a message. As soon as it becomes apparent that the meaning and the interpretation of a message are no longer the same, the communicator can reshape the message to drive home the point. Even if the setting is not conducive to spontaneous receiver feedback, the communicator can monitor the interpretation of his or her message by asking questions.

This involves the receiver in the communication process and takes advantage of feedback potentials in the interpersonal setting. Teachers use this approach all the time. "What do you think about this issue?" "Do you see how this process works?" Such questions help keep the receiver involved and focused on the topic, and they help the communicator bear on the receiver's understanding of that topic. Since selective exposure and perception occur in the context of a communication event, the communicator can affect them directly. Selective retention, on the other hand, occurs after the communication event, and so control is more difficult. However, features of the interpersonal setting can improve the chances a receiver will retain information.

At the outset, remember that when the communicator improves the level of exposure to and perception of a message, he or she has advanced the likelihood that the receiver will retain the information. Obviously, if someone never gets the information or misunderstands what is said, he or she carries little away from the communication event. Note also that receivers express an initial level of interest in a topic when they choose to engage in the interpersonal communication event. We might expect that such an interest would result in a higher retention of related information. As suggested, give this point to interpersonal communication, even though it is a function of selection rather than of any feature in the interpersonal setting itself.

Specific features of the interpersonal communication environment improve the retention of information in several additional ways. First, when receivers become actively involved in the communication process, they are more likely to retain the information. Their active participation creates a stronger image and results in better recall. They are more likely to retain information from an event in which they have participated than one that they have just observed. The communicator also can motivate a receiver to retain information. First, he or she can encourage the receiver to link information with everyday events, thereby creating an association between the new information and familiar experiences.

One electric utility company used this technique with success when it encouraged customers to shift power consumption to less costly evening and early morning hours. In the interpersonal portion of the campaign, for example, company representatives suggested that every time the receiver took a shower or ran the dishwasher, he or she should think about what time it was. These behaviours then were linked to thoughts about "timeof-day (TOD) rates," which was the company's name for a new billing programme. In this example the receiver linked objectives of the programme with everyday behaviours, thus stimulating better retention of the information. Another way of overcoming selective retention problems is to arrange with the receiver a specific time for a follow-up contact. Let the receiver know that the process is not over with the first meeting. In a designated number of days or weeks, the receiver can expect a phone call, letter, or visit to pursue items covered in the interpersonal setting. In this way, perceived need for the information is projected onto a future setting where the receiver can expect to draw on the information he or she has obtained during the initial meeting. Although we hardly expect people to prepare by studying the information, we can anticipate that they will retain at least an awareness of the issues discussed.

The final method of dealing with selective retention problems is an adaptation of the previous technique. In this case, we ask the receiver to accomplish some task within a specified time. We may ask him or her to complete a questionnaire, contact a representative, or inform us about a decision. We may encourage compliance by offering a premium or other inducement. Here, we provide the receiver with a reason to retain the information. He or she has engaged in an interpersonal encounter with someone who has requested something. It need not be much-just to fill out a postcard or make a call yet this simple behaviour compels retention of the information from the conversation.

We can use a variety of techniques to develop messages that overcome the natural defences receivers use to avoid the full impact of a communication. In the interpersonal setting, a communicator can examine the ongoing feedback and so assess the reception of a message. He or she can then employ strategies to draw in the receiver, to promote an accurate understanding of the issues, and to project a need for the information in the future. Inasmuch as any form of communication can deal with selective exposure, perception, and retention, designs available in interpersonal settings have the strongest possibility.

Social Features

Earlier we proposed that the receiver's involvement in the give-and-take of interpersonal communication contributed to the success of information exchange because it helped overcome selective blocks. We believe the receiver's involvement in social relationships, also part of the interpersonal communication setting, advances the same purpose. The bond established between two people in an interpersonal environment offers a major advantage over mass communication programmes for reasons as suggested, examine.

Two aspects of the social features in interpersonal designs concern this discussion: personal attraction and personal responsibility. In the first case, we are referring to the simple notion that people enjoy other people, particularly if the other person is friendly, knowledgeable, and interested in the well-being of others. Whether the other person is on a telephone, drafts a personal letter, or meets with us in person, it is the person-to-person contact that makes a difference in our reception to a message.

We can walk out on a television programme. We can even walk out on a televised presidential address without concern for hurting anyone's feelings or breaching any social rules. On the other hand, it is difficult for many people to break off communication with another person. In telephone surveys when people are called by total strangers, it is not uncommon for a respondent to stay with an interview for fifteen to twenty minutes. If someone does not wish to participate in the survey or has other pressing matters at hand, he or she will generally provide an explanation for discontinuing the interview. Sometimes people even apologize because they do not wish to hurt the caller's feelings.

It would be simpler to hang up the phone; and while some do, most do not without first explaining their reasons. As a comparison, some polling firms have attempted to automate the telephone surveying process. They have machines place the call and pose questions to a receiver who has a specified time in which to provide a response. In these approaches the portion of uncompleted interviews, as compared with human-administered surveys, is vastly larger. People will talk to people but not to a machine. Bem's observation that people are the greatest influence on people is valid for reasons that are helpful in specialized communication programmes.

People will usually listen to another person, at least for a while, and so this human delivered message has a much better chance of avoiding the selective gates that so often block mass media messages. Granted, they may allow only a few moments for the person to make the point, but for that time they will probably listen to the message. If the topic is relevant and the pitch is well crafted, then perhaps the receiver will stay with the entire message. Where the receiver selects himself or herself into the communication event, there is a strong chance the communicator will have his or her message heard.

If we like this person talking to us, as suggested, probably look favourably on the message. If what he or she says is interesting and a logical argument is provided, as suggested, likely listen to the message. Moreover, the developing relationship will allow us to feel comfortable about expressing our doubts and reservations or raising questions about the message. This social environment promotes the feedback so important in interpersonal settings. Misperceptions of the message are less likely where feedback abounds, and feedback is most likely when a good social relationship is established. This interpersonal contact is not desirable just because it is pleasant, but because it is productive. The communicator can engage the receiver's attention, then shape the message to make his or her point.

The social context of interpersonal communications is beneficial in staving off problems of selective retention. The receiver departs the communication event not only with content or subject cues, but also with social cues. In other words, the message and the messenger become linked. If the social encounter is pleasant, we can expect thoughts about the topic also to be viewed positively. Consequently, the relationship between the communicator and the receiver has a direct bearing on retention of the message. An indirect effect of the relationship also occurs beyond the confines of the communication event. We can expect a higher response rate to follow through portions of the programme. The communicator or the receiver initiates some action in the aftermath of the initial communication.

People are more likely to complete and mail a questionnaire or to continue discussions when such action has been requested by a source with whom the receiver has established a social rapport. We do not want to let down someone we know and like, someone who may be disappointed if we ignore a simple request. Consequently, the selective retention matter—how long and how accurately someone keeps an active mental file on a communication—is enhanced by the social nature of interpersonal communication settings.

We have described how social relationships are important in overcoming the barriers to successful communication. Consider yet another feature, known as the "focusing of responsibility." In order to describe the meaning of this term, it is helpful to understand first what is meant by the "diffusion of responsibility." Consider a situation in which a large number of people gathers in a single place—say, one thousand troops standing at attention on a drill field.

Suppose an officer addressing the troops asks for a volunteer to participate in some dangerous mission. We can expect a request of such a large group to yield a relatively low percentage of volunteers. As each soldier thinks about the appeal and weighs the advantages against the dangers of volunteering, he also is aware he is just one of a thousand being asked. Maybe someone else will raise his hand, and even if no one does, each soldier is just one of the many who hold back. There is safety in numbers. The responsibility to volunteer is diffused among all these soldiers and does not rest on the back of any one.

This diffusion of responsibility theory has been used to explain what appears to be apathy among people who view a crime committed in public. Latane and Darley explain that the costs of nonintervention are spread among all observers, so no one feels particularly responsible to aid the victim. Here, too, bystanders believe that perhaps.someone else will lend a hand; and even if no one else does, the accountability is divided, so no one feels culpable. The responsibility and so ultimately the guilt for inaction are spread among many. While large numbers allow each person to find refuge in the crowd, small numbers or one-on-one encounters pinpoint the responsibility. If a sergeant asked each soldier individually to volunteer for the assignment, we would expect a much higher response rate. If only one passerby saw someone being assaulted, it is more likely that that person would intervene. The same idea of responsibility focusing applies to interpersonal communication settings.

We are less likely to daydream or discard a message if we are the sole receiver. We sense a responsibility to maintain our attention to a message in these communication events. If the communicator asks a question, who else can respond? No one else can share the burden. In a mass media environment, it is easy to ignore requests. Tens of thousands, perhaps millions of other people may respond to pleas for assistance or support. No single viewer is on the spot, and no single viewer feels the weight of responsibility.

MASS MEDIA/INTERPERSONAL CONNECTIONS

Fortunately, in most communication campaigns, we do not have to choose between mass media and interpersonal programmes. The two can work together well in augmenting the impact of a programme. Each reinforces the effects of the other; one picks up where the other leaves off. As suggested, describe the relationship between mass media and interpersonal phases of a communication campaign and show how each contributes to the overall effectiveness of specialized communication activities.

In these discussions, we expect that companies becoming involved in specialized communications will want to reach a large number of people. They may wisely choose to divide the larger audience into smaller units for individual treatment, but their primary objective is to reach more than a handful of receivers. It is therefore given that the mass media will be involved in all programmes, even those that plan to reach people on a one-on-one basis. Since as suggested, assume one or some combination of media will be employed in all campaigns, we must view the use of interpersonal programmes in the context of the mass media scheme.

With this in mind, let us make clear that adding an interpersonal feature to a communication campaign is not just like adding another car to a train. Do not view an interpersonal component as an addendum to a mass media programme, but as an integral feature of it. In a campaign that has an interpersonal component, mass media will be used differently than in cases where no interpersonal feature is planned. Our discussions here will be confined to the use of media that support an interpersonal component.

In this context the mass media serve two essential functions. First, they help familiarize the audience with basic concepts and issues involved in a campaign. They provide information that enables the audience to recognize how the service, product, or idea relates to them personally. They familiarize the audience and make people comfortable with the subject of the campaign.

The second function of the media deals specifically with the interpersonal element: They inform people about what they should do to become involved in the interpersonal programme, and they persuade target audiences to take this step towards involvement. They may also incorporate more substantive persuasion elements dealing with issues, although major persuasive efforts will likely be reserved for the interpersonal programme.

Introducing Concepts

Whether a company is introducing an innovation that is unknown to an audience or presenting a familiar issue in a new wrapping, it is important to familiarize the audience with basic concepts. Audiences need access to fundamental information on which they can base decisions. We cannot expect people to invest personal energy in an interpersonal programme if they have no idea about the relevance and importance of the topic or product being promoted. Mass media are used as the primary means of acquainting audience members with these issues.

Take, for example, one of the many innovations in the computer industry. A company by the name of Cauzin Systems, Inc., has introduced a clever method of data storage for business computers. Unlike tape and floppy disks that store information on a magnetic medium, Cauzin's system uses a simple strip of paper with markings resembling three-dimensional dots that are read by a light beam. The company has a valuable product and obviously would like to market it to a specialized audience of business computer users.

In its initial advertising phases, the company bought space in major business computer magazines where it described the central features of its "Softstrip" technology. It provided the audience with basic information about how the product worked and suggested that businesses could use such an innovation in their operations.

They avoided technical discussions (which might have frightened their audience), and offered just enough information to help potential customers understand the concept of Softstrip technology and recognize its application to their activities. In this case, magazines provided the initial contact with primary target audience groups. They introduced the product name and described its basic functions. They also explained how the product might be used in business computer applications, showing the relevance of the product to potential customers. The Cauzin ads went one step further, however, by leading interested readers into the interpersonal phase of the communication programme through the magazine ads.

Interpersonal Link

In most interpersonal programmes, customers need to be invited into the programme, and the mass media are best used to extend the invitation. The media tell people something about the information available in an interpersonal programme, and they tell them how to go about obtaining this information. The best techniques for drawing mass media audiences into interpersonal programmes involve a few simple principles. First, requirements of the receiver should be minimal and easy to fulfill. As long as someone is not obliged to invest much energy or spend much time, he or she is more likely to take that next step.

This is why many companies have obtained toll-free 800 lines to accommodate customer requests for further involvement. Although a number of businesses still use postage-paid, returnable post cards, among many that rely heavily on interpersonal customer contact, the 800 lines have become an efficient alternative. It is easy to dial a few numbers, particularly for people who have grown comfortable with using the telephone for so many business and personal applications. Despite the technique eventually chosen, observe this basic rule: Keep the method of contact simple.

The second principle concerns the value of a reward. People will seek to become involved further in communications with a company if they recognize a value in doing so. What do they get for their efforts? Some companies offer a nominal prize or gift for continuing the communication process, and for many audiences some tangible premium may be necessary. For your efforts, many computer software companies will send a free demonstration diskette that exhibits basic features of a programme without providing the full power of the product.

Other companies send buttons, photos, or free samples of soap or perfume. We know of one company that even sends along samples of stained glass. Such premiums allow the potential customer to sample the wares before purchase, but they also serve as an inducement for the receiver to send in a bid for continuing the communication process. Rewards need not be physical products. Often the dividend for investing one's energy will be the information itself. Receivers may not need more than the promise of becoming further involved in learning about a product, service, or idea. Based on what they see in the mass media, they may develop only a genuine interest in learning more—not the hope of acquiring some prize. The information itself is a prize. In this case, of course, the company must make the promise of information attractive. Receivers must be assured their efforts will result in something of use to them. Perhaps they will receive an attractive packet of information that will further describe a product or a telephone call from someone who will answer their questions and provide additional details. People rightly expect to get something for their efforts, and the mass media can best describe the reward.

The final technique of bringing people from a mass media environment to the interpersonal setting involves safety and respondent obligation. People have grown wary of becoming too involved too quickly. They may be willing to have a company mail information or even have a representative phone them, but when it comes to a personal visit, they may feel pressured and so shy away from making the initial reply. Whatever the company plans for a follow-up interpersonal contact, it should be certain not to imply a threat. Assure the receiver that he or she is not obligated to buy anything or do anything chosen not to do as a result of taking the next step. With these features in mind—require little time, give fair rewards, and promise no hassle—the bid made in a mass media message will have a stronger chance of acceptance by potential customers. Such an approach requires minimum effort, promises a reasonable expectation of some return, and guarantees relative safety—three important characteristics of any business transaction.

Although we have discussed designs in which a single type of follow-up interpersonal programme was implied, nothing limits companies from offering several of these programmes. A company may use the media to suggest a few ways to follow through, for instance, phoning the company, filling out a postcard, or visiting a shop or office. Each offers a different level of commitment by the receiver and a different intensity of interpersonal contact. By offering several such possibilities, the company can sort individuals into those who prefer to proceed slowly, minimizing initial involvement, and those who are ready for a more intensive interaction. Such an approach has been well used in the magazine advertisements of Cauzin Systems, which we cited as an example earlier. This company markets a product that stores computer data on strips of ordinary typing paper and has chosen to promote this product to specialized audiences through targeted business computer magazines. It also has planned to reach customers with well-designed interpersonal components detailing the innovation.

Three interpersonal communication programme options were presented in the Cauzin ads. First, customers could write in for additional information. Recognizing that some people might be reluctant to write or might not wish to wait for a reply, Cauzin published an 800 number by which receivers could request the same information or talk directly with company representatives about the Softstrip product. In this second application, the company escalated the level of communication. For those ready to move more quickly with their decision or who had no need for the intermediate step of reading additional descriptions, the phone call offered more direct and immediate access to company representatives. A clever inducement was used to urge receivers into the final interpersonal programme.

A printed strip, about five and one-half inches long and five-eighth inch wide, appeared along the outside margin of the magazine page—it was a functional example of a Softstrip programme. Instructions beneath this oddlooking column of three-dimensional dots suggested the reader take the advertisement to the nearest computer store where the programme could be "read." The ad claimed that this strip, no bigger than three and one-half square inches, contained a large amount of interesting information.

For a computer aficionado, the enticement was compelling. For the company, the potential payoff was substantial. Here was a fairly simple, high-reward, and relatively low-threat inducement to attract audience members willing to become involved more quickly. Of course, while customers were having their strips read, they should have been prepared for the sales pitch. Most people who would take the ad to a computer store probably would be willing to hear what the salesperson had to say. Those who were not might have opted for one of the less intense interpersonal programme alternatives—the postcard or the phone call. At the bottom line of this discussion lies the relationship between the mass media and interpersonal portions of a communication campaign. They work together, not in opposition. The mass media set up conditions of, announce the features of, and provide information about procedures necessary to take the step into interpersonal portions of the communication programme.

Programme Considerations

Think of the combined mass media/interpersonal communication programme as a series of steps that ratchet upward the level of involvement between message source and receiver. We begin with a general information forum and step up to more specific, refined, interpersonal transactions. In the early phases, a company seeks the audience through public channels. In the later phases, the receivers seek the company through private channels. We move from information to persuasion, from audience-passive to audience-active formats. At each level, as the receiver's involvement increases, the inherent strengths of interpersonal communications simultaneously expand; the potential for successful persuasion becomes greater.

Communicators must keep this perspective in view. The mass media involvement is a prelude to the interpersonal portions of the campaign. The media serve as lures and bridges to interpersonal programmes. They function as lures by attracting receivers to the issues and providing sufficient information to stimulate an interest and perhaps a curiosity about the message. They performance as bridges by furnishing details that enable receivers to pass from the general mass message environment to the specific interpersonal environment. They tell how the receiver may become involved further in the communication process.To use the mass media, follow several logical guidelines:

- Identify media that pinpoint desired audiences.
- Time delivery of the mass media message to coincide with the availability of interpersonal programmes.
- Determine product and programme features that hold the greatest lure for target audiences (strategy features).

TARGET AUDIENCES

We cannot overstate the importance of targeting audiences through appropriate media. Obviously, there can be little hope for a successful interpersonal programme if the invitations are sent to the wrong audience. Media selection should be as specific as possible, providing access only to audiences of particular interest. Not only will it cost less to place a message in an audience-specific medium but also one can tailor the message with precise appeal to the target group.

We noted that mass media can stimulate interest in interpersonal programmes, involving audience members further in the communication process by increasing their level of involvement. The same notion can apply, however, within the selection of media channels. In such cases, use general audience media to point audiences towards more specific media. A television message, reaching general audiences, may suggest that viewers read a local newspaper or magazine or look for a direct mail piece describing specific details about some issue.

Here, general audiences are sorted into specific audiences, and these specific audiences will in turn be sorted into yet more narrow audiences when they are given the opportunity to join interpersonal programmes. The process is one of continuing focus—mass audience to target audience to oneon-one communication. Audiences may arrive at the same interpersonal programme through several media paths. Various audience groups may be drawn into an interpersonal programme through different messages. These messages may offer different inducements and be carried by different media. A community college wanting to increase adult enrollment for evening classes might use direct mail for businesspeople, radio ads for homemakers, and inserts in local magazines for young professionals to announce an 800 number for registration information. In each case the message can be specific and direct. Appeals to each group can focus chiefly on issues of greatest interest, yet converge on the same interpersonal response—calling the 800 number. Thus, media use can be simple, targeting one group through a single medium. Strategies also can employ layers of media, narrowing audiences at each step. Additionally, different media can be used to bring different audiences to the same interpersonal programme, allowing audience-targeting features to determine the most appropriate strategy in each case. Despite the approach selected, the role of the media is essentially unchanged: to get out the word about the interpersonal programme and encourage audiences to take the next step.

TIMING THE MESSAGE

Timing of the mass media message involves mostly common sense. Before the media persuade people to become involved in the interpersonal programme, the programme should be staffed and ready for business. Phones should be installed and trained company representatives should be prepared to field a variety of anticipated questions. Face-to-face scenarios should be rehearsed. Coordination among employees and participating retail outlets should be arranged.

On the other hand, the cost of maintaining such support facilities can be substantial, so it is equally desirable to avoid delay of the media portion of the campaign. Study the customary lag times in message preparation and production and the lead times necessary for purchasing media time and space. It is no small task to bring the two together at the same time. Poor coordination may result in the loss of money, but serious miscalculations may throw off the tempo of a programme and result in its failure.

STRATEGY CONSIDERATIONS

Programme planning draws from a complex set of variables addressed throughout this book. How we design our message to attract receivers to the interpersonal portion of a campaign depends on the receivers, on our product, and on our company. As we have said, answers provided by research suggest a proper mix of elements. If we are introducing an innovation, we may need to provide an opportunity for the receivers to see the product in action. Research will suggest if audiences prefer to see the new product or want first to learn more about it through printed descriptions. As suggested, also learn if people will be ready to make purchases quickly, without programmes that add time and company expense. Research will examine different audience segments and suggest in which media we should promote which interpersonal programme.

In the Cauzin Softstrip example, we saw a company that recognized three groups of customers: (1) those with a general interest in the product, for whom Cauzin provided an address and phone number to obtain printed material; (2) those with more urgent interests in the product, for whom it provided a phone number where a company representative could be reached; and (3) those who were sufficiently curious about the product to want to see it in operation, for whom it provided a live demonstration at local computer stores. The company determined the strategy in each by assessing the predicted level of interest within various audience segments. It attempted to accommodate each group with an interpersonal programme announced in magazine ads. Readers could see the range of possibilities and could select the one that best suited their needs.

Research identifies audience segments that will be interested in other aspects of an interpersonal programme. Suppose, upon examination of research data, we discover large industrial customers are reluctant to buy our products because they know little about our new firm. They tend to restrict purchases to well-known manufacturers and avoid dealing with unknown fledgling companies. In such a case, we may want to promote an interpersonal programme in specialized trade magazines or through direct mail, which initially would promote our company and not our products. We may make it easy for these large customers to invite our company representative to visit their facility or to learn about us through telephone conversations or brochures. After we have satisfied these customers that our company is sound, then we may begin to promote our products.Notice that in each case we rely on research to suggest the need for information by receivers. Once our research has identified the need, then we promote that portion of our interpersonal programme in targeted media to address concerns of the attending audiences.

The lure to recruit receivers relies on the same targeting principles that guide selection of topics and media throughout the specialized communication process: We discover the needs of receivers, and we seek them out with specific messages through the media to which they attend.

INTERPERSONAL PROGRAMME EXAMPLES

As suggested, describe examples of three interpersonal programmes that have successfully extended the reach of mass media activities.Each involves a different level of contact between company representatives and receivers, and accordingly provides a range of opportunities for interpersonal contact with target audience members. Furthermore, these programmes range widely in cost and commitment of company resources. In presenting these examples, we emphasize various features of interpersonal programmes that have a history of success. These descriptions do not provide a blueprint for programmes, although certain portions may be adaptable to a wide variety of conditions.

Energy Demonstration Centres

Note: A composite of several programmes conducted by public utility companies, federal and state governments, and private energy conservation companies. We have combined some of the best features of each into a single programme for our purposes here.

Setting and Background

During the energy crises of the mid-1970s, government agencies in cooperation with electric utility companies stressed the need for energy conservation. Residential and small company buildings were major energy users because of poor insulation, inefficient appliances, poorly adjusted furnaces, and other problems related to building design or practices of the occupants. In several communities, electric utility companies experimented with public communication techniques designed to increase general awareness of conservation issues. Companies realised it would be difficult to mandate conservation practices.

Instead, government and industry thought that escalating energy costs would prevent waste. They also believed that Americans felt a spirit of civic responsibility to reduce their dependence on foreign oil. To capitalize on these natural motivations, the government and participating utility companies determined their primary role was to provide the information people needed to begin saving energy. They also felt that in the early phases of this work, it would be necessary to use persuasion techniques to motivate people to take those initial conservation steps.

Programme Design

The electric utility conservation campaign involved integrated mass media and interpersonal communication phases. In the mass media portion, utilities ran general announcements about the problems electricity customers were facing with higher energy costs. Ads described the relationship between the rising price of imported oil and rapidly increasing electricity rates. They said that utility companies were as much plagued by high fuel costs as were customers, explaining that power companies were forced to pass on their increased operating costs.

By design, this portion of the campaign demonstrated that electricity companies were not the villains but the victims of oil-pricing policy. If the companies ever hoped to influence their target audiences, they had to fortify their own images and not be seen as scoundrels. People naturally blame the companies that send them higher bills. Along with this image building, companies used the mass media to alert customers to the likelihood of continued high energy prices. They warned that high energy prices were likely here to stay and suggested that wise customers would change their habits and modify their homes or businesses to increase their energy efficiency.

The specific "how-to" portion of the information campaign began at this point. Some of the media ads were devoted to a single issue, say, reminding family members to turn off lights or explaining that laundry could be washed just as well in warm as in hot water. Other media ads listed conservation practices that would help save power and lower the energy bill. Electric companies also used bill stuffers to get information across to customers. What better time to explain energy- and cost-saving techniques than when someone has to write a check for a large electricity bill!

The final feature of this mass media programme involved methods of preparing a home or company building to be more energy efficient. Media messages explained how the installation of storm windows, seals around doors and windows, insulation, and more efficient furnaces could reduce the power required to heat and cool.

They discussed power-saving appliances such as energy-efficient hot water heaters, refrigerators, and dishwashers. They showed how timers on thermostats could reduce energy consumption without causing discomfort to occupants. Moreover, federal tax laws implemented during this period provided tax deductions for the purchase of energy-efficient windows, doors, insulation, and other products. Utility company advertisements explained the logic of installing these items for immediate savings on tax bills as well as for long-term economic payoffs.

Interpersonal portions of the campaign concerned primarily this last set of issues dealing with the installation of equipment such as insulation and thermal windows. Research revealed that most people who planned to put in these items wanted to do the work themselves. Utility companies felt they could be most effective in assisting their customers by setting up centres that displayed these products and described installation techniques. Model conservation demonstrations were designed as follows. Depending on the size of the community, the utility set up model homes or model rooms in company-owned buildings. They equipped display centres with a wide variety of conservation devices. They showed how the products could be installed, how they operated, and how they could be used.

Trained workers explained how to operate and install equipment. Retrofitting, or installing products such as insulation and thermal windows in older buildings, was an important subject of the model demonstrations. People wanting to put insulation in their walls or attics could discuss the procedure with trained representatives who would point out shortcuts and identify pitfalls.

These centres provided excellent face-to-face interpersonal communication forums. People could see working models of energy-saving equipment, and they could talk directly with company employees. The information flow was rich in these settings, and the persuasion components were strong. The person-to-person contact effectively motivated people to adopt energy conservation practices advocated by the utility company.

All of the interpersonal communication characteristics are evident in this design. Audiences are self-selected. They are attending these centres because they have a personal interest in the subject. Audience members also play an active role in the communication. They have spent time to drive to a centre and so have invested something of themselves. Feedback potentials are unlimited. Company representatives can monitor the progress of their arguments through the many cues available in face-to-face-settings and respond accordingly. Source and receiver can establish a rapport that would be difficult in other settings.

The mass media campaign, meanwhile, was in full swing. Ads run in local media told customers about the model conservation demonstration centres. They provided a limited amount of information about the products and encouraged audiences to visit the centres for specific details. Media ads further supported the interpersonal programme by providing operating schedules of the centres, maps depicting centre locations, and lists of features one could expect to find at each centre. Without support of the mass media, it is doubtful the demonstration centres would have had any success. How else would people have known the centres existed? How could they have been persuaded to seek additional information? As in most campaigns, the mass media and the interpersonal programmes worked together. The media provided basic details, then sustained the interpersonal portion with a continuing flow of information.

TELEPHONE BANKS

Setting and Background

A small industrial city in the southeastern United States was having serious teenager delinquency problems. Drug and alcohol usage measured higher than state norms, and pregnancy rates per capita were higher than for most other locations in the region. Teenage crime and school dropout rates were above the average for cities of comparable size. University studies revealed many youngsters had poor family lives. They had little parental support, and many were unable to seek professional assistance because they feared the system and peer and parental pressures.

Steps taken to deal with this problem included these: The state funded programmes to work with the most serious cases. The school system set up peer counseling programmes that had been used with success in other locations. A hospital, with financial assistance from local businesses, established a telephone tape hot line to deal with special adolescent problems. This discussion deals with the telephone tape hot line.

Programme Design

State and city government and private sources of funding provided for extensive research on the teenage community. Data were gathered from three sources. First, researchers from a major university conducted a comprehensive survey of community adolescents. This research examined the youngsters' family life, academic achievement, leisure time, drug and alcohol usage, and media consumption, among other items. Data from this study provided a valuable snapshot of adolescent life in the target community. Researchers also gathered data from teachers, counselors, church leaders, and others in the city who regularly worked with youngsters. Finally, they assembled published statistics from human services and law enforcement agencies on the levels of pregnancy, child abuse, arrest rates, drug overdoses, and other conditions that signal community problems.

These data were examined by city officials and consultants and used as a basis on which to develop several programmes, including the telephone tape hot line. The hot line worked as follows: A youngster who wanted information or had a particular problem could call a well-publicized hot line number. The call would be answered by an operator who would ask what tape the caller wished to hear. The caller would select a tape from lists published in the media and elsewhere and provide the name or code number of the tape to the operator.

Tapes lasted from one to two minutes and concluded with directions for obtaining additional information from appropriate service agencies. Callers also learned that if they needed immediate help, they should stay on the line and the operator would connect them to a counselor. These calls were patched through to a twenty-four-hour counseling agency located elsewhere in the city. In cases where the operator felt it was a life-or-death matter, he or she referred callers to an ambulance service or to the police for emergency aid.

Several features of the hot line made it attractive for use with a teenage audience:

- It offered privacy for the receiver.
- It was relatively inexpensive.
- It was flexible (a variety of subjects could be covered).
- It allowed the receivers to determine how much information they received.
- It had a rapid start-up time.

Privacy

The tape bank dealt with issues that were most difficult for teenagers to discuss with adults, or even with each other. For instance, drugs, sex, and parental problems were covered in fifteen of the twenty-two titles available. Other subjects concerned suicide, depression, and parental abuse. These are serious topics, yet they are among the most difficult for youngsters to discuss openly.

Privacy was guaranteed with the tape bank. Operators never asked for a youngster's name, except in a crisis when it appeared there might be risk of serious injury or loss of life. Even then the caller knew he or she could hang up the phone and remain anonymous. Because there was no risk, youngsters could obtain information from the hot line that they could get comfortably from no other source. Fear of recognition, which drove away youngsters from so many other information sources, was not a problem with the hot line. Follow-up studies found that users recognized privacy as a major advantage.

Cost

The hot line was simple. It had only a few components. Usually a single operator could handle the calls, so staffing was minimal. Although operators screened calls for the serious, life-threatening cases, they did not offer counseling. It was unnecessary to have a licensed psychologist on duty. Hardware consisted of several phone lines and a cassette tape deck that could play several tapes simultaneously. This equipment was rugged and handled thousands of calls, requiring no maintenance. Scripts for the tapes were developed at a nearby university, which minimized expense and provided the opportunity to build in local references. Recording of the tapes required little more than a reel-to-reel tape recorder and a quiet room. All messages were dubbed to cassette.

Flexibility

Because the tapes were so inexpensive and simple to produce, city planners could provide messages on a wide variety of topics. Initial research disclosed several dozen subjects of concern to these youths. Nearly all of these topics were treated in the first round. This way, even though a topic might have only a limited audience, nothing prevented development of a tape to help these few youngsters. As time went on and the popularity of issues changed in the community, it was simple to update the tape bank to reflect emerging concerns. The tape bank was always current and relevant to the target audience.

Receiver Orientation

As with all the interpersonal communication designs we offer, those who used the hot line had chosen to do so. They were a self-selected audience and were calling because they recognized the personal relevance of the issue. With this system, the receiver determined at what level the interpersonal communication would operate. Perhaps the taped message would be adequate to answer all questions, in which case the caller could choose to go no further. At the cease of each tape, though, it was strongly suggested that the caller continue the communication process by staying on the line and talking directly with someone about the problem.

Communication continued only if the caller chose. Such a design guaranteed time would be spent with those who really wanted additional information and not with someone who would rather have been elsewhere. As long as the receiver determined the level of contact, the system remained efficient and ensured the best use of resources. Rapid Start-up. The limited equipment and personnel requirements of the tape bank allowed it to begin operation with a short setup period. While the hospital staff was waiting for equipment to arrive, they recruited and trained operators and arranged for script development and tape production.

They also arranged for the mass media portion of the campaign that would support the interpersonal communication functions. Within six weeks from its inception, the hot line was up and running. No doubt such a programme could be set up even in half the time if it became necessary to do so. The mass media played an essential role in the success of the telephone hot line. Thirty-second spots on local radio stations announced the purpose of the hot line and provided the phone number to call.

Television stations ran ten-second ads that told the name, basic purpose, and hot line phone number. Newspapers printed a list of the topics covered by the tapes and described how the system operated. All media stressed the privacy of the programme and explained that anonymity was guaranteed.

In addition to the mass media, sponsors developed informational posters that were put up in local stores, churches, and schools. They also produced wallet-sized cards that had the phone number, instructions on using the services, and a complete listing of the topics covered by hot line. Here, too, the card stressed privacy.

Business Application

The telephone tape bank offers an excellent means of interpersonal communication that extends beyond the limits of a mass media programme. Several features make it attractive for business applications:

- It requires little capital outlay and office space. Depending on the number of phone lines and the sophistication of the tape equipment, it may cost no more than a few thousand dollars to set up.
- By offering two levels of communication, it allows the company to concentrate its resources on the best customer prospects. The tapes alone may satisfy some callers' need for information. Company representatives can spend time only with those who wish to go beyond the tapes and discuss specifics about a product or service.
- The company may be able to operate the hot line with existing personnel. While many factors must be considered, a company can conceivably handle information requests without a staff increase. Remember, those calls going beyond the taped

session likely will be more promising prospects and will make best use of time spent by staff members.

- The tape bank concept is widely adaptable to a variety of applications. Although we have described a system that uses a simple cassette recorder, more advanced equipment can expand considerably the possibilities of a tape bank design. For instance, an operator may not be needed with totally automated systems. By following signals provided by the caller, computers can transfer calls to sales representatives, other company personnel, or even other tapes.

COMPUTER COMMUNICATIONS

We have thus far avoided mention of the budding computer communication industry that, without doubt, will have a major impact on the ways businesses communicate among themselves and with clients. Cost of equipment necessary for computer communication is beyond reach of the average person, and applications for such a service are limited to professional settings.

Nonetheless, there are two reasons why this discussion is relevant to our purposes. First, there are immediate uses for computer communications among many specialized audiences.

Businesses, educational institutions, political organizations, and others have already adopted the equipment necessary for computer communication and are now in a position to utilize computer-based interpersonal programmes. Second, as costs are reduced for computer equipment and the technology diffuses further into the population, audiences and uses for such programmes will expand.

The design we describe here is only an early prototype that will probably go through many modifications to accommodate expanding audiences and improvements in technology. This example draws positive features from several existing computer communication programmes and thus represents an amalgam of the best components rather than a single programme currently in operation.

Setting and Background

A political consulting firm in Arlington, Virginia, spotted a trend in the use of professional campaign assistance by candidates running for small state and local offices. As campaigns have become more sophisticated with extensive use of mass media, direct mail, and polling technologies, candidates have had to supplement their small campaign staffs with help from professional consultants. Market analysis revealed that candidates often had difficulty locating such help, and when they did hire these specialists, they often had to pay for more services than their small campaigns really needed. The firm decided there was a national market for one-stop shopping for campaign consulting services. Candidates around the United States could turn to this outfit for assistance in audience measurement, campaign strategy design, media purchases, fund raising, and other political campaign features. They could buy an entire package or use only those services they needed at any given time.

Moreover, the company believed it could provide most of its services directly from Arlington and avoid spending a great deal of time on site. Although company specialists would travel to the field if necessary, the plan called for most of the work to be done from the main office in northern Virginia. The essential communication link between the company and clients would be the computer. Data could be sent back and forth, problems could be examined and discussed, budgets could be debated, media could be planned. In fact, communication required for all activities could be accomplished quickly, accurately, and efficiently by exchanging information between computers over the telephone lines. For instance, a client in Missouri could send telephone survey data to Arlington where they would be processed and analysed. Within hours, results complete with charts, graphs, and recommendations could be sent back to the client. The computer system would allow transmission of complex material that could otherwise be sent conveniently only by mail. In the heat of a political campaign, even overnight mail is too slow. The computer links made this consulting plan possible. Information could be exchanged quickly with virtually no limitation on the complexity of data that could be sent. Since computers were so important in the operation of this service, the company decided to involve them in the interpersonal portions of the promotion. This consulting firm established initial contact with potential clients through mass media and direct mail. They would then demonstrate the capacity of their system to engage in an interpersonal dialogue using the computer connections.

Programme Design

It is typical for such consulting firms to work exclusively with one political party. Such was the case in this instance. Consultants who work exclusively with one party enjoy the confidence of candidates and party officials. They also find it easier to obtain general information about people who plan to run on that party's ticket. With its party connections, the Arlington firm was able to get a mailing list for the direct mail portion of the campaign.

The company firm generated personalized letters to several thousand announced candidates. It prepared several versions of the letter based on the office sought, incumbency status of the candidate, region, previous party successes in the area, and probable campaign issues. Computer-typed letters were addressed to each candidate by name, and letters were further personalized by using the candidate's name throughout the text. The firm advertised this service in political party magazines received by large numbers of party regulars, officeholders, and staff members.

Interested readers were given an address to which they could write and a toll-free number to call if they wished additional information about the company's services. Through either channel, the receiver was placed on a list that would bring a copy of the personalized letter (the same one sent out in the direct mail phase). Only the letter, and not the mass media ads, contained specific information about the interpersonal portion of the programme. Significant programme costs made it necessary for the company to limit inquiries, where possible, to serious prosp-ects. If a receiver was sufficiently stimulated by descriptions in the letter to make the inquiry, he or she would have some reasonable level of interest in the service. The letter provided simple step-by-step instructions for the receiver to become involved in the interpersonal communication programme—called the "demonstration." Receivers were told what hardware and software they would require and what they should expect when they had established contact for the demonstration. First, they were to call an 800 number. A company representative would answer and review with the caller the basic design of the consulting services being promoted. In other words, the caller was given a standard sales pitch. But the programme went beyond that. The caller was prompted to ask questions, discuss problems, or deal with any relevant aspect of these consulting services. When this interaction played out, the caller was asked for several items of information that were used by the representative to prepare the demonstration programme. The caller was asked to turn on his or her computer, printer, and modem (equipment that enables computers to communicate over phone lines), load the communication software, and then observe the computer screen.

Using the information provided by the caller, messages appearing on the screen showed colour charts, budgets, and other information selected for their substance and visual appeal. For the grand finale, a message on the screen instructed the receiver to turn attention to the printer that typed out three pages of statistics, charts, and a radio script. The printer then produced a final message wishing the candidate (by name) success and expressing the consulting firm's desire to assist in the campaign. A message flashed on the screen directing the caller to pick up the phone for further conversation with the company representative. At this point, talk turned to specific commitments to the service, follow-up demonstrations, and additional discussions. This computer communication system is an example of a truly specialized, interpersonal communication approach, posses-sing many of the features we look for in one-on-one communi-cations:

- It provides for feedback. Interactants first make verbal contact and establish a rapport, then they communicate through computer keyboards and other computer devices (such as sending data contained on a disk) in an iterative fashion. The same channel allows information to flow back and forth between sender and receiver.
- Information exchange is rapid. People can send and receive information instantaneously, avoiding the serious problems that result from delayed transmissions. In some applications this feature may be critical.
- Receivers are self-selected. Clients who use the computer to interact with a business choose to do so. They are inclined, therefore, to have a particular interest in the topic and so are stronger business prospects.

As we said at the beginning, the use of computers is just now being explored for interpersonal business communica-tions. Technology within the next decade will no doubt considerably expand these uses for specialized interpersonal programmes. Businesses stand to save time and money.

They will be able to do a great deal of work from a single location, reducing travel requirements and enabling a single employee to handle a greater number of accounts. An accountant in New York can work on the books of a client in Seattle without leaving his or her desk. Moreover, he or she can discuss intricacies of these books with as much ease as if everyone were in the same room.

A small automotive engineering firm in Albuquerque can review details of its new windshield design with prospective clients in Detroit who have decided to see what the distant firm has to offer. Companies may conduct sales, respond to queries, and generally engage in the give-and-take we have come to expect with interpersonal communications. Although there will still be need for other forms of interpersonal contact, we expect computer communication to be an increasingly important addition to the available repertoire of approaches.

6

Strategy and Design of Targeted Programmes

The plans and practices of a public communication campaign. It reviews four essential stages of planning and discusses the rationale for each. Principles of persuasion, media usage, interpersonal communication, audience feedback, and other components into a coherent, effective communication programme is demonstrated.

Few would dispute our need to communicate. We accept the importance of communication as we accept the value of exercise and the power of knowledge. We chant slogans about the need to communicate and believe we can find the solutions to many problems in the process. We have added our voice to those proclaiming the value of communication. We believe businesses can do much through communication to strengthen their market positions, to improve their efficiency, and to stave off problems.

. Specifically, we have strongly advocated targeted communications, because communication effectiveness increases with audience specificity. Now our concerns move beyond preparatory discussions, as valid and essential as they are, to review the means of developing concrete plans for communication campaigns.

As suggested, examine how a company can evaluate its communication needs and how it can establish a priority among those needs. As suggested, look at how the company should study its audience in order to allow receiver information to factor prominently into communication plans.

Finally, as suggested, consider how a business communicator can translate general concerns into specific messages. This process enables the company to look at itself, its audience, and its communication programme in a single frame. It is a well-developed, comprehensive, and flexible approach that has been used successfully under a variety of field conditions.

Before we describe the planning process, it will help to examine two broad categories of reasons for which companies may engage in communication campaigns. The approach one takes to reach target audiences will have much to do with the purpose of the programme. A company responding to negative conditions, such as bad publicity or a groundswell of customer dissatisfaction, will likely employ different tactics from one preparing to introduce a new product or publicize its recent successes. Let us examine several of the reasons for which companies may engage in specialized communicaton programmes.

SELLING A PRODUCT, SERVICE, OR IDEA

Promotion is a major reason for engaging in targeted communication. Even well-established products require sustaining programmes to keep them before the public eye and to defend them against assaults of the competition. People need to be reminded that a product is good, is available, and is better than alternative choices. The introduction of new products or of existing products to new audiences involves a good measure of communication work.

Audiences must become acquainted with the product and learn about its features. Through the mass media or through an interpersonal programme, they also must be persuaded to purchase the product for the first time—to give it a try—to see how it can meet their needs. If the competition is formidable, audiences need to be convinced the new product is better than the old, that this product has something the others do not. On the other hand, while a truly innovative product may have little competition to fear, it may become necessary to convince potential customers they really need the product. Why else would consumers buy something that, so far, they have done without? Although in some dimension the promotion of an idea may be akin to the selling of a product or service, several features set it apart. First, the response we expect from a receiver may be different. When we sell a product or service, our ultimate aim is to have audience members make a purchasing decision. We have been successful when receivers respond to our messages and buy what we are selling.

In some campaigns when we are promoting an ideology, the receiver's behaviour may be equally decisive. For instance, we may witness the results of our efforts to encourage the use of seat belts when members of the audience buckle up. We measure the effectiveness of our programme to promote a school bond referendum when people pull the right lever in the polling booth. Objectives of many programmes promoting an ideological issue may not be as evident. In such cases, goals that drive a communication campaign may be illusive and less well defined. If the nature of the goals is different, then the strategies, too, will be different.

Consider objectives of the Sierra Club, which seeks to promote public awareness of conservation and protection of the environment. Although occasionally there may be a clear programme objective, the organization has an ongoing mission to increase public regard for natural resources. Such sustaining communication programmes attend more to long-term attitude modification and less to specific, observable behaviours. Political parties, public interest organizations, and religious associations are other examples of groups with similar objectives—to promote an ideology that has long-term implications often without immediate, measurable goals.

COMPANY IMAGE BUILDING

Ample evidence demonstrates that a strong company image is essential to maintain sales. There is an inevitable link between the company and its product or service, with the obvious implication that if customers like the company, they will buy its product. A tarnished image decisively reduces the customer's likelihood of purchase. The Procter and Gamble

Company, for instance, recognized image problems when groups of customers interpreted its century-old logo as a satanic symbol. They started boycotting Procter and Gamble products. California grape growers suffered image problems in the 1960s because they were accused of underpaying migrant laborers. The sale of California grapes dropped dramatically. In both of these examples, nothing was wrong with the product, only with the company (or organization) image.

New companies can develop an image where none before existed. Those starting with a clean slate are in a comfortable position, because they can project whatever image they feel best supports their marketing intentions. Established companies, on the other hand, may sponsor sustaining programmes to fortify an existing image that has worked well. Such routine image maintenance is part and parcel of any active communication programme.

But there are also established companies whose images have not fared well among target audience groups, and in these cases there is yeoman's work to do. Correcting a poor image is a formidable task at best and an impossible one at worst. Depending on a variety of circumstances, including why the company's image has been tarnished and how extensive the perception is among audience groups, improving the damaged image involves time and a skillful use of communication techniques.

Ethical considerations also cannot be ignored. Does the company reform its image to reflect accurately its way of doing business, or is the image itself the sum and substance of its programmes? Does the company make changes to correct conditions that might have brought about the negative image, or does it change only the way its messages characterize those conditions? Within the context of these two general categories, there is clearly a great deal of variance in the specific conditions that underlie public communication campaigns.

These considerations, campaigns vary according to available resources, time limitations, and many target audience factors such as predispositions, media usage habits, and behaviour patterns. Such great variability in the conditions makes it impossible to use an off-the-shelf design. Each strategy must be developed in view of characteristics unique to the individual case. We arrive now at a point where we become more prescriptive. Thus far, the reader has been acquainted with a wide array of information concerning elements of the communication process.

We have looked at how people process information and how communicators can shape their messages to be as effective as possible in bringing about favourable audience response under a variety of conditions. We turn now to how these considerations can be used in a communication programme. Furthermore, we examine how planners can place communication designs in the larger context of overall company operations.

A communication programme is not an adjunct to other events in a company, but integral to them. Demonstrated is how to provide structure and order to the planning process. The procedures we recommend involve four phases:

Situation Analysis

Before a company can engineer its communication solutions, it must understand its problems. We pose five questions the communicator should consider to define these problems and to understand their scope and implications.

Variables Specification

Here we refine the information obtained in the first phase and gather new information from target audiences. We consider company goals and audience needs in a single frame and generate a composite list that will serve later in message planning and media strategies.

Programme Specification

With the information obtained thus far, planners will have sufficent information about company needs and audience concerns and attitudes to develop a plan that guides message development, sets the tone of the campaign, and establishes criteria by which to gauge effectiveness of the efforts. The final plan resulting from this step provides specific directions for the content of a campaign.

Programme Implementation

In this final stage we use all the information we have gathered thus far. Audience research data provide the information for cross-matching the responses, personal characteristics, and media consumption patterns of our target audiences. We select mass media and interpersonal communication programmes to carry the messages to specific audience groups.

SITUATION ANALYSIS

Identification of a company's motivations for engaging in a communication campaign is vastly more important than the academic drill it initially appears to be. At the outset of this phase, company planners explain why they have decided to spend company resources on such a venture. Thereby, they force themselves to deal with concrete issues.

If this accounting stands close scrutiny, and planners agree that communication is appropriate to deal with a problem or to achieve stated goals, then the communication-planning process continues. On the other hand, examination may suggest the problem is fundamental to the company's operational programmes or policies and is not communication related or cannot be solved by communication approaches. In such a case, the company must seek other remedies before it can pursue a communication solution. When we conclude that communication is the answer, the follow-up element of this planning phase must be to look carefully at specific concerns of the company and target audience members. Finally, the company must examine the extent of its commitment: How much money and personnel resources can it commit to the campaign? As suggested, examine each of these steps in turn.

Communication is Necessary

In this first step, the company examines the rationale for proposing a communication programme. It provides a simple initial test: Why communication? Sometimes the answer is obvious. For instance, a company may wish to promote a new product or to increase its market share of an existing product. Both evidently would involve a communication programme. A candidate running for office or a group wishing to generate support for a public referendum also has obvious reasons to initiate communication programmes and take action to accomplish their objectives.

In such cases where conditions are unambiguous and free of clouded objectives, one need not dwell further on this matter. Motivations are clear, and a programme involving communication seems appropriate. Sometimes, though, answers to this question are obscure. For example, a company may decide some sort of communication programme is necessary because its market share for a product is shrinking. The thinking here is that if the company can publicize its product, it can regain its market position. Such a cease may overlook a number of essential alternatives.

A communication programme is not the panacea for all problems. Before someone decides to commit resources to a communication strategy, he or she should consider first another line of inquiry. In this case, why is the market share shrinking? Has the quality control slipped so that the product is not what it once was? Has the competition introduced a superior product and lured away customers? Have market conditions changed, making the product obsolete? Or, in this trendy world, is the product a fad whose time has passed? Before committing to a communication strategy, investigate these fundamental conditions. It may be necessary to change the product before promoting it.

Perhaps blame lies in the public image of the company and not in its product. A tarnished company image may have rubbed off on its products, and this may explain the drop in market share. Although communication programmes can go a long way towards recovering a respectable company image among target audiences, little can be done over the long term if reasons for the eroding image remain unchanged. In such cases, good public relations require a change in substance—

not only in image. What the company does about itself will be more important over time than what it says about itself. For example, a large grocery store chain in the southeastern United States recently came under fire for exploiting its workers. Detractors claimed the company, owned by a Scandinavian corporation, underpaid and overworked its employees and refused to allow union organizing. Furthermore, the chain was accused of drawing money from the U.S. economy and funneling large amounts of cash overseas. On the other hand, these grocery stores were popular among consumers and held large shares of the grocery market.

Nonetheless, claims of anti worker and anti-American practices are not well received in these conservative areas. The American South in the mid-1980s was not the place or time a company, and particularly a foreign company, would choose to be so labeled. The heat was on, and the company obviously needed to take action to head off an awkward and potentially debilitating company image problem.

Wisely, the company chose not to embark on a titfor-tat communication programme. Rather, it asked fundamental questions of itself about its practices. It examined its policies and made changes. It conducted several high-visibility programmes that dealt forthrightly with the challenges raised by the opposition. It revised its work and pay schedules for employees (although it did not encourage unionization). The corporation donated large sums of money to community organizations and became a more conspicuous benefactor of poverty and human services activities. In other words, it changed many of the conditions that drew fire from critics. Only then did it escalate its communication efforts. Its media ads discussed these programmes and provided empirical evidence of a changed company outlook on its responsibilities to employees and its role in the community.

Before all other planning activities, it makes sense for companies to ask themselves why they feel communication is appropriate. Ultimately, communication may be desirable, but we feel it is important to consider instituting more fundamental changes first. A slick communication campaign cannot save products outshined by the competition or overcome by obsolescence or companies out of touch and out of favour with customers. It is better to recognize one's frailties at the outset and avoid wasting precious resources on programmes with scarce hope of enduring success.

Communication Programme Produce

Once communication is deemed appropriate, ask several global questions that provide definition to the task. Begin with the most encompassing of all: If this communication programme were to work flawlessly, what would it achieve? Would it increase our sales? Get me elected? Create a sufficiently strong positive image to stop assaults on our character? These are the large and sweeping issues that ultimately drive a communication campaign. It may seem unnecessary to ask such obvious questions, and yet we have found it often helps provide initial structure to articulate even these basic and visible objectives.

The next level of questions examines more immediate goals of the communication design that ultimately contribute to those big objectives. For instance, will communication create an awareness of a product or service? Will it teach target audiences about product features? Will it contain a persuasion component and convince receivers to buy a product or service or adopt a point of view?

It is helpful, at various stages of a campaign, to see when portions of a communication strategy will be called upon to accomplish specific, identifiable tasks. The purpose of this study is to provide structure. One of the biggest problems faced by business communicators is to recognize order in these often large and confusing problems. One person assigned the organization of a campaign to marshal support behind a public referendum remarked there was so much to do and so many things to consider that he had lost his perspective.

Everything seemed disorganized. There was no order and no obvious place to begin because there were no priorities. Numbering these interim objectives helps provide such order and structure. These temporary goals help identify specific tasks that later become milestones in a campaign. In simple communication problems, discussing these points may be unnecessary. In more complex designs, the task is indispensable. Three months before election day, a group of businesses in North Carolina initiated a campaign to repeal the blue law in their county.

The state provided for local option, which meant that laws allowing stores to be open on Sunday were determined on a county-by-county basis. Three months is little time to accomplish such a task, so organizers had to move quickly. In their initial planning sessions, they laid out the overall and interim objectives. Clearly, the overall objective was to see voters rescind the blue law. Everything else would contribute to this goal. First, supporters would need signatures from 10 per cent of the registered voters to place the issue on the November ballot. If they failed to obtain these signatures, there would be no chance to rescind the law.

A communication programme would contribute substantially to this task:

- *Communication Objective #1:* Make community residents aware that the campaign was underway.
- *Communication Objective #2:* Tell residents that the law required signatures from 10 per cent of the voters.
- *Communication Objective #3*: Publicize the location of signature booths.

In this first stage of the campaign, it was not important to persuade people about the need to rescind the blue law. With early polls showing well over 10 per cent of voters already convinced, the matter was more of information and logistics than persuasion. The second phase of the campaign, though, involved a good measure of persuasion.

Knowledge was necessary but not sufficient to guarantee a positive result. People had to be convinced to vote down the blue law. In order to make the best case possible, planners identified several issues they felt would be important for their communication programme. Note that these are general framing issues and will not be specified and expanded until a later portion of the planning process.

- *Communication Objective #4*: Familiarize voters with the economic benefits of Sunday store opening.
- *Communication Objective #5:* Educate voters about the importance of Sunday opening to many shoppers.
- *Communication Objective #6:* Remind people they needed to vote if they wished the law rescinded.

The basic campaign structure derives from these general communication objectives that serve as goals for later parts of the planning process. These objectives usually change with the introduction of new information and further consideration, but they serve an important function in these early discussions. They organize and structure what otherwise might be ill defined and help to start more substantive evaluations.

Specific Company Objectives

The objective of the situation analysis is to provide order, structure, and perspective to the fundamental issues of a campaign. In order to be as thorough as possible in the early planning phases, consider these issues from various viewpoints. We have already examined the general programme objectives. Now as suggested, consider goals of the campaign first from the company's perspective, then from the audience's.

Companies engage in communication campaigns because they stand to benefit in some way. They may realise direct benefits, such as an immediate increase in sales, or indirect benefits, such as an improved image among customers or better relations with certain portions of the target audience. A company rarely will identify itself with a campaign and expect nothing beneficial.

The company should articulate the anticipated advantages to itself in order to confirm its planned use of communication. If it expects the campaign to increase sales, it should state so and then focus the communication programme to achieve this goal. On review, the overall communication programme objectives may not be entirely compatible with stated company goals and expected benefits. In such a case, draw basic campaign objectives into line with specific company objectives.

At the heart of this study is alignment. Do objectives of the communication programme align with specific company objectives? Consider, for example, a small electric utility company planning a summer communication campaign designed to reduce customer use of air conditioners during peak power usage periods.

With an assortment of mass media messages, the company expects to stress the need to curtail heavy air conditioner use between 4 and 8 p.m. It will explain this request and describe techniques for staying comfortable without heavy air conditioning usage. The principal communication programme objective is to reduce air conditioning use during peak power periods.

The anticipated company objectives are not the same. Consider the following. Under normal conditions the company can supply adequate power using its large, relatively inexpensive, coal-fired boilers. With a surge in usage, though, the company must turn on costly gas-powered generators. On hot summer days, this nearly always occurs between 4 and 8 p.m. During this time, people typically increase use of their air conditioning units and so add to the use of other high-power appliances. The company loses money with sustained usage of the smaller peak-load generators. The company objectives, therefore, are to reduce usage of these high-cost generators.

We are suggesting here that the communication programme objectives (reduce air conditioner usage between 4 and 8 p.m.) be examined in light of company objectives (reduce usage of costly peak-load generators). Are they compatible? Will the communication programme contribute to basic company objectives? In this case it appears they are compatible, although it may be argued that the communication programme can go even further in achieving company benefits.

At this point the communication objectives deal with only a portion of the company objectives. Perhaps the communication programme can expand its concerns beyond air conditioning usage into other conservation areas. It may describe additional ways of reducing power usage during the peak period. For instance, it may promote a reduction or shift in the use of hot water, stoves, and other high-power appliances, all of which will contribute to the basic company objectives of curtailing peak-load generator usage. The communication programme objectives will thus become even more supportive of company objectives.

An examination of anticipated company benefits then places the overall objectives in perspective. It determines the compatibility of the two and suggests early modifications to make the programme more effective in the long run.

Receivers Stand to benefit

As communication programmes are shaped to fit company requirements, there is a danger that they will become less responsive to audience needs. Tunnel vision may develop. We may see only those issues of concern to the sponsoring company. The theme expressed throughout this book: A communication strategy that overlooks audience positions is bound to be less effective than one that integrates these positions into the basic design. In our efforts to predominate the communication programme with our own agenda, we may fashion something unacceptable to our target audience. Audience considerations should be imposed early in the planning process.

The importance of human motivations must never be underestimated. Why should audience members want to comply with suggestions offered in a communication campaign? If they recognize some personal benefit, they may investigate the matter further. It is unlikely they will bother if it appears they have nothing to gain. At the outset, then, one must assume the viewpoint of target audiences in order to develop a balanced strategy—one that accommodates both company and audience needs.

Consider our example of the small electric utility. Overall communication objectives have been rewritten to be more encompassing—now they are to curtail peak-hour energy consumption rather than just reduce air conditioning usage.

Company objectives are to save money by reducing the need for costly gas-fired generators. But what are the consumer benefits? Why should they have to modify behaviours to accommodate a power company? Why should they care if it costs the company more to supply increased power during certain hours? The company can tell customers how to cut power usage, but it also needs to tell them why. What is in it for them?

If planners cannot find the answer to such questions, they may wish to redesign the programme to sweeten the deal for customers. In other words, build in a component that customers will recognize as a benefit. At the very least, planners should examine the programme to discover any existing features that may provide the necessary motivational components. We can exemplify both of these positions by our electric utility example.

As the programme now stands, customers may realise two general benefits. First, conservation practices on particularly hot days when electricity demand is greatest will reduce chances of blackouts (total power loss) and brownouts (diminished strength of delivered power). This suggests an interesting benefit of compliance with conservation requests, but not a particularly persuasive one. It offers a negative reward. If customers do not comply, they will lose electricity. If they do comply, they will simply maintain the service they usually receive.

Also, there is no guarantee of a link between individual efforts and individual reward. Even if someone does his or her best to conserve power, unless others also comply, he or she will lose electricity. The second customer benefit may be lower electricity rates. If people save energy, rates can remain low. If they do not, rates will increase. The company will have to recover its losses from sustained use of the gas generators, and no one but the rate payers will pick up the tab.

The company may suggest lower rates as a benefit of conservation, but this is unlikely to have much persuasive effect. Individual efforts may not translate into individual benefits. There is no guarantee that any person who conserves can expect a rate reduction. Such a benefit is derived from group efforts, and no one can be certain what others are doing. These community effort designs have little history of success. Another problem with this proposed benefit comes from the complexity of the rate-making process. Rates go up and down because of many conditions, only one of which is the cost of auxiliary peak-period generators. The effects of conservation on the rate scheme are difficult to recognize. Customers will never know if their efforts really translate into lower bills.If the company is serious about providing an incentive for customers to conserve, it may need to redesign its policies and practices, not just its communication plans.

It will need to demonstrate an observable and measurable benefit for those who comply. Several companies have done this by installing special meters that show when a person uses power. They then charge different rates according to the time of use. They charge lower rates for off-peak hours and higher rates for on-peak hours. Between 4 and 8 p.m., customers may run an air conditioner, take showers, and use the oven, but they will pay premium rates to offset the cost of add-on generators.

Other customers may save money by shifting their energy-consuming activities to low-rate periods. Here the company has provided a clear benefit for the consumer. It has built into its operating programmes a feature that customers will recognize is a personal benefit.As this example demonstrates, customer concerns may involve just communication matters, or they may suggest more substantive policy and practical considerations. Whatever results from the analysis, planners must examine these issues from the audience perspective. If substantive changes are indicated but cannot be accomplished, at least the communicator will be aware of the obstacles likely to evolve.

THE COMMUNICATION CAMPAIGN

Presumably, issues high on the company agenda will command greater resource commitment of personnel allocation, financial support, and management attention. High-priority campaigns are given technical input from programme personnel and receive the weight necessary to move a programme through the company hierarchy. Heavier funding allows more sophisticated market analysis and message development, and provides for the purchase of more frequent messages with better placement in the media.

If a company cannot commit the resources necessary to develop and sustain a mass media campaign, then planners should question the importance of the communication need and either drop the programme or decide on a diminished programme. Whatever the case, it is better to know in these early stages just where the company places the programme among its priorities. Specifically, the communication specialist should know the level of company commitment for these resources:

Financial Support

Those uninitiated to communication campaigns may be surprised to learn what it costs to produce messages and purchase time and space in the mass media. Costs for interpersonal programmes, too, may raise eyebrows. Although it may be difficult to arrive at an accurate cost estimate so early in the campaign, it is essential to determine the magnitude of commitment by the company.

How much does it plan to spend? It may be possible at this time to determine the nature of a campaign based on the available funding. For example, do not consider television and magazine advertising if funding is particularly low. Or, with moderate funding, one might wish to trade off duration of the campaign for the use of the more elaborate and costly media. Again, before the campaign progresses further, determine the available budget.

Facilities and Personnel

In large companies, support facilities and personnel often may be used in a communication campaign. Writers, graphic artists, statisticians, public relations specialists, and others may assist the campaign staff. In-house planning and production may improve the quality and reduce the costs of a programme. Moreover, by pledging such resources, a company demonstrates a high level of commitment to the project. It cares enough to give its very own to the campaign.

One word of Caution

Planning a communication campaign and producing messages require experience and special skills. Unless the company has facilities and personnel equipped to handle the demands of a communication campaign, they should go elsewhere for those who can. In an effort to save money, people sometimes try to make do with something or someone who can come close to meeting the needs of the job.

This is not the place to trim a budget. Use proven specialists, not well-meaning, but ill-equipped people to do the work. A person who writes scientific papers for a living may not do well writing a thirty-second television spot. Someone with a nice speaking voice may not have that professional sound needed on a radio or television spot. Welcome specialized company resources; leave almost-fits alone.

Executive Attention

This, too, is a concern limited to large companies. How accessible to people working on the communication campaign are the decision makers? When planners must make initial judgments or changes during the course of a campaign, how difficult is it to locate someone who can provide a ruling?

Two problems are likely when the communication specialists are far removed from the decision maker. First, they may waste time waiting for request and response messages to work their way through the organizational pipeline. It takes time to pass memos from desk to desk and even to relay phone calls from person to person. A direct line to the decision maker clearly allows a rapid exchange of information.

The second problem is more serious. Messages that pass over several desks are subject to scrutiny by people who often feel they need to make changes, if for no other reason than to justify their place in the organization. As a result the decision maker may not receive the original message, but some altered version of it. Another problem with a long chain of command results when there is no advocate for the position. If the communication specialist wishes to support one particular resolution to a problem, he or she cannot plead this case directly to the decision maker but must instead rely on his or her memo or on someone else making the point.

All of this is sloppy communication. Communication specialists should gain direct access to those authorized to make campaign decisions. They should be able to talk directly without gates and filters that impede the message flow. Whenever possible in communication projects of large organizations, planners should negotiate such access at the outset before cumbersome patterns become established.

AUDIENCE ASSESSMENT AND VARIABLES SPECIFICATION

If communication specialists have followed these guidelines so far, they should now see the main features of their communication strategy taking shape. They should be defining clearly their problems and goals. They have determined the boundaries of the campaign. They are forming an agenda and evolving a priority for the issues constituting the campaign. Moreover, they should have some feel for the dimensions of the programme.

They have confronted these important questions: Will there be adequate resources for an elaborate media campaign and to set up an interpersonal component? Will they need to plan a scaled-down, limited design? At this point the communicator should recognize some basic structure and feel that nothing significant has been overlooked in the initial evaluation of conditions for the campaign.

In this next phase, we continue to refine and shape the campaign structure. This process will yield at the end a composite list of items comprising the content of messages. Three steps make up this phase. First, we reexamine concerns of the company relevant to the campaign, but this time we do so with considerable specificity. We seek to articulate all features that may be of interest to the sponsoring organization. Next, we take a close look at the target audience. We tried to speak for the electricity consumers, here we allow them to speak for themselves. As suggested, listen to their collective voices through audience research. Here is where we obtain that audience-specific information we have discussed so often throughout this book.

Finally, as suggested, develop a composite list that represents the combined concerns of the company and the target audience. This list ultimately will serve as the basis on which we develop campaign objectives and construct mass media and interpersonal messages.

Specify Issues Important to the Company

The primary objective of this procedure is for the campaign managers to elaborate on general company concerns identified in the situation analysis. We need to develop a list that reflects every possible matter related to the overall company objectives. The process is simple. Develop a short description of the overall communication programme and company objectives. Distribute the description to designated people throughout the organization, and ask them to comment and elaborate on the points contained.

Ask them to view the issues from their organizational perspective. They should consider each item from their viewpoint as an attorney, an accountant, a salesperson, or whatever their role in the organization. What would they like the target audiences to know about these issues or to be persuaded to do about these issues? They can do this in writing or during a round-table discussion.

People should be able to defend their rationale and show the relevance of their comments. Remind everyone that suggestions are advisory and may not ultimately appear in the campaign. Since as suggested, have to trim the list because of economic and strategic considerations, naturally as suggested, have to cull some items. When we have collected this feedback, we should synthesize the comments and, when possible, cluster them into categories. The final product should provide a comprehensive company-based study of the issues and represent all positions on the topics. In small organizations this task is obviously simpler but important nonetheless. Even a one-person business should go through the same examination of issues. Despite the size and complexity of an organization, it is important that this process be observed. This work will yield a product that ensures against omitting important considerations or overlooking necessary perspectives in the campaign.

In larger organizations this process serves several other functions. First, it provides an opportunity for everyone in the organization to make a contribution to the process. In many companies this is no small matter. Political expediency may demand that everyone have a chance to participate. So communication planners feel compelled to involve people and office divisions within the organization, but may wish to do so without inviting unwanted advice on all aspects of the programme. Here is an excellent opportunity to obtain valuable information and satisfy the need for others to participate.

Ask people to perform a specific task that will contribute to efforts of the campaign. Do not give them an open-ended assignment that might bring more general recommendations than one may care to deal with. This technique also ensures against overlooking major company concerns. Particularly in large organizations, it is easy to see only one side of an issue or one set of issues. This process helps break that fixation on a single perspective and introduces other angles and other issues. It is much easier to add new dimensions to a campaign at this early stage than later when plans have gelled and programmes have gotten underway.

It is better to toss out a wide net early in the campaign than to recognize later that an important company concern has been overlooked. Finally, this process allows debate in the developmental stages of a campaign. Here is the place for discussion—before the company has made plans. Debate at this point helps install items on an agenda and fix priorities.

Debate clarifies issues and brings about a consensus. Many substantive benefits from this process have long-term payoff for the campaign. Consider the electric utility example we discussed earlier. Here the small power company wished to reduce energy consumption during peak power periods because of high electricity production costs. It decided to launch a communication campaign to encourage time shifting. It also agreed to make available special meters to customers willing to pay differential rates for power according to time of use.

To examine all features of this issue, communication planners developed a short list of the overall and company objectives and showed them to staff members at the planning group meeting. They asked participants to consider the list and reflect on the implication of these items for their area of responsibility. Planners also asked if there were any related matters that might have been overlooked.

During this meeting a number of ideas emerged, some of which promised to be helpful in the campaign. A few heated discussions broke out. One in particular dealt with the value of getting into TOD pricing. At the end, advocates of the procedure won out. From all of this, communication planners developed a list of issues that proved to be important within the group. All consensus items were included. Most items logically defended were similarly added to the list. They pared down issues and categorized them under general headings. Since the purpose of this exercise is simply to record specific thoughts, the items may be in the form of questions or statements.

The final list included the following:

- *Prevent Blackouts and Brownouts:* Do people understand blackouts and brownouts? Explain what they are.

Do they see how their behaviours contribute to these conditions?

Explain the notion of shared responsibility.

Give them a list of things they can do to alleviate drain on the system—Keep Rates Lower.

Explain how power usually is generated by our large coal-fired boilers. Show how we need to kick in the costly gas-powered generators during peak demand times. Show how turning on auxiliary generators increases total costs. Will they recognize their individual contribution to this population-wide problem? Explain it.

Time-of-Day meters: Explain the concept of TOD pricing. (Use long distance telephone-billing procedures as an analogy.)

Link production costs with purchase costs.

Explain pass-through concept.

Describe how the meters work.

Show the advantages of the meters to the customer.

Explain time-shifting practices.

What are procedures for obtaining a TOD meter? Explain payment plans.

This is an abbreviated list, but it demonstrates the features necessary to record thoughts of the company staff. Arguments are trimmed and presented in a bullet-point format, and the list is organized according to each major feature anticipated for the campaign. We expect a number of these points to be discarded later when priorities are assigned and cuts are made to fit the dimensions of the communication programme.

At this point we are concerned only with thoroughness and structure. The list must be complete and contain every major concern expressed by the staff. It also must be orderly and logically arranged to permit easy interpretation and analysis. This will be valuable later when planners make final decisions about what subjects are to be discussed in the communication programmes.

Specify Issues Important to Customers

This may well be the single most important feature of programme planning and at the same time the most routinely overlooked. Too often, communicators substitute their intuitive estimates for objective audience-specific information. Their reasons are rarely convincing. Some believe that they know the target audience so well, they have an instinctive sense for what people feel about an issue. Others find the costs of audience surveys to be expensive and would rather spend the money on more visible portions of the programme. A third reason concerns the sophistication of survey information. In this case, people believe audience research will provide more detail and more information than they really know how or care to use. Reasoning in each of these instances is flawed.

Intuitive Sense for the Community

It is difficult to imagine conditions under which anyone can have an accurate and detailed sense for public thinking on an issue. We may be able to suggest how the majority feels about large, popular matters, but we are bound to overlook the sentiments and intensity of feeling among many population subgroups.

In specialized communication campaigns, these subgroups are particularly important. We must be able to understand in detail their outlooks on an issue. Yet unless someone has ongoing interaction with a representative cross section of this special audience, there is no way to anticipate such information. That person simply will not have sufficient exposure to monitor the audience adequately.

It is also unlikely that one could gather the array of details necessary to understand this audience. Survey procedures yield a large amount of information about the audience. We can obtain details on how people feel about an issue and about the intensity of those feelings. We can examine their attitudes towards collateral issues.

We can obtain their demographic statistics and their media consumption patterns. Survey research can provide this kind and more of the information so necessary for programme planning. It is unlikely even well-placed community leaders can furnish such necessary details.

Cost of Survey Research

A communicator trying to save money by doing without survey research is like an airline trying to save money by doing without a flight plan. Both survey research and the flight plan cost money, but are indispensable. Much more can be lost in "flying by the seat of our pants" than by obtaining the information necessary for the job. The costs of media production and time, interpersonal programmes, and other features of a communication campaign can be substantial. Usually, these costs far outweigh survey research expenses.

It is penny wise and pound foolish to trim research costs that will prevent unwise expenditures in the most costly portion of a campaign. One may buy more costly media than necessary, and this may yield no better or even poorer results than lowercost alternatives. Survey research is money well spent. We know of a real estate firm that decided to expand its market into a nearby town.

It planned a large media campaign and a costly interpersonal communication programme. Owners of the company felt they knew the market well and, despite warnings, declined to contract for market research because they felt it was too expensive. Savings on the cost of survey research in this region enabled them to air a prime-time television spot three additional times. After six months the company abandoned its efforts to break into the new market. Their ads generated little new business, and the interpersonal programmes went begging.

Early market research would have suggested that they either avoid this venture entirely or attempt to cultivate a different audience, offering different services. Survey research may not be as ironclad as insurance in guaranteeing campaign success, but it goes a long way towards increasing the odds.

There Is Too Much Information

We believe this argument comes from people who have never seen survey information. To them, research conveys images of statistics, charts, and algebraic equations, all too difficult to understand. Survey research is an enigma to many people. Let us clear the air about this.

Findings from audience research can be made simple to comprehend. The raw data resulting from survey research can be difficult to decipher, but let the consultants deal with these complexities. Any good researcher can analyse the data and provide an understandable interpretation of what it all means. He or she can describe what the overall sample feels about an issue and how that issue is handled by subgroups, say Republicans versus Democrats or people who have graduated from high school versus people who have not. Nothing is difficult about the results of survey research. If a client cannot make heads or tails of the results, the researcher is not doing his or her job.

Even the most detailed aspects of a survey can be expressed in understandable, usable terms. Newspapers often translate national surveys into descriptions that the average reader can understand. Television news departments have become particularly adept at presenting survey results using graphics and verbal descriptions. There is no reason why the average business communicator cannot work productively with survey findings.

We should add that surveys range from simple designs providing a quick look at a population to more complex reports exploring audiences in considerable detail. For most communication campaigns, the simpler approaches work just fine. They provide the necessary details for programme design and media planning. They cost less and are adequate to meet task requirements. Particularly with such survey designs, the user unfamiliar with survey techniques has little to fear. In a few minutes, a research consultant can explain how to interpret the findings and how to apply them to specific tasks of the communication campaign.

Reasons for supplanting research data with intuitive estimates of population characteristics are difficult to defend. Hunches rarely provide the accuracy or scope necessary to guide a campaign. In the long run, hunches do not save money and often may be wasteful. Finally, a good survey will yield accurate, usable information that answers important questions in a straight forward manner. Fears of threatening, uninterpretable data are ill founded. Survey research helps communicators to understand an audience. There is no other viable way of gathering important feedback data from target audience members. In the strictest sense, feedback is information obtained from the receivers of a message. We extend the meaning of the term here to apply to information gathered from intended receivers even before we deliver the first message. As we prepare to shape details of our strategy for the communication campaign, we must make decisions in light of audience positions and needs. We examined issues from the company perspective. We wanted to ensure that we had not overlooked important details that might affect company operations. Here we look at the issue from the perspectives of the receivers who are partners in the communication process.

Exactly how do we go about this task? How do we examine the issues from the receivers' position? In survey research, we get answers by asking questions. The usability and usefulness of the answers we receive depend on the selection of questions that set the agenda for respondents. From this it follows that the value of the feedback data depends largely on the agenda we establish through our questions. Well, then, how do we go about asking appropriate questions? How do we recognize this agenda ourselves in order to develop questions that will yield usable information?

Here we describe an approach that derives its structure from the intersection of two features. The first is the Berlo model of communication: source, message, channel, and receiver. The second is our orientation to a subject: knowledge, where we obtain information about it; attitude, where we develop feelings and dispositions towards it; and behaviour, where we may engage in some activity relating to it. When we examine these two categories together, we discover a valuable guide to developing our agenda for audience research.

In this description as suggested, discuss (1) each element of the Berlo model (SMCR) in relation to (2) receiver orientation towards a subject (knowledge, attitude, and behaviour). As suggested, make a few substitutions along the way to serve our particular purpose, but wherever possible as suggested, adhere to the original design. As we get into this discussion, we remind the reader of our goals. We are examining a procedure that will provide structure in developing the survey instrument for our audience research. We wish to deal with all relevant matters and therefore ask appropriate questions. We want to overlook nothing important, include nothing irrelevant.

The source is not necessarily who developed the message but who the audience believes developed the message. So the source may be the company sponsoring the campaign, or it may be the individual on camera who delivers the message. Both may be important in this phase of research.We may wish to examine audience perceptions of the company. We also may wish to look at audience evaluations of a spokesperson we plan to use in the campaign. In both cases our considerations are the same.We should examine two features of the source. We want to find out the receivers' knowledge of the source, then their attitudes towards the source.

Knowledge

We stated earlier that knowledge is a precondition for any subsequent reaction. People must know about the source before they can generate attitudes towards it. Without knowledge about a source, there can be no response. It is therefore important in an audience survey to get an accurate picture of what receivers know about the source. Their knowledge will fall into four general categories: As we develop an accurate composite picture of our receivers, it is important to know what they know.

We may wish to improve their knowledge about our company before we attempt to promote our product. Perhaps they know nothing about us, in which case we may wish to provide background information. They may have inaccurate information that has contribu-ted to problems faced by the company. Consider the Procter and Gamble case we described earlier. Many customers inaccurately believed the Procter and Gamble logo signified satanic affiliations. Attitudes that will be examined next are founded on a knowledge base, and that knowledge base may be distorted or incomplete. In these cases the company needs to correct the information available to audiences as part of its campaign. If the information is complete and accurate and based on the knowledge that people are forming poor impressions, the company may be advised to make substantive changes in its policies and practices to correct the problem.

Without such changes, we can expect few lasting effects of a communication campaign. Whatever the implications of such observations, it is first necessary to obtain this information through research. This may be accomplished with a survey instrument designed to elicit such data from target audiences. Specialists in instrument construction can develop items that will determine the level and accuracy of information within target audience populations. It is up to the communicator to identify such issues for inclusion in the survey.

Attitudes

Questions in this category examine impressions that receivers hold about a source. They look at overall perceptions, such as positive and negative sentiments towards a source, and at specific categories of attitudes. Of the specific concerns, information about receivers' perceptions of source credibility may be most valuable.

Trustworthiness

This deals with the extent to which receivers believe a source to be honest, dependable, and reliable. In other words, how much confidence can receivers place in the source?

Expertise

How much does the source know? When a source is seen as having the skill, knowledge, or credentials necessary to perform a task, he or she will be viewed as expert and qualified.

Charisma

Although operational definitions of charisma are difficult to provide, we generally use the term to describe the ability of someone to hold sway over other people. It is a composite of personality, appearance, voice, and style that enables a person to affect others. In a company, we look for creativity and innovativeness.

Companies facing declining sales or direct customer opposition should consider dealing with these attitude issues in their research. They should develop a profile of audience perceptions both of the overall company image and of specific features. An examination of credibility issues in particular may suggest ways to improve audience impressions. Trustworthiness can be fortified through media techniques that concentrate on the honesty, care, and concern of a company for its customers.

A company can bolster public images of its expertise by promoting its staff specialists, advanced equipment, and management concerned with excellence. Before communicators can find solutions, though, they must first identify the problems.

An examination of public attitudes towards a company can provide a more complete perspective on how that company and its products are viewed.

THE MESSAGE

An issue may be a product or service, an idea, or an ideology. It may pertain to the company or to an individual. Here we examine the audience perspectives on campaign issues that should be included in a research design. We look at what one needs to know about audience perceptions of the issue at hand.

Our concerns for the research design must always be driven by our objectives for the communication programme. If we plan to teach an audience, we need to know what they already know. If we wish to persuade them to do something or to accept some position, we need to know their sentiments and outlooks before we begin. What do target audiences think is important about an issue? What are they likely to reject, accept, or ignore? As suggested, look here at respondent knowledge and attitudes. As suggested, also explore the implications for behaviour or how audience members will be likely to respond (or have responded) with actions to an issue. Thus, the structure of a survey instrument might consider what people know about an issue, how they feel about the issue, and what their behavioural responses are.

Knowledge

The basic knowledge concerns are similar to those for our discussion on the source. It is important to ask questions that assess respondent understanding of an issue.

We should gauge their level of knowledge and the accuracy and thoroughness of that knowledge. However, we also should look at collateral features of the issue we may not have anticipated.

Attitudes

We use different communication strategies with friends than we do with adversaries. If audiences believe as we do, we use techniques to gel support and rally the faithful. When we are among those who do not agree with our position or who are undecided, we use different persuasive devices to convince them of our viewpoint. In public communication, strategy requirements demand that we learn about our audiences' attitudes.

Survey research is well adapted to gathering such information. We can ask people to tell us how they feel and how strongly they feel about an issue. We thus can obtain information on the direction of feeling as well as the intensity of their reactions.

Consider a moderate-sized southern city thinking about holding a public referendum on the selling of liquor by the drink. Supporters of the measure need to convince the majority of voters to allow liquor sales. In order to get some idea of how people feel about the issue, planners conducted an early public survey. Among the items was this question: "How do you feel about permitting the sale of liquor by the drink in restaurants? Do you strongly support, somewhat support, somewhat oppose, or strongly oppose selling liquor by the drink in restaurants?"

They obtained the following results:

Strongly support	35 per cent
Somewhat support	18 per cent
Somewhat oppose	37 per cent
Strongly oppose	10 per cent

Notice there are 53 per cent in support and 47 per cent in opposition to the proposal. This is a close call. But look at the distribution of intensity 35 per cent strongly support while only 10 per cent strongly oppose. These represent audience members well entrenched in their positions who may be moved only with considerable persuasive force, if at all.

The "somewhat" categories are less committed, and thus more easily swayed to the other side. In this case, supporters of liquor by the drink have reason to be optimistic. There are more supporters than opposers. There are more strongly supporting than strongly opposing. Moreover, there are more people in the somewhat opposed category who might be drawn into the support side than those in the somewhat support category who might be drawn into the opposed side. From this we have information on the direction of respondent attitude (53 per cent support, 47 per cent oppose), but also a measure of intensity (how many "strongly" and "somewhat" in each category).

In this particular case, the intensity information gives more reason for supporters to celebrate than the direction information. In planning a public survey, then, one should look at issues on which gauging respondent attitudes is important. Such information enables the communicator to evaluate the campaign climate and determine the best persuasive strategy. In gathering attitudinal information, researchers should look at both the direction and the intensity of these attitudes.

Behaviour

Identification of likely behaviours may be important to some campaigns. In political campaigns as suggested, wish to know how voters plan to behave at the polling station. In a product promotional campaign, we may want to know if consumers plan to purchase a certain product or to shop at a certain store. We consider any contingent action by audience members as a behaviour. Voting behaviour, purchasing behaviour, striking behaviour (for unions), and joining behaviour are typical examples. We may not always need to ask people to anticipate a behaviour. We have discovered that if we ask about present behaviours and past behaviours, we can make predictions about possible future behaviours.

Past Republican voters tend to be future Republican voters. Present Chevy owners tend to be future Chevy owners.In most cases we are interested in future behaviours and use whatever information we can to help predict these behaviours—direct questions about anticipated actions, the respondent's history of actions, even the actions of others in the respondent's social circle. We must extend a word of caution. Depending on the topic, there is great variance in the accuracy of research to predict behaviours. Many things can weaken the relationship between survey results and observed behaviour. As suggested, review just a few here:

Intervening Events Can Affect Respondents

Circumstances may change what one expects to do and what one actually does. A candidate may bungle a debate or not kiss enough babies. A product may be found to have flaws. Any number of things may cause persons to change their mind. They may have believed they would behave in a certain way when they reported their expectations, but unforeseen events may have altered prevailing conditions.

Respondents Do Not Always Tell the Truth

Researchers know that respondents sometimes lie. Sometimes they lie because they are embarrassed to tell the truth. When asked if they plan to vote in the next election, some respondents may report they will just to appear to be good citizens. People often will provide the socially acceptable answer to avoid discomfort. Sometimes people lie because they enjoy giving researchers a hard time. *Chicago Tribune* columnist Mike Royko once asked his readers to lie to interviewers at exit polls conducted in various Chicago voting precincts. Large numbers of people went along with Royko's prank and falsely reported their voting behaviours. The data gathered in these polls did not reflect accurately the collective behaviours of Chicago voters for this election. Respondents Can Be Uncertain. Survey questions may deal with behaviours about which the respondents have not given any thought. On a whim they might say they will behave in a certain way, if only to satisfy the interviewer who is expecting a response. Perhaps later, when the matter has become more important on the people's agenda, additional thought will bring about a different behaviour. Summary. Let us consider all of these concerns for the issue in a single example. Take a hypothetical political situation in which a candidate, the incumbent, wishes to shape a reelection campaign around three themes:

- His voting record on taxes, the environment, and automobile safety legislation;
- His constituent assistance programme during the last two years in office;
- His major new proposal for increased economic ties with China.

In anticipation of a political campaign, like most candidates, our congressman wisely conducts a poll to see how his constituents feel about these three issues. He wants to know if he should make a big point of them in the campaign or play them down. In planning his research, the candidate and his staff may construct a set of questions such as these:

Voting Record

- How much do respondents know about my voting record on taxes, on the environment, and on auto safety legislation?
- Do they have an accurate understanding of what we have accomplished?
- What sorts of things have I overlooked? What related concerns on these matters do they have?
- Do they agree with my decision on each of these matters? How strongly do they feel about my decisions?

Constituent Assistance

- Do they know about the assistance programme we have implemented in the last two years for constituents of this district?
- Have they personally used my constituent services? Do they know personally of anyone who has used them?
- What else do they feel I should do to improve these services?
- Do they feel we have done a good or a bad job—how good/how bad?

China Ties

- Have they heard about my work on increased economic ties with China?
- What do they know about this work?
- Is their information accurate and complete?
- What do they feel about the plan? Do they think I should pursue this?
- Is there any other related issue on their minds?
- Do they feel I am dealing with things that draw too much of my attention from problems in the district? Do they think it is prestigious for their congressman to be dealing with such global issues?
- How strongly do they feel about these matters?

In each case the congressman has examined the knowledge, attitudes, and, when appropriate, behaviours of constituents. Researchers will translate this list into survey items appropriately worded to gather the necessary data. With this approach the congressman will have thought about all relevant aspects of the issues and developed a comprehensive picture from the constituents' perspective.

Obviously, not all constituents think alike, although they often think in patterns. Answers to certain questions cluster together, as do groups of people identified by certain characteristics. Information generated in this part may be analysed with other data in the survey to reveal these important patterns.

THE CHANNEL

Here we are interested primarily in behaviours and are less concerned with knowledge and attitudes. We have a specific application for the information we obtain about the channel: To reach our target audiences, we must know what media they use. For reasons as suggested, describe, published media usage data, such as Arbitron and Nielsen, are inadequate to meet the needs of many specialized communications programmes. These standard ratings services provide general information, while we require specific, pinpoint data on audience subgroups.

We can obtain such precise information only in our own research. As suggested, examine reasons for which we need such precise information in a moment. First, it will be helpful to review two categories of channel information relevant to survey planning.

MASS MEDIA USAGE

Here we audit the repertoire of media used by each respondent. Some call this the "media inventory." In specialized communication programmes, we are particularly concerned with respondent use of targeted media such as magazines, journals, newsletters, and perhaps even radio stations. These media may become the major channels through which we reach such audiences; consequently, our planning will be aided by as much detailed information as we can øbtain. We may wish to consider the following categories related to media usage:

- Which media do they use?
- How regularly do they use each of these media (weekly, monthly, annually)?
- How do they obtain these media (subscription, pass along)?
- Do they pass along these media to others?

Although we have said our interests were primarily in media behaviours, occasionally we may need to examine attitudes towards the media as well. Such information may be helpful in deciding between two media or in allocating resources among a list of media. When the need for such data arises, consider the following categories:

- Why do you use this medium?
- What are your opinions towards this medium (you may use the credibility sequence here—trustworthiness, expertise, and charisma)?
- How do you use information contained in this medium?

INTERPERSONAL CHANNELS

In this category we are concerned with the likelihood of our audience participating in certain kinds of interpersonal programmes. How probable is it that they will visit a model home? Do they think they would ever use a tape bank? What do they feel about sophisticated demonstrations? Such information may suggest the feasibility of using certain interpersonal approaches.

Our survey can identify programmes most likely to draw target audiences and those most likely to attract little interest, thereby preventing the waste inherent in hit or miss planning strategies. As we have noted, it is up to the communication specialist to raise questions about these issues, and up to the research specialist to provide answers. Researchers may require a more sophisticated instrument design.

People may be unfamiliar with the techniques proposed. They may be unwilling to report their interest for fear of being given a sales pitch. They may feel the interviewer is becoming too personal with such questions. All of these responses pose blocks, but not insurmountable problems. Communication planners should identify the information they need and let the research people worry about how to obtain it.

It is evident that information on interpersonal programmes is specific and probably not available from other sources. But what about mass media channel information? Why not just use a commercial media research service such as Arbitron and Nielsen? Do they not tell how many and what kinds of people are watching which television stations and listening to which radio stations? Obviously they do provide this information, but for our purposes it is inadequate. In large audience campaigns designed to reach a cross section of the entire population, published data such as these may be sufficient. Communicators can concentrate their media purchases on the most popular station for consumers, say, between eighteen and forty-nine years of age, or those most patronized by people over fifty-five.

They also may buy space in the largest newspaper to reach as many people as possible with a single message. In specialized communication campaigns, though, we approach our task with more precision. We look carefully at small subgroups.

We examine unique needs of audience members partitioned into clusters identified by special characteristics. We also attempt to reach our receivers through channels that provide the most specific audience selection. There is considerable value in gathering in a single frame all data relevant to target audiences. We can identify audience subgroups not only according to demographic traits (as do published sources), but to source- and issue-related responses as well.

We can concentrate messages reinforcing the position of those supporting our proposal in the channels they most favour. We may reach opponents of the proposal with different messages through a different, specific set of channels. This ability to combine survey information provides the specificity we need in targeted communication. We need to sort audiences on more than just a few simple demographics. We need more specific information on their attitudes and beliefs on a range of issues. Once we have identified our target audience groups according to these traits, we can link them to specific media. Published sources cannot provide the detail necessary to meet these needs.

THE RECEIVER

How to retrieve the thoughts of the receiver has dominated this discussion. The purpose here, after all, has been to obtain the thoughts of those who would be the recipients of our messages. We have seen the problems characteristic of a programme devoid of audience input, and so we have built in this important research feature.What is left to know about our receivers? We have looked at their interests, concerns, and impressions towards the source and the issues. We have a pretty good idea about what they know and how they feel and have made some reasonable predictions about their behaviours. We know their media usage patterns.

We are missing information only about the receivers' personal characteristics. We think about identifying audience groups according to personal traits.Development of this list is based on common sense. Apart from obvious physical characteristics, what features would we use to describe a man we have just met? We would probably report the person's age and gender. We might note where he lived, his occupation, and perhaps his education. Depending on our reason for describing this person, we might also discuss his religious beliefs, political party affiliation, and something about his family life. Is he married?

Does he have children? Is he a grandparent? Depending, again, on our purpose, we might note that this person owns his own home, lives in a city, and generally considers himself to have a liberal political outlook.We use a similar approach in developing our list of personal traits (generally called "demographic traits") in planning our survey. Several characteristics are nearly always included: age, gender, occupation, education level, and income. These are standard because over time they have proven to be a basis on which to sort audiences.

For instance, in reviewing a handful of public surveys, we have seen the following:

- Young people are significantly more likely than older people to favour increasing highway driving speeds.
- Older people more than young people are more likely to favour higher taxes to deal with the national debt.
- Women are more likely than men to favour cuts in military spending.
- People with higher education levels favour serious

discussions with the Soviets on the limitation of nuclear weapons.

- People in higher income brackets are more likely to vote for Republican candidates.

Survey researchers know well the predictive capacity of these standard demographic traits. They form natural audience subgroups. For many topics in a specialized communication campaign, sponsors would send a different message through different media to different groups identified by these demographic features. It is standard practice to include them in a survey.

Apart from these traits, the communicator must decide what other features of his or her audience would be helpful in identifying subgroups. The researcher may offer some ideas on the topic. Many communicators will come up with recommendations based on their experience. Receiver traits in this category are issue specific and should be considered on a case-by-case basis.

In political polls, one may wish to include political party affiliation and registration status. In polls of business leaders, we may ask about civic group membership, years of residence in the community, and participation in the chamber of commerce and other advocacy organizations. Each of these features may help sort audiences into smaller, more like-minded groups. Each group then may be treated with approaches specifically designed for their needs.

PROGRAMME IMPLEMENTATION

Much of the work that puts the communication campaign into place requires the input of specialists. In a large mass media/interpersonal campaign involving several audience levels and a variety of topics, we expect to involve researchers and statisticians, media experts, a host of production people, advertising agencies, and strategy consultants. Company representatives serve to oversee the activities of these specialists and to watch out for interests of their organization. Since they have been involved extensively in the planning process, which outlined the intentions and objectives of the campaign, they can speak with authority on the campaign goals. Activities of the planning process put company representatives in the middle of the project rather than on the edges of it. The organization does more than pay the bills. It takes control of the process and imposes its interests on the support staff. This ensures the company's best interests are observed and its needs met by the chosen strategy.

In smaller operations, programme implementation will assume a less elaborate design, but one no less important to the company. Even in these cases, it may be advisable to seek the counsel of a research specialist and an advertising agency to guide in the final steps of media planning. Buy from these consultants only what you need. You have already done the planning and market analysis. Tell them precisely what you want them to do.

Do not pay for unnecessary services. Because of the individual nature of these final activities, we cannot become too specific in our review of procedures. As suggested, provide just a brief outline of tasks that complete the implementation phase of a campaign. As suggested, also identify the specialist who may help with each portion of this work.

AUDIENCES, AND MEDIA

A research consultant will be able to look for response patterns across families of issues. Computer programmes can identify characteristics of respondents who answer in certain ways to substantive issues and reveal the nature of target audiences. These characterisics may be based on receiver response to other substantive issues (for instance, people who are interested in buying TOD meters may also feel their utility bills are too high) or on demographic traits (age, income, etc.). In our electric company example, the researcher may note that a large number of people who are interested in buying TOD meters recall experiencing a blackout.

They also already have a reasonable understanding of the differential pricing concept (substantive issue). Furthermore, findings may disclose the majority of these people are over forty years of age, earn more than $35,000 per year, and have at least some college education (demographic traits). This may be sufficient information with which to suggest ways that messages may be developed to reach those customers who have a high probability of purchasing the product. Other groups that may demonstrate little interest in the product can be approached from a different angle or may be avoided altogether.

Once the researcher has identified target audiences based on responses to substantive issues, he or she must examine their corresponding media consumption patterns. Here information is obtained that enables him or her to pinpoint delivery of the messages. Messages designed specifically to reach those who have the greatest potential to purchase the TOD meters must be carried by the channels to which these consumers are tuned. Perhaps they usually listen to the same radio stations and subscribe to the same magazines. Media usage patterns within such groups may be disclosed using simple matching techniques known to the researcher.

We can use the same approach to identify the likelihood of target audience participation in interpersonal programmes. The second category of channel usage considered in the research design that involved respondents' interest in becoming engaged in specific follow-through programmes. With this information the researcher can identify the interpersonal approaches most likely to attract target audience segments.

For example, the high-probability group may show interest in telephone conversations with company representatives about TOD meters, but report little likelihood of visiting a demonstration centre. Such information can help the company make informed decisions about costly interpersonal programmes.

SELECT THE MEDIA

The sophistication in planning for media selection is directly proportional to the complexity of a communication programme. As the design increases in geographic area, numbers of target audiences, and message levels, so, too, do considerations for media selection. In smaller, limited campaigns, planners may wish to make media selections and buys on their own or with minimal aid of a local advertising agency or media consultant. We suggest they become familiar with the principles involved in the process by reviewing one of several good texts on the subject. For larger programmes we nearly always recommend the assistance of a specialist. Media selection may be complex. It is nearly always expensive.

Consultant fees add to the cost of a campaign, but will pay off in the long run. As suggested, review just the highlights of media selection. We leave the details to texts specializing in the topic.Media selection is based on several considerations. First, target audience media consumption patterns must be considered. If audiences tend to cluster around certain channels (specific magazines or radio or even television stations), these media should be given priority.

This becomes particularly valid in the case of small, specific audiences focused on a narrow topic. For example, take the narrow customer group that may be interested in buying a new altimeter for small, private, commuter aircraft. The altimeter company would be wise to concentrate its promotional efforts on those specific media identified by research to interest this audience. As audiences grow larger and the topic takes on more general audience interest, there is more latitude in media selection.The next consideration has to do with the communication task.

What do we wish to do with this message? Inform? Persuade? Stimulate interest? In any given circumstance, one medium may be better able to achieve the communication task than any other. Consider these sample purposes:

Display a Product

Some products may require a visual component to make a point, in which case print or television may be appropriate. In some cases, sound may be important, suggesting the broadcast media. In a political campaign where voters must feel they know the candidate, television may provide the most useful format.

Get Across Details of a Product

Information about details and specifications of a product are best disseminated through print media. Readers can study the information, become familiar with the data, and compare these facts against those of competing products. Radio is a poor choice to communicate more than just a few specifications because people quickly become lost in the recitation of numbers.

Television, too, can flash numbers on a screen only for short periods, and does not permit detailed study by viewers. All media can handle a few details. Print is ideally suited for extensive lists.

Build an Image of a Product

Any of the media can contribute to building a product image. In specific circumstances, some of the media may be more adept at the task than others. With sight and sound, television can set a mood and evoke emotional audience responses. So, too, can radio, with its capacity to stimulate the imagination. Print media are limited in stimulating emotion and generally are better able to elicit an intellectual response.

It is impossible to anticipate all the reasons that one may wish to communicate with target audiences.

As a general consideration, we suggest the communicator examine the basic goals of the message and look to the media that may best meet them.

The immediate needs and will probably have the intended impact. Also, consider the way media work together. One channel may acquaint audiences with a topic and another pick up with persuasive messages. Television may build the image of a product or service, and newspapers might provide details. It is unusual to place all messages in a single medium. Consider the synergistic effects of a family of messages carried in a variety of formats.

Another consideration is cost. Although somewhere there must have been a campaign run without cost constraints, we have not seen it. In most cases, we make final media decisions in light of what we can afford to buy.

It is important that costs not become the driving element in media selection. Naturally, with some general budget constraints in mind, work first with other variables to lay out the media design.

Then allow specific financial limitations to enter the process. Use the suggestions proposed earlier. Before eliminating entire media from the programme, try various economizing techniques. There are messages and media short of the ideal that can be effective with target audiences.

INTERPERSONAL PROGRAMME

Research data already available should suggest programmes that will likely be effective with target audiences. Certain audiences may be inclined to visit a showroom or ask a representative to visit their homes or businesses, while others will go no further than a telephone call. Plan the programme around the audience. If there are doubts, start with less costly approaches and build when an audience need becomes apparent.

Use the mail or a tape bank before getting into face-to-face techniques. Setup costs for these programmes are expensive, and their payoff should be ensured before too much is invested. If the phone bank works, and later there is an indication that personal visits would be even more effective, then set up the more elaborate programme. At least you will have tested the waters before making such a large commitment.

Consider the link between a mass media and interpersonal communication programme. The information necessary to see the relationship between these two approaches. By teaching, alerting, and persuading target audiences, the mass media support the interpersonal efforts. Interpersonal programmes extend the notion of targeted communication to its natural cease. Media and interpersonal programmes should therefore be considered in a single frame. Both contribute to company goals and should be integrated at every step of the planning process.

7

Assessing the Mind of the Public

A theoretical framework for the process of attitude formation. By understanding the psychological underpinnings, he argues business communicators effectively can reach their target audiences with persuasive information. He discusses methods of routinely monitoring public attitudes and of conducting ongoing communication with the consumer community.

He also offers a variety of valuable suggestions for dealing with events that are likely to receive negative public attention. What does the public think about my business? Whether your business is large or small, service oriented or production oriented, public or private, the question of how the public views your business is important to the management process. Does the public have a favourable impression? Do people like the way the store is decorated?

Are people concerned that my plant might be adding to pollution, or are they pleased that my plant is going to be hiring more people? Effective managers have always been interested in public opinion, and have devised many ways to assess what John Q. Public thinks about their business. The questions about public opinion that should concern business managers. How important is public opinion to the manager of a business? Can public opinion be changed? How does the public acquire the opinions it holds? Before addressing these and related questions, it may be helpful to note that the American public is capable of dramatic changes in attitude.

In the past the result has frequently meant equally dramatic changes in the way the public behaves. When the increased efficiency of the diesel locomotive meant fewer stops for fuel and water, the small towns across our western plains that had depended on the regular stops of the steam locomotives for their economy became ghost towns. The people in those towns became concerned, and local ordinances attempted to force the railroads to make stops.

The oil embargo in 1973 produced almost immediate changes in public opinion and public behaviour. People stopped buying large, gas-guzzling automobiles. The public began to pay close attention to any business that had a relationship to oil and its use. Few people before the oil embargo, for example, paid much attention to our public utilities. Public opinion is usually neutral or mildly favourable towards the utility business when the lights work, the heat comes on automatically, and the water flows unimpeded from the tap.

Public opinion is seldom aroused when stories do not appear in the newspaper and when the monthly bills for utility services are but a minor part of the monthly pile. But public opinion can be expected to change when paying the utility bill may mean that the clothing bill does not get paid. Public opinion can be expected to change when the six o'clock news reports that the local utility shut off the heat of a little old lady because she did not pay her bill. Public opinion can be expected to change when the newspaper urges people to turn down their air conditioners because of the overuse of electricity.

Whether oil companies, railroads, utilities, cereal companies, universities, or businesses of any type are affected, the process is the same. Whenever there is some major change in the way people live, equally major changes in public opinion can be expected, and changes in behaviour will occur. The effective manager must know how to assess public opinion and how to adjust to changes in what the public may think about the business. Before addressing the question of what managers can or ought to do about public opinion, it will be useful to see just how such opinion is formed.

DEVELOPMENT OF PUBLIC OPINION

The "public" in the United States is composed of all of its people, some 240 million people. In general, all we mean by "public opinion" is the views held by a majority (or very large number) of the people in the country at any one time about any event or series of events. In order to determine what public opinion is about an event, we simply ask a large number of people how they feel about a particular topic.

If we find that most of the people we ask feel generally the same way, we usually can write statements that begin with "Public opinion seems to be united on this topic." If we find great differences of opinion, with some people favouring the topic, some opposed to it, and many neutral, we might find the report beginning with "Public opinion is divided on this topic."

Knowing the level of public opinion, however, is not enough. We still need some insight into how the opinion process works. For that understanding, we turn to the individual and examine the process of attitude formation. All we mean by an "attitude" is the feelings of liking or disliking we all have towards people, places, events, and ideas.

We have attitudes about dogs, cats, gasoline, rationing, and businesses. We have attitudes about friends, coworkers, wives, children, and legislators; about movies, education, politics, and religion. We form attitudes about all of the events that occur in our daily lives. The actual attitudes we hold will generally be the result of our experiences with people, ideas, and events. If we meet a teacher who is helpful to us, we are likely to hold favourable attitudes towards teachers. If we were bitten by a dog when we were very young, we may have a negative attitude towards dogs.

Attitudes can range from highly favourable to neutral to highly unfavourable. They can also be held with various degrees of intensity. I may be highly favourable towards a certain product, but it does not fill all my thoughts. I do not try to sell the product to others, do not try to have it adopted by my company or to convince others to use it. I just do not hold a very intense attitude towards the product. In another case the situation might be different. I might be highly unfavourable towards abortion and also feel highly intensely about the subject. I might well write letters to the newspaper, try to get a new law passed prohibiting abortion, avoid socializing with people who favour abortion, and vote only for candidates who favour antiabortion legislation. Clearly, it is important to distinguish between the nature of the attitude held, that is, favourable or unfavourable, and the degree of intensity with which the attitude is held.

As managers we might become concerned if we found that a large number of people held unfavourable attitudes towards our company. But we would become greatly concerned if we found that many of those same people were filing petitions to increase our taxes by increasing our assessed valuation. The latter group is not only unfavourable, but holds its attitudes intensely enough to operate in accordance with them. We have said that individuals hold attitudes towards all of the people, objects, events, and ideas that they meet in their daily lives. Those attitudes do not seem to be held completely in isolation from one another.

Instead, we tend to "group" attitudes into larger sets that we can term "frames of reference." When individuals build up a pattern of attitudes towards a set of objects or ideas based on past experience, they then tend to use this frame of reference as a way of assessing events or experiences or messages that may appear in the future. Thus, we might expect that an individual would develop a reference frame based on all the experiences he or she may have had with similar businesses. There may be some favourable experiences and thus favourable attitudes towards the water company.

There may be favourable attitudes towards a telephone company repairman. There may be unfavourable attitudes towards a service representative at the telephone company. That total set of attitudes towards utilities can be called the individual's frame of reference about utilities. Why is the frame of reference important? There are two main reasons why behavioural scientists think this is so. First, the existing reference frame that an individual possesses tends to govern the ways in which new experiences are perceived. Thus, the individual who has had a whole series of negative experiences with one supermarket is very likely to approach any new contact with that supermarket in a negative manner. Such an approach may be neither logical nor rational, but behavioural scientists are inclined to think that rationality is not as important to attitude development as the kind of past experiences we have had. The obvious implication for a manager, for example, is the importance of long-range programmes. It is not enough to make an individual happy on the first visit to a store or when a product or service is first purchased. Efforts must be made to continue the flow of favourable experiences to the customer.

The second major reason why frames of reference are important is that they tend to govern future behaviour. The frame of reference is composed of a set of attitudes. An individual who is exposed to a new situation and who has a favourable attitude towards the situation is likely to behave favourably. An individual who approaches a new situation with an unfavourable attitude is likely to behave by avoiding the situation.

A simple example will emphasize this relationship between attitudes and behaviour. Imagine two children. One child was bitten by a dog when he was three years old. The other was given a puppy for Christmas when she was three and has always loved it. What happens when the two children are approached by a large police dog on the streets? The child who was bitten is likely to run away. The child who loves her own dog is likely to pet this new dog. Note that neither behaviour may be "rational." This dog might be friendly, in which case running away is not an appropriate behaviour. Or the dog might be unfriendly, in which case attempting to pet the dog is not appropriate. But the children behaved as their set past attitudes dictated. The frame of reference they had developed helped govern behaviour.

We must hasten to note that not all behaviour is directly governed by attitudes. Many people are prejudiced against members of minority groups. But that does not mean that someone meeting a member of a minority group on the street will automatically run over and hit the person. Our behaviour is also determined by laws, customs, fear of retaliation, and other influences. That we may not always behave as our attitudes would indicate, however, is important to the individual attempting to make an assessment of public opinion and its possible consequences. For example, suppose we hold a series of public meetings and find very few people who say anything negative about a bond issue.

But when the vote is taken, the bond issue fails miserably. What happened? The fact is that few people are willing to express themselves in public meetings. They worry that they may be the only ones opposed to the bond issue, so they keep quiet. They may not want to offend the individual conducting the meeting, so they say nothing. In the privacy of the voting booth, their behaviour is governed more directly by their attitudes.

The fact that not all attitudes lead directly to behaviour should not lead to the cease that attitudes are not important. Making a careful assessment as to the state of individual attitudes, and thus the attitudes of a population, is one of the best ways we have to predict the eventual outcome of a proposal, a law, a bond issue, or a price increase. One other matter should be understood about the frames of reference we possess. We have said that we tend to group all of the attitudes we hold about the ideas, events, or people associated with an area into similar reference frames. Thus, we might expect an individual to have attitudes about a product, about the manufacturer, and about expenses incurred from purchase of that product.

The same individual might not have strong attitudes towards managers of that company, if only because there may never have been an association between a manager and the company he or she represents. However, if that association is made, and the manager is featured in a newspaper story or radio feature or television announcement, it is likely the manager will now be perceived in a fashion similar to that used to perceive the other events in the frame of reference. If the individual has a generally favourable reference frame, the likelihood is that the manager will be initially perceived as favourable. If the frame of reference is negative, the likelihood is that the manager also will be initially perceived as negative. In other words, new ideas, new events, and new people are viewed against the backdrop of the reference frames that people possess.

This is one of the central reasons why it is important to send messages stressing the positive aspects of everything connected with the affairs of a business. If someone is exposed to a series of messages in the local newspaper that are constantly negative towards a business, its employees, and operation, it is not likely that one or two positive contacts with that business will be able to undo all of the negative information. However, if that same person picked up the local newspaper, found the negative stories, but had a positive frame of reference for the business based on a long history of positive contacts, the effect of the newspaper story should be quite different. The positive frame of reference should mean that the negative story will not have the same effect on the reader as it might if the reader had a negative frame of reference or had not developed a strong reference frame.

We are now ready to move to a discussion of public opinion and of ways of helping to modify or to maintain certain levels of public opinion. We know individuals form attitudes as the result of contacts with their environment. We know people tend to group their attitudes into reference frames. And we know that people tend to react to new ideas, new experiences, and new people in ways that are dependent on their reference frames.

PUBLIC OPINION

The term "public opinion" has a long history. In 1922 Walter Lippmann published his famous book entitled Public Opinion. Lippmann utilized the concept of a stereotype to build a definition of public opinion. People utilize the experiences they have, the books they have read, and the messages they have received to build a "picture in their heads" of how the world is. The picture may be right or wrong, but it is this individual picture that people use to govern their behaviour. Only when sufficiently strong contradictory information is encountered will people change their stereotype. Lippmann suggests that those people who have had similar experiences will tend to have similar stereotypes, and thus public opinion can be determined by looking at people of similar socioeconomic class, similar education, and similar geographic area. Lippmann's concept of stereotype, of course, is very much like the frame of reference concept we have already used. We prefer "frame of reference," because the term "stereotype" has come to have a negative connotation.Today, there are many ways of measuring or assessing what attitudes are held by individuals within the society. We can use those methods to get an estimate of the attitudes held by a random sample of the people in a community, a state, or the entire country.

We define public opinion as the majority opinion or set of attitudes held by the members of a population. This procedure is used every day by market opinion research firms, political polling firms, and social psychologists. Many of these studies are done on a national basis, and are intended to give a picture of what the general public may feel about governmental policies, political issues, or foreign affairs.Many managers, of course, will not find these general studies very useful in the daily business of managing a supermarket, a plastics-manufacturing plant, or a restaurant. For example, presumably we could ask a number of people about their attitudes towards coffee tables, or sliced bread, or blue rugs. We would certainly be able to determine what the majority attitudes were towards each of these three objects. But the probability is that none of these attitudes will be held with any degree of intensity.

It is also likely that most people will be either neutral towards these topics or only very mildly favourable or unfavourable. Unless we happen to be in the business of selling blue rugs, the time and expense of trying to find out what public opinion is for relatively minor topics or issues are seldom worth it.As managers, the fact that people are seldom interested about blue rugs or any other events that are not of crucial importance poses a dilemma. If we do not monitor public opinion in some way, before we may recognize it, a very minor matter may be blown into a major event. On the other hand, spending the money to make constant analyses of public opinion in a community may not be justified. What is needed is some way of cheaply monitoring public attitudes such that potential crises can be identified in time for more adequate measures to be taken.

- Set up a Procedure for Systematically Logging and Classifying Letters and Telephone Calls from Clients, Customers, or Citizens.
- Most of these calls and letters will fall into common patterns and will deal with service or rate or payment problems. But problems of a potentially more serious nature can sometimes be identified by changes in the flow of letters and calls. When this happens, the manager can implement more accurate research about the state of public opinion in the community.
- Encourage Public Comments by Providing Space on Monthly or Quarterly Bills. You will typically receive very few such comments, but those that are received can sometimes lead to the identification of emerging issues before they become a major problem.
- Use Suggestion Boxes or Feedback Letters to Solicit Comments. Many motels and restaurants provide forms that people can mark and send back to evaluate the nature of the service. Relatively few people ever send back such forms, but those who do usually identify problems previously unknown to managers, who can make corrections. There is no reason why such suggestion boxes and feedback forms should be confined to hotels and restaurants. Many businesses would benefit from these attempts to tap into public opinion.
- Monitor the Opinion Leaders in a Community. Every community has individuals who are influential with certain groups of people. They may be ministers,

labour leaders, local store owners, or even local politicians. They are members of the community who see and talk to a lot of people. Frequently, problems that may arise in the community are identified and passed on by opinion leaders. Attendance at civic functions, labour picnics, church groups, and other such meetings can frequently provide information of real value about the potential state of public opinion in a community.

One caution needs to be added. One of the most frequent mistakes made by managers is attending only those functions where they know everybody and are, in fact, opinion leaders for those groups. Such groups are comfortable places to be, but will probably add little new information and almost never provide disturbing information. An attempt must be made to get information from all segments of the community.

MONITOR THE LOCAL MEDIA IN A SYSTEMATIC FASHION

Many large companies subscribe to a monitoring service that provides newspaper clippings. I urge all companies to do the same even if the service is on a smaller scale. Stories in news columns, editorials, and letters to the editor will frequently be forerunners of major problems that can arise in a community. The business that has a carefully planned monitoring service may well be able to anticipate problems from the local, state, and national news and comments. Monitor Legislative Bodies and Potential Legislation. Many large companies already monitor such activities, but there is no reason why even small businesses should not do so.

It may be possible for a number of interested firms to join together to hire an analyst who will inform member firms about potential legislation that could affect business success or failure. The activities of legislators may not seem directly related to public opinion. Usually, however, there is a fairly direct relationship between legislative activity and the state of public opinion about an area. Legislators do have their fingers on the pulse of the majority of the voters or are influenced by those voters in a city or state who are most influential. Activity on the legislative front is almost always an excellent barometer of public opinion about any topic. These suggestions are designed to let managers identify potential changes in public opinion before they emerge as serious and difficult problems. This kind of monitoring effort, however, cannot exist in isolation. If companies are to establish a favourable image and thus have potential problems viewed from positive frames of reference, communication and public information campaigns must be conducted on a continuing basis. Most frequently, that is not what is done. The company "goes into action" when a price increase is needed or when something negative appears in the press. Much of the rest of the time, there are relatively few efforts to establish dialogue with a community.

A real example, but with the name of the company omitted, emphasizes the situation. A major utility was in the midst of requesting a major rate increase because of the increased cost of supplies. The case generated considerable public interest, and the public response to the increase was strongly negative. The response included marches on the Public Service Commission, threats of lawsuits, organized letter campaigns, and the other accompaniments of aroused public opinion. The outcome of the case is still in doubt, but the utility's behaviour leading to the rate increase request was not. I examined every local newspaper for a two-month period prior to the news release announcing the request for a rate increase. I found exactly three stories that pertained to the utility itself. One announced a minor change in personnel. Two were good public relations stories about the company, picked up by several area weekly newspapers.

In none of these stories was there any mention of activities of any company top management or any suggestion of problems that might cause a rate hike.The point is that this company went into a major rate situation with a public image that could, at best, be described as "neutral." In such a situation, the announcement of a major rate increase cannot help but be viewed as negative by the public. There was no backlog of goodwill built up. There were apparently no credible individuals within the utility that could have explained the situation. If a steady public information campaign had taken place over the three- or four-month period prior to the announcement, the probability is that the public furor would have been far less. I would not want to argue that some negative public reaction would not have taken place at all, but I will argue that the level of objections might have been considerably lessened if the company had engaged in an effective public information campaign before making the rate announcement.

MAKE USE OF ALL THE LOCAL MEDIA IN A COMMUNITY TO GIVE INFORMATION TO THE GENERAL PUBLIC

This is a principle that is frequently forgotten. The local daily newspaper is flooded with feature stories and announcements. Much of what is sent to them is tossed away. But in almost any community of even fair size, there are weekly newspapers, "shoppers" of various types, union newsletters, college papers, local magazines, board of education publications, local library bulletin boards, and other potential outlets. Many of these are excellent sources for stories about local people and local companies. Local television stations are usually inundated with stories. But the local radio station may well use feature stories and do local interviews. The local cable network is frequently open to local industries. The communications specialist should attempt to make use of all potential media.

Become as Publicly Visible as Possible. What we know about attitudes and attitude formation suggests that people form stronger attitudes about people than they do about ideas or events. But when there are only weak attitudes held towards people associated with an idea, an event, or a company, the evidence suggests that the negative idea can also "rub off" negatively on individuals associated with it. If, however, there are strong positive attitudes towards the individual, it is possible to propose even negative ideas and have them accepted without seriously damaging the credibility of the individual. For many managers this is an unusual idea to accept. Individuals are usually selected for top management positions because of their technical expertise, and not because of their ability to "make friends and influence people." I am suggesting we ought to encourage top management to take stronger interests in civic affairs, be willing to make speeches and be interviewed by the press, be available for interviews, and take a stronger interest in the state of public opinion within their community. Only in such fashion can individuals build personal credibility and have at least a chance of overcoming negative publicity.

MAKE POSITIVE USE OF ALL EMPLOYEES AS CHANNELS OF PUBLIC INFORMATION

Many companies recognize this principle and systematically give their employees information about upcoming events, problems, and proposals. Many other companies do not, and employees read about a new idea in the local newspaper along with their neighbours. This failure to inform employees is a mistake. Imagine the attitude of an employee who goes home after work and is greeted by his next door neighbour with the words, "Hi Jim. I see in the paper where you guys are going to raise prices again." If the employee knows nothing about the increases, he is made to feel like a dunce in front of his neighbours.

A far better situation would obtain if the employee could answer, "Yes Bob, but they aren't going to start until next month, and we're going to have a sale next week. The cost of raw materials just won't stop climbing." This ability to answer makes the employee more credible to the neighbour, and also increases the employee's loyalty to the company. It is difficult to see why more companies do not make better use of their employees. Up to now, our suggestions have been concerned with attempts to conduct ongoing public relations campaigns in such a fashion that a company can build its credibility and thus mitigate the effects of negative actions. However, events may still occur that will be perceived as negative by the public, and public opinion may be expressed through negative attitudes on the part of the general public. What should the stance of the manager be?

WHENEVER POSSIBLE, HANDLE THE RELEASE OF ANY INFORMATION

It is seldom the case that any given piece of information is entirely negative. Frequently, there are positive aspects to any event. If the news media are allowed to make the presentation through the mechanism of a press conference, the manager has very little control of what they will present. If, however, a manager can release the information through a press release or a personal appearance, there is some opportunity to present positive as well as negative aspects.

MAKE USE OF CREDIBLE SOURCES TO RELEASE NEGATIVE INFORMATION

Too frequently, the company president announces only positive things, and negative announcements are relegated to the public information officer. In my judgment, this is a mistake. If the president has built up credibility over time by participation in civic affairs, help to the community, and announcement of positive measures, that same credibility can be used to "soften" the blow of having to announce a price increase or a serious accident.

The president may well lose some credibility, but that temporary loss can be made up:

- Whenever Possible, Involve Community Opinion Leaders. It can be very helpful to give briefings to labour leaders, church leaders, city council members, and other influential groups. Opinion leaders are inclined to talk to anyone who asks their opinion. If they do not have any special information, they are most likely to reflect that frustration in a complete lack of support for a new idea. If, however, they have been briefed ahead of time, they can give more accurate information. This tends to increase their credibility with their followers and to make them more receptive to further announcements. Obviously, care must be taken in using opinion leaders, but they can prove of immense benefit to a company manager who must transmit information to the general public and have most of that information understood and accepted by the public.

- If Possible, Time the Release of Negative Information to Coincide with the Announcement of a Positive Piece of Information. If a natural gas utility has to raise rates, it may help to mitigate that announcement if the utility can also announce the discovery of a new gas source that will have positive effects on customers. Certainly, this combination of announcements is not always possible, but when it is, the company should take advantage of it. It may not eliminate the formation of negative attitudes on the part of the public, but it may help soften the blow.

USE EMPLOYEES TO TRANSMIT INFORMATION

We have suggested this for longrange public information programmes. It is even more useful when a company has a public relations problem. Members of the general public usually want to hear "the inside story" after reading a general news story about a problem or viewing a television account. Many people do not read their newspapers carefully, nor do they always trust them.

If they know that their next door neighbour works for a certain company, they will turn to that source for information. If the employee has no idea what is going on, his or her answer is likely to be one that blames the company and its managers for not telling him or her what is happening. In such a situation, the company takes a double blow—once from the bad news and then from its own employee.

USES OF COMPANY RESOURCES

Many companies can use inserts that are sent with the monthly bills. Others have newsletters that are sent to customers. In many cases it is possible to use these means to transmit new information to the public. This list is not exhaustive, but it should give some indication of the ways in which companies might help meet demands for public information in situations where negative information has to be given to the public or in which a high level of public concern has been voiced.

I must offer one final bit of information about public opinion. Although the management of a company may feel that the "public" will become outraged about information that appears to be inimical to their interests, the chances are that most of the members of the public feel far less strongly than do the managers. We are all inclined to react strongly to anything about ourselves that seems to be going badly. The fact of the matter is that most members of the public will feel far less concerned than will company managers.

There are always a few who will raise their voices, but most people simply accept change without reacting in a negative manner. This is particularly true when a company has established goodwill through a long campaign of public information activities before negative ideas or proposals must be transmitted to the public. If the company has done its job well, the intense pressure placed by a few members of the public can be overcome by the larger mass of real public opinion.

8

Layout of Information

It is not possible to set out here just one ideal way of organizing and laying out reports or papers. The tactics of arrangement and physical layout must be varied according to the task involved and the needs of the audience. We tried to discuss the specific tactics of layout to be used in every type of report, paper, or other document, it would require almost a book by itself. So we propose here to discuss the best tactics for organizing and laying out detailed technical reports and papers, such as progress reports, project reports, and research papers.

THE INITIAL IMPACT

The first thing to realise is that your papers begin to produce a response from the readers-begin to work for or against you-as soon as they land on those readers' desks. Indeed, it is possible to argue that reports and papers begin to work for or against their writers even before that.

Readers' over-all responses to papers are influenced by the ease with which they can identify the papers they want and retrieve them from libraries or information storage systems. We begin by emphasizing that there are at least *two* broad groups of readers to consider; those who have asked for the paper, and those who have not been expecting the paper or report that has arrived.

The first group, who have asked for the report or paper to be sent to them, want to know immediately 'Is this the right paper?'; 'Does it have the information that I wanted?'; 'Should I read it now or later?' The second group, who have not been expecting the paper, have at least four questions that run through their minds:

- What's this all about?
- Is it of relevance to me?
- Does it contain significant new information?
- Should I allocate time for reading it now?

Both groups are looking for *information* to help focus quickly on the orientation and content of the document. They want a prominent, succinct and apt title. They want to find quickly a terse but reliable summing up of the essence of the work, showing the points that touch their interests or needs-the reasons why the paper has come to them.

They want a clear summary of the ceases drawn from the work and of the recommendations consequent upon those ceases. If your paper is to get off to a good start, give your readers the information they want in the quickest and most accessible way. Do you need to take all this trouble, especially when managers have asked you to write the paper, and your readers are being paid to read it? The answer is 'yes'; because no matter whether they are being paid to read your paper or not, your readers are unlikely to seize it with excitement and enthusiasm.

All of us complain that we have too much to do, especially that we have too much paper to read. Any new document that arrives must compete for attention. Consider our own response to most papers we receive. Do we settle down to careful reading at once? Usually not. We pick up the paper and weigh (sometimes literally!) and consider it. We look at its size and organization.

We glance at its cover and 'headlines' and riffle quickly through to get a sense of its organization and density. We debate the attractiveness of reading the paper and-of great importance-we estimate the resources of time and effort that will be needed to deal with it. As we do this, an attitude to the paper begins to form-we begin to respond to it.

Our response-to-papers meter begins to register on a scale such as:

- That really so, how interesting!
- Looks very interesting.

- Interesting.
- Could just be interesting.
- I wonder if this is worth reading.
- Looks damned heavy going.
- Have I really got to read all this?

THE FRONT PAGE

The very appearance of a report or paper should begin the campaign to win the attention of both groups of readers. Does it look heavy, dauntingly thick and covered with dense black type? Does the design of the front page draw the reader's attention immediately to the answers to the questions that have crossed his or her mind?

Most readers who see the front page complain that their eyes are drawn immediately to information of secondary importance. Others notice first the heavy black prominence of the company's name in the top left-hand corner. Yet others see first the large part devoted to the distribution list. Most have to *search* for the title, which gives the main answer to the question: what is this paper about?

Of course, a note on confidentiality, or the company's name, or the circulation list has every right to appear on the front page of a report. Those items are too prominent. Our point is that the secondary material has been given a prominence that it does not deserve-a prominence that *should* have been given to the title and the information of principal importance and use to the reader.

FACTORS THAT GIVE EMPHASIS

Three factors that are important in achieving prominence for items of information on a page: position on the page, size of the area allocated to the information, and size of the type faces used in the printing of the information. These three factors can be used alone or in various combinations to draw readers' eyes to those things that you wish to highlight.

To give the title of a paper maximum prominence, it is best to place it as near as possible to the position that breaks the page into ideal proportions-the 'golden section'. As *The*

Penguin Encylopaedia states, the golden section is not easy to define exactly: An ideal proportion used by architects and artists which cannot be resolved mathematically; expressed by a line divided so that the smaller part is to the greater as the greater is to the whole; very roughtly. In classical times and during the Renaissance it was supposed to provide a key to the harmony of the universe, and architects and artists sought to compose their works in accordance with it.

In Western civilization, readers expect to find titles 'balanced' comfortably on the page, and this means that their eyes are inclined to go first to a position about one third of the way down from the top of the page and in the centre. It helps if the title is in larger type than the rest of the information surrounding it on the front page; and if possible, it should be separated from all other information by ample areas of white space, which will make it stand out. Another device for giving emphasis is the use of underlining and ruling. But combination of several devices is usually overwhelming. Titles that are in large type and are clearly spaced do not need underlining as well.

Readers need to know a job number and a report number-where this paper fits into a sequence of information. They need to know the date on which the paper was written, to know what currency it has. They will be helped by having a distribution list readily accessible on the front page, because it tells them who else has received the information and is therefore 'in the know'. Though all persons reading internal documents should be well aware of the name of the organization for which they work, it is reasonable that the organization's name should appear on every document that is circulated. A recognizable house style helps to build a sense of identity and 'belonging'.

It is certainly important that readers should know which department, part or group the paper emerges from. Likewise, it is vital to know who has written and who has approved the circulation of the paper. And if a paper must be kept confidential, that is one of the first things readers must be told. All these *are* relevant pieces of information and should, if possible, appear on the front page of the document; but they should be kept in subordinate positions so that the principal emphasis is always thrown on the title of the paper. This can be done without producing the cluttered effect. It is often possible to give readers even more information on the front page without the cluttering effect.

WORDING OF TITLES

We want to make two further points about titles, both designed to help make a sharp impact on readers: titles should be short, preferably on one line only; and they should specify exactly what the paper is talking about, not simply name a whole subject. First, they have to inform readers about what is in the document.

Second, they have to distinguish one document from another. If readers are flicking through piles of documents in their in-trays or in the reference part of a library, they want a brief title which can be taken in at a single glance, and which will distinguish one document from all the others.

POSITIONING THE SUMMARY

So far, we have been discussing what we call the orientation part of the report-the part that influences the readers' initial attitude to and interest in the paper. We have said that the summary plays an important part in this part. At this point in our discussion of how to organize information effectively, we wish simply to emphasize that most reports and papers need a summary on the title page or on the page immediately following.

And since the main aim of the summary is to emphasize what is new and interesting to potential readers, the principal emphasis in the summary should be on findings, ceases and recommendations. Of course, if your report is to be only one or two pages long, a separate title page and summary will seem over-elaborate. But even in those circumstances, get your paper off to a good start by ensuring that the heading of your first page is comfortably spaced and incorporates a sharp, focusing title. If you decide against having a separate summary, at least bring your attention-catching information forward into a summarizing opening paragraph.

THE BODY OF THE REPORT

The title page and summary-comes the body of the report, in which you present the full 'story' for readers who want complete details.

We suggest that the following arrangement will be effective for most reports:

Table of contents
List of symbols, abbreviations, definitions
Introductory material
Report of the work done
Results/findings
Discussion/analysis/argument, leading to ceases
Ceases
Recommendations
Acknowledgements
References
Appendix for tables, figures and graphs
Other appendices

These headings represent a full format; not all reports will require all these parts and a selection must be made for the particular reporting task on hand. Never write a part under each heading just because the headings are there. We have seen a report, written according to a rigid 'house' format, which duly went through every part. In the introduction it said that the test equipment available was inadequate, and the tests had to be abandoned without results. This fact was repeated under 'report of work done'. The 'results/findings' part contained a rephrasing of the same information, as did the 'discussion of results' part. Finally, the ceases laboriously repeated that no results were obtained because the test equipment was not up to the job. Such absurdities arise when writers slavishly follow rigid formats. Every reporting task needs its own format; the writer must be prepared (and free) to delete, or reverse, the order of parts to produce the most effective reporting of his or her particular information.

Table of Contents

It is sensible to begin by providing your readers with a detailed table of contents which will show the pattern of ideas through which you are about to lead them. The table of contents is not provided simply to enable people to find a page on which they will be able to read about a topic. Just as most of us like to have some idea of the route we are to follow when we set off on a journey, so most of us like to know the general pattern of ideas through which we are to be led in a paper or a talk. A well-designed table of contents, showing main headings and all sub-headings, and showing the relationship of those parts by indentation and a clear numbering system, provides readers with this overview of the document they are about to read. Standard titles like 'results' are uninformative; such a list of headings could be used for almost any report ever written. Certainly it does neither the job of giving readers an over-view or map of the territory they are about to enter, nor the job of helping them find any particular part they are interested in.

Contents	*Page No.*	
1.	Introduction	1
2.	Method	3
3.	Requirements	10
4.	Recommendations	16
5.	References	16
6.	Appendices	17

CONTENTS

Informative Contents Page

1. Introduction	1	
2. Method Of Treatment		
2.1	General	3
2.2	Survey Of Reducing Agents	4
2.3	Survey Of Precipitating Agents	6
2.4	Chemical Treatment Procedure	7
3. Plant Requirements And Usage		
3.1	Pre-treatment Storage Tank	10

Notice that sub-headings, as well as main headings, are included. Notice too that most headings are full and informative, and only two are single standard words. Finally, notice that a decimal numbering system, indentation, and varying weight of type all contribute to the ease with which we can see the sense, shape and content of the document. Some writers worry about how long a document must be to need a contents list. Other writers always put one in, even if the document is only two pages. Clearly, adding 50% to the length and bulk of the document in this way is unnecessary. As always, consider how the reader will use a contents list, and use this to decide if it is needed. In a short document, it is probably just as quick to flick over two or three pages looking at the headings as it is to glance over a contents page.

If the document has only a few obvious parts, then a contents page is probably unnecessary, even if the document is five or six pages long. But in a short document, with a number of disparate parts, some of which will be isolated and picked out by readers not interested in the rest of the text, a contents page is needed.

LIST OF SYMBOLS, ABBREVIATIONS AND DEFINITIONS

Next, it will help your readers if you provide a list of new symbols, abbreviations, and definitions used in the report. Of course, there may not be any new symbols to list at this point. Also, we must emphasize that your main obligation is to explain each new term, symbol or abbreviation at the first point in the text at which you introduce it.

But it is often helpful to your readers, if a new term is used infrequently. And that is best placed at the *beginning* of the report, not at the end, so that readers know where they can remind themselves of definitions that they have forgotten since they first read them in the text.

INTRODUCTORY MATERIAL

Once readers have been shown the pattern of ideas they are to be led through, it is useful to set out the background to the report in full. Readers who want a fully detailed account of your work find it helpful if you state in full the problem you were aiming to solve or the aspect you were setting out to investigate.

Why was the work undertaken? That scope was given? What limitations of time, personnel and materials were imposed? It may help readers if you give an outline of previous relevant work at this point-a survey of the history of related work and a theoretical analysis of problems related to your topic.

Anything that fills in the background up to the point at which the work began is relevant to the introductory part. Any material that you now know as a result of having done the work that you are about to describe. A common source of distraction in introductions to reports is failure to distinguish what had been done *before* the work to be reported was started, and the inclusion of information that the writer could have known only after he had completed the work. Consider the following example:

This report relates to work on the active rudders on HMS Park Place during 1987. The work was undertaken because of problems in the past of ships losing propellers and breaking drive shafts. In the past this loss has been prevented by securing the active rudders to prevent rotation, but this was not satisfactory due to the time and effort required. To try and prevent further loss, a new design was instigated and at the same time, measurements were to be made of the various forces present when operating normally.

These measurements were made on one of the modified shaft/propeller combinations and whereas the stresses measured would not be the same as the original shafts, the forces acting on the various components would be representative of the original system.

Corrosion affects the materials used in constructing chemical plants, the main areas of attack being crevices, welds, and bimetallic contacts. Undue stress and vibrations must be avoided. Many expensive materials can be profitably used as thin linings supported by cheaper, more corrosive, stronger materials.

This technique decreases corrosion in plants which handle chlorides. The change can be hampered by cost, but as the technique improves, the cost will decrease. Linings of tantalum, zirconium and titanium are the most satisfactory. The work to be reported in the paper was an exploration of which materials would be best for use as thin linings.

Did the writer know before he started that linings of tantalum, zirconium and titanium would be most satisfactory? No, that is the cease he came to as a result of doing his work; but that became plain to the reader only after reading the whole report.

You will help yourself get the right perspective on writing an introduction if you consider that you are trying to say to your readers, 'this is the position as we saw it before we began our work'. That leads naturally into the body of the report in which you say, in effect, 'so this is what we did and this is what we discovered'.

Here is an example of a better introduction: Development Department is interested in the possibility of using resin cloth for electrical insulation. As overheating of electrical equipment could cause heating of the resin cloth, which could lead to the evolution of flammable gases from the resin, they asked us to investigate the pyrolysis products of the resin.

We decided that it was necessary to approach this task in two stages:

- To establish a reliable analytical procedure;
- To identify and measure the products from pyrolysis of resin cloths A and B.

We could find no helpful literature on the thermal decomposition of resin cloths or on directly suitable analytical procedures.

We therefore decided to attempt to modify the 'Rapid Combustion' method of Belcher and Ingram. This report describes our experiments to establish a reliable analytical procedure. A later report will give details of the pyrolysis products from resin cloths A and B.

ACCOUNT OF THE WORK DONE

The account of the work you did will probably be the longest part in your report. It is difficult for us to discuss in general terms what should go in this part.

The precise data that the reader will find helpful will vary according to such factors as whether you are describing a design, a survey procedure, a test method, or an experimental procedure. But here is a helpful check-list of what readers in an industrial setting will want to know in various types of papers.

WHAT READERS WILL WANT TO KNOW

- About new products: the potential uses, the risks, the commercial requirements, the technical requirements, if any more work needs to be done on problems, manpower requirements, financial requirements, material requirements, the probable life of the product or project, the relative importance of the product or project compared with other products or projects, and proposed schedules for development.
- About technical problems: just what the problem is, how big and important it is, whether it has arisen before and what has been done and by whom, whether the problem is temporary or permanent,

whether the solution being put forward in the report is the only solution and if not, what others were considered and why they were rejected, what should be done now, who and what will be involved in the recommendations, and whether any redesign will be called for.

- About surveys of materials or processes: the properties, characteristics, and capabilities of the material, its limitations, whether its properties vary in varying conditions, where the material could be used and how, whether the materials are readily available or are to be made by the company, the costs of the materials or processes, the costs of plant required, if any, to handle the materials or processes, the materials and/or processes which the new materials or processes would compete with, how the new materials and processes would fit in with present company plans, processes, and future programme.

The way in which you arrange a description or explanation of your work will inevitably be related to your decisions about the aim and audience for your paper. There are many ways of organizing even an apparently simple description, depending on your readers' orientation or interests.

For some readers, a description may be best arranged to guide them 'from the outside in'-reflecting the real order of perception as a person approaches an object for the first time; but for other readers, who have some understanding of the object you are describing, it may be better to write in a way that reflects the hierarchy of components-starting with the 'heart' of the machine or process, and gradually explaining how ancillary elements are related or how your work involved modifying customary structures or procedures.

If you have information to present about activities at three sites, A, B and C, and if you want to describe the ways in which you experimented with variations in manpower, machinery and materials, you have at least two patterns of organization available:

Arrangement 1

Site A	-manpower
	-machinery
	-materials
Site B	-manpower
	-machinery
	-materials
Site C	-manpower
	-machinery
	-materials

Arrangement 2

Manpower	-site A
	-site B
	-site C
Machinery	-site A
	-site B
	-site C
Materials	-site A
	-site B
	-site C

But we want to emphasize again here that your choice must be dictated by your readers' principal interests and by the particular impact you wish to make with your account.

ORDER OF ARRANGEMENT

In our discussions so far, we have been advocating that you arrange your reports and papers in order of importance *from the readers' point of view*. We have been advocating a *descending* order of importance, presenting the new, most important information in outline at the beginning of the paper, and giving the supporting evidence or detail afterwards. This is not simply to help focus and orientation.

It is also because readers find it easier to assimilate detailed information if they have first been given a general framework into which to fit the detail. Imagine a man who is called for jury duty, and finds himself watching a grave be-wigged figure rise to open the case: 'My Lord, the accused is a man of previous good character; he is married, My Lord, and has been married for eighteen years. He has three children, My Lord, lives in a detached house in a good part of town, and has worked for his present employer in the same capacity for over twenty years...' As the barrister drones on, ask yourself, is the defendant guilty or not? The question is unanswerable, because much depends on whether he is accused of speeding or of murdering his wife. What the evidence is *for* determines our view of its importance.

Unless we know what case we are trying, we cannot assess each item of information as we receive it. If it does not fit into a pattern or framework, it is rapidly lost in a confusion of formless detail. Yet such confusion is often caused by writers who give detailed evidence before stating their objectives and ceases. Readers do not know what the evidence is for, or where it is leading, and so are unable to make it do any work in their minds.

PYRAMIDS OF EVIDENCE

Evidence, in a document which is explaining, proving, or arguing a case, must be marshalled to support that case. And it will be of use to the reader only if he or she is clearly told what that case is. Too often writers let the evidence swamp the case.

We must emphasize again that there is a difference between the order of discovery and the order of announcement. And that the thoroughness necessary to make and check discoveries is opposite to the parsimony needed to explain them without confusion. We are aware that there are some types of writing that can make use of *ascending* order-starting with minor matters and gradually building to a striking climax.

In theory, this technique can be psychologically effective: it makes use of the readers' curiosity and encourages them to read on to learn the final outcome. It is the detective story style, with clues dropped here and there to intrigue us and a final dramatic revelation of where responsibility and innocence really lie. But we think it is rarely appropriate for professional reports and papers to use this 'intriguing' technique. Perhaps if you have a particularly delicate topic to broach, it may be appropriate to approach it obliquely: but most readers of reports and papers are looking for a more open and rigorous approach. They will be at least suspicious and at worst hostile to your apparent reluctance to 'come to the point'.

Most reports and papers, then, will be best organized in a pyramid structure, in order of importance, with a summary at the top and a gradual expansion into greater detail within the body of the paper. The base of the pyramid will be your appendices, containing the most detailed information.

This arrangement has the advantage of making readily accessible the information wanted by the majority of readers. Readers can stop reading when they have obtained as much detail as they need. Perhaps only a few will read right through to the appendices. Your readership will probably be an inverted pyramid:

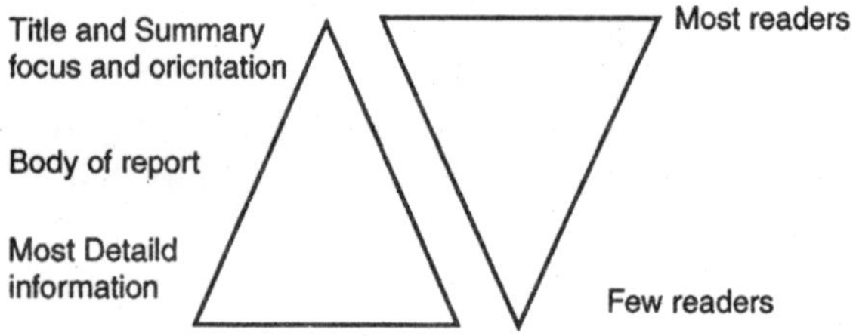

However, *within* your order of importance, it is possible to arrange parts of the account in many ways, to reflect, for example:

- Spatial or topographical arrangements;
- Experimental or manufacturing sequences;
- Fault-finding or operating sequences;
- Order of discovery;
- Existing patterns of information in libraries or other stores.

Each one of these ways of organizing a paper is 'logical' in its own terms. But the internal logic of such organizational structures is of little interest to readers. The logic which matters to them as they read is the logic of their understanding. This starts from the familiar (which may be the old process, or the desired end-product, or a familiar part of the machine which will be retained intact in modification), and moves onwards to the unfamiliar. Just what is familiar or unfamiliar depends on what the reader already knows, not what the *writer* knows. Many writers hand information over to their readers like a dinner-table guest passing a knife with the sharp end pointing outwards. Polite people turn it round, offering the comfortable handle first. So with information. In most cases it has to be turned round, so that the reader can grasp it comfortably.

AMOUNT OF DETAIL

The amount of detail in your account must also vary according to your purpose in writing and according to your audience. Are you aiming to assemble and write about all available information for permanent record or are you aiming simply to describe how and why you came to a particular set of ceases? In our experience, junior staff frequently misjudge what their supervisors want from them.

A major complaint from managers in business and industry is that new recruits stlll think they are writing school and university, emphasizing *how much* they know about a topic. Report-writing in business and industry is mainly a *management* activity, and not part of the academic activity of generating and making available new knowledge for anyone who may be interested.

Report-writing in business and industry should focus more sharply on what needs to be said in order *to get something done,* and details in reports and papers should be sorted and selected with that objective uppermost in mind. Note, however, that it would be simplistic to set up too sharp a contrast between 'writing to get something done' and 'writing for the record'. A good paper will often need to contain both types of writing. Indeed, you may find that you have to write at three levels: in outline in your summary; in greater detail as you present evidence supporting a particular cease in the body of your report; and in very great detail in your appendices. It may be desirable to record in your appendices your false starts, negative findings and test details, for the benefit of just a few readers who might otherwise waste time and money in the future by re-exploring ground you have covered already. It is important to provide a clear signalling system within your report to help readers find the details they want-to find their way around. To do this, make liberal use of headings and sub-headings that performance as sign-posts signalling routes and announcing the content of parts.

You may feel that this uses more paper. But the disadvantage of increasing the amount of paper must be weighed against the advantage of making it possible for your reader to get a sense of rapid, comfortable progress through the story. Normally, this sense of comfortable progress will be helped by the division of the work into logically related, manageable parts, and by the liberal use of headings and sub-headings.

RESULTS AND FINDINGS

The results part in the body of your report should rarely by bulky. Bring forward into the results part just the main facts and figures that are necessary to support and explain the argument you are presenting. Do not 'clog up' the centre of the report with a mass of data that it is not essential for readers to consider as they follow the description or argument.

We are not saying that you should not present all your findings, negative and otherwise: we are suggesting that these findings *in detail* should be presented in appendices to the main report. In the main text, give the reader just the pieces of information that are necessary to make the argument logically acceptable and technically persuasive.

It is too easy to swamp a clear argument, which requires underpinning with carefully selected facts, with a mountain of detailed evidence. Readers should not be expected to repeat all the sifting the writer did in arriving at his or her ceases. Our experience is that the urge to be complete often leads writers to ignore the readers' need to have a *manageable* argument to grasp. *Less* evidence is usually needed if the reader is to *understand* the point. To record and discuss every result is overkill or in your filing cabinet.

DISCUSSION AND ANALYSIS

After the statement of your findings, it will be natural for you to discuss the ceases to which these lead. What is implied by the data that has emerged from your experiments, surveys or evaluations of material? In your discussion, you will state the inferences you draw from your observations.

Drawing inferences means talking about results, not simply repeating them. Many report writers let themselves down badly at this point by failing to state implications, to recognize trends and changes, to draw attention to comparisons and contrasts, and to sum up differences. Repetition of readings should rarely be necessary: a discussion will normally require speculation about causes and effects, and analysis of implications for the future.

A discussion of what the facts imply must include a statement of the ceases drawn from the premises laid down. For this reason it is not essential in all reports to follow the discussion part by another part re-stating your ceases. A well-written report will have included the ceases and recommendations at the front in its summary; its ceases again in the course of its discussion; so it is not essential to state the ceases a third time after the discussion part. However, in a long and detailed report, it may be desirable to have a full statement of ceases in a separate part after the discussion within the body of the report, and to give a summary of the ceases at the beginning.

Footnotes

Distinguish between references and footnotes. References are statements that help readers find source material that is referred to in a text. Footnotes are additional comments, details or notes that the writer chooses to place outside the main stream of the account.

Footnotes at the bottom of the page are usually a sign that the writer has not thought out carefully what he or she wanted to say, or what importance to attach to each piece of information. Broadly speaking, if a piece of information is relevant to your readers' understanding of what is being said, that piece of information should be included within the main text, not slipped in at the bottom of the page. The placing of items at the bottom of the page is an irritating distraction to readers, especially when they find that there is *no* additional information in the footnote or that it is information they did not need.

After skipping to the bottom of the page, readers have to go back to the main text, find the appropriate place and pick up the threads of the argument as best they can. If the information you are tempted to put at the bottom of the page will be useful to your readers, put it in the main text. If the information is not important enough to be included in the text itself, that information is probably not worth including anywhere.

We are not arguing that all information is of equal importance. All writers occasionally find it helpful to offer their readers an 'aside' or parenthetical remark. But the most comfortable way to present such remarks is in parentheses, at least preserving the linear sequence for readers. Footnotes almost always introduce a sense of 'choppiness'. They should, therefore, be reserved for special circumstances.

PLACING OF ILLUSTRATIONS

Sometimes, you may feel that you can make your points most clearly by using non-verbal techniques of presentation. If so, place your tables or illustrations as close as possible in the text to the point at which you want readers to refer to them. This will cause difficulties when you are producing a text simply in typescript. You will not always be able to include your graph, diagram or picture in a convenient place in the text. It may be necessary to collect all your graphs and figures in several separate pages at the end of a part of your report. If you do this, remember to tell your reader where the illustrations are.

You can also consider presenting your illustrations on fold-out pages, to minimize the amount of turning to and fro that the reader has to do. Or, if you dislike this lay-out because fold-out pages can get tattered, consider the possibility of using two spiral bindings. Beware of the temptation to include graphs and other illustrations in the body of your report simply because you have drawn them during the course of your work. Each time you are thinking about including an illustration, ask yourself whether that particular illustration will most effectively make the point you wish to press home to your reader.

Are you being tempted to include the illustration simply to duplicate something that you have already said in words with adequate clarity? It is an irritating distraction for a reader to be encouraged to look at an illustration that provides no information in addition to that already in the prose text. For example, one often reads statements such as 'the results show that as the temperature rose, the viscosity decreased, until at point X there was no further change. The reader then dutifully looks and after a few moments' scrutiny can see that as the temperature rose, the viscosity decreased, until at point X there was no further change.

The reader, having gained no additional information from looking at the illustration, has then to go back and find the place in the prose text, pick up the threads of the argument and go ahead. Concentration on the argument has not been helped, rather hindered, by the writer's direction of the reader to look at the illustration. Of course, if your readers *can* gain additional information by looking at the illustration, for example by extrapolating beyond given points or readings, then it will be beneficial for you to urge them to look at the illustration; but beware of the temptation to provide illustrations in scientific and technical papers simply to 'make it look scientific', or simply to show that you have been assiduous in drawing graphs and making tables as your work progressed.

Remember, too, that there is a difference between tables and graphs that are designed to make a point in an argument, and tables and graphs that are designed to make available a mass of information so that readers can scrutinize it at leisure. In this discussion of organization and lay-out of papers, we wish simply to emphasize that, wherever possible, masses of data and supporting. Give your reader a smooth, uninterrupted passage through the argument or description in the body of your report.

Appendices

Use appendices, then, to clear supporting information out of the way of the readers' concentration on the main theme. Is it necessary to include in the main text the specifications for materials and equipment used? Is it necessary to include in the main text your inspection-test data? Do you need to include in the main text the mathematical calculations by which you derived formulae?

Do you need to include start-up procedures? Most material of this sort can reasonably be placed in an appendix where it is available if necessary but where it will not interfere with the progress of readers who do not need it.

STRUCTURE FOR OTHER TYPES OF DOCUMENTS

This discussion has concentrated on structure for reports and papers. The same structure, a pyramid starting with an incisive title, expanding gradually through a summary to the main story, and based on fully detailed appendices, normally works effectively for most other scientific and technical documents. In using the pyramid structure, you make it possible for readers to stop at various points on their way through the report, having accumulated as much as they need on their way up to that point.

A well-written journal substance makes it possible for readers to do the same. It provides an effective, orienting title and summary. It then expands into full detail for those who want to know more about a procedure or survey method, or the advantages and disadvantages of various materials and activities. If the journal editor can find room for full details of matters such as specifications or experimental procedures, they are best left at the end for those readers whose interest continues to this level of detail. Instruction sheets, specifications, and most other technical documents benefit from the same structure. A well-written set of instructions preferably starts with a statement of the overall aim of the procedure or an outline of the various steps or stages in the instructions. A well-written handbook for maintenance of equipment preferably starts with an orienting part which at least describes the remainder of the text.

Sales documentation is not the subject of our advice in this book-it calls for special techniques. But if you have to write technical information documents to be used in conjunction with sales literature, remember that new information is what readers are interested in. They will not welcome a laborious repetition of first principles, known to everyone in the industry. Nor will they welcome having to wade through detailed descriptions of the mode of action of a type of machine they know very well.

What *they do* want to know is how this particular product differs from familiar and established ones. Other types of document include requests for capital, and recommendations for the purchase of machinery or services. Here, again, make sure readers know clearly *what* you want, before swamping them with details as to *why* you want it. Recognize that they may not want *full* details of all the alternatives, although they will need to be assured that you have checked all other possibilities before recommending one.

However, they do not want to re-do your job, and go through all the possibilities again themselves. For example, if you have eight possibilities to choose from, by all means give brief details of all eight in an appendix. But in the text, dismiss most of them quickly on the basis of their obvious inadequacies, and discuss in detail only two or three. This gives the assurance of a realistic choice, without the confusion of too much detail.

Even documents which group information according to physical location or manufacturing procedures are most effective if the whole document (and probably each part within it) starts with a summarizing sentence or paragraph outlining what is to come. It is a basic tenet of all good communication that one starts by presenting an audience with some orientation material, an outline of the whole, before beginning to discuss the parts. Only in documents that aim at presenting a chronological account is it preferable to depart from an order of importance such as we have described; and even in such documents, it is probably best to start with some orienting information explaining why the historical account is being given.

First, choose an order for your information which works from main points downwards to details, and not the other way. Second, always be flexible in your choice of organization and lay-out. Resist the temptation to categorise each writing task, and then to squeeze and distort the information into a recognized and stereotyped format. Choose your path through the facts you have to communicate with a careful eye on the readers' convenience. Each task requires an individual structure.

THE USE OF HEADINGS AND NUMBERING

FORMAL AND INFORMATIVE HEADINGS

Usually, it helps if you make generous use of headings and sub-headings. Headings break text into manageable parts, and help by increasing the 'white space' around the blocks of type, especially when the type is single-spaced. They also performance as signposts, pointing out what is to be found in each part. Formal headings such as *Problem,* or *Experimental,* or *Discussion* are neither informative nor useful, because they do not focus attention on the essence of the following paragraphs. Better headings, such as *Updating Operation Flow Charts* or *The Influence of Sunlight on Linings,* convey real information about the content of the part. In word-processed text, there are four ways in which the relative hierarchy of the headings can be shown:

- Numbering;
- Indenting;
- Using capitals and lower case letters;
- Bolding (use of heavy type). (In typewritten texts, underlining has to take the place of bolding.)

To ensure that readers grasp the relationships at a glance, documents that use all four systems are best.

The usual hierarchy of size and letter forms is:

- Capitals Bolded (or Underlined)
- Capitals Not Bolded (or Underlined)
- Lower Case Bolded (or underlined)
- Lower case not bolded (or underlined)

A decimal numbering system helps further, but note the effect of the following layout:

- First Level Heading
- Second Level Heading
- Third Level Heading
- Fourth level heading

Because a number like '7.2.1.2' is longer than the single '7' it seems more important. So it is preferable to use indenting as well, in order to complete the visual representation of the hierarchy of parts.

Some writers (or their typists or managers) will not use indentation because they believe that progressively increasing left-hand margins wastes paper. We think that nothing is a waste of paper that helps the reader. In any case, if the indentation is only two or three spaces each time, the margins never get very wide.

But if managers insist that indenting the text is wasteful, a good compromise is to indent the headings only, leaving all the text on the margin. The use of decimal numbering, differing weights of type, and indentation for the headings shows the reader the 'shape' of the information.

SYSTEMS OF NUMBERING

Three systems of numbering are widely used in business, industrial and research writing:

- The decimal system;
- Mixtures of numbers and letters;
- The HMSO system.

The *decimal system* is generally accepted as the clearest numbering system available. In this system, the headed parts and sub-parts only are numbered, not every paragraph. There can be any number of paragraphs in a part or sub-section. When you have sub-divisions, your first sub-division number and heading should always come immediately after the division number and heading. Numbering to three or four places of decimals is usually a sign that grouping and sub-division of ideas need to be reviewed. If you wish to set items in a list within your sub-sections, use simple numbers. Remember that the decimal numbering system is for *headings* only.

ALGORITHMS FOR COMPLEX POSSIBILITIES AND PROCEDURES

Another aspect of organization which we wish to discuss separately is the need to arrange information physically so that readers can easily find their route through a mass of information that must be made available, but will not all be relevant to all readers. It is often necessary to present information which has complex inter-relations, and to show how those inter-relations can lead to various outcomes. Similarly, it is often necessary to explain that various combinations of conditions can produce a particular state (perhaps a fault), and to explain that various actions must be taken according to which conditions exist.

From reading tax guides or instruction manuals for equipment, we all know that prose accounts of this sort of information can be extraordinarily complex. They often read like conundrums. Though the sentences may be short and simple, the complexity of the relations is confusing, principally because we have to read about all the possible situations. Normally, however, readers are interested in only one set of conditions, and wish to know the outcome from these only. They want the information presented in a way that will help them sort out the possible relationships or conditions and isolate the set relevant to their interests.

In these circumstances, it is not enough just to 'present' the complex information-to make a mass of data available to any reader prepared to work through it. For effective communication, the writer must enable readers to find their way quickly and easily to the decisions they need, which means helping them to ignore information not relevant to them. The writer must make the right information available for use, yet make minimum demands on the readers' time and attention.

Often, the best way to meet these objectives when writing about procedures is to use an algorithm. An algorithm is a carefully planned sequence of statements, questions or instructions arranged in a logical hierarchy and requiring readers to read only the starting item and such subsequent items of information as are relevant to their needs. The most common forms of algorithms in engineering and scientific work are list-form algorithms, flow-charts (logical trees) and MAP layouts. All achieve the same purpose: they enable readers to concentrate on finding a clear path through a complex set of relationships or conditions by ignoring anything that does not apply to their situations. They

Before the adapter test can be carried out it is essential to check that there is a gap of 0.13 to 0.25 mm between the card reader lamp and the optic surface at the bottom of the lamp holder screw-hole. If there is no gap or if the gap is not within the specified measurements, disconnect the card reader lamp terminals, screw the lamp out of the lamp holder and inspect the optic surface beneath the lamp holder screw-hole for dirt, dust or damage. If the optic surface is in good condition (shiny), the lamp can be reinstalled, ensuring that the gap between the lamp and the optic surface at the bottom of the lamp holder screw-hole is between 0.13 and 0.25 mm.

Use a card strip to check this gap. If the optic surface is dirty or dusty, clean the surface with lint free cloth (and alcohol if necessary) and then reinstall the lamp, ensuring that the correct gap is present between the lamp and the optic surface. If the optic surface is not dirty or dusty but is in unsatisfactory condition for some other reason, exchange the fibre optic assembly and then reinstall the lamp, ensuring that the correct lamp-to-surface gap is present. When the lamp is reinstalled, reconnect the lamp terminals. Then press the FAD button to signal that the card reader is ready for the adapter test. They reduce distraction caused by unwanted information and reduce the load on memory because readers do not have to hold in mind previous questions or previous decisions. Examples of a complex piece of prose, and of three algorithmic presentations of the same information are given. The original prose text is shown.

The list form algorithm presents the same information using simple numbering. It is clear and to the point and takes less space than the flow chart or MAP layout. The need for the reader's eye to jump from item to item is, however, a disadvantage. The flow chart algorithm is equally explicit but takes more time to prepare and more space in the document. It has, however, the advantage of using lines to guide the reader's eye from one item to the next.

Also it can use different symbols (squares, rectangles, diamonds, circles) to emphasise the distinction between instructions, questions, comments and ceases. The MAP format is explicit and takes less space than a symbolic flow chart algorithm. It also has the great advantage that it can be produced entirely by typewriter.

All the elements can be typed in from a normal alphanumeric keyboard. A disadvantage, however, is that it has less visual impact than a symbolic flow chart. Complex, inter-related items of information are almost always communicated most efficiently to scientific and technical readers if presented in flow charts or logical trees, but once again it is necessary to emphasise that the most suitable choice of communication tactics will depend on the aim, audience and context of the document you are writing.

Research has shown that the speed and accuracy with which readers can find their way through complex information vary according to:

- Whether each reader is able to decide easily which items of information are relevant and which irrelevant to his or her situation;
- Whether there are so many interdependent contingencies that some display formats are automatically precluded.

Wright and Reid explored the comparative effectiveness of presenting complex information in four ways-complex prose, a list of simple short sentences, a table, and a flow chart. Their main cease was that details of the user's background experience and situation influence the relative effectiveness of the different formats.

However, conveying exactly the same information, may nevertheless be better as a logical tree if it is being used on a do-it-yourself basis by the homespun car mechanic. These findings emphasize the need for writers to choose their visual tactics with as much thought about their aim and audience as they use in choosing their verbal tactics.

9

Presentation Techniques

VISUAL SIGNALLING

In turning to consider the use of tables, graphs, diagrams and other illustrations in the presentation of information, we are not changing our topic. Our subject is still clear communication, and we are still discussing how to make precise, manageable statements using language. Words, graphs and drawings are all visual patterns used to symbolise or represent meaning. In both graphic statements and verbal statements, we use a variety of hieroglyphics-dots, dashes, and other marks on paper-as symbols to carry information.

Words, after all, are made up of letters which are composed of combinations of lines and circles; for example, the difference between 'o', 'p', 'd', and 'b' lies only in the positioning of the line tangential to the circle. So words and drawings are not conflicting or competing modes of expression. They are, at most, extremes on a continuum, with words at one end making minimum use of the visual appearance of the signals, and with drawings and graphic presentations at the other end making maximum use of the visual appearance of the signals.

We have discussed how statements in words often cause difficulty for receivers because they contain unfamiliar vocabulary or signals, because they are too long and complex, or because they require the reader to hold in mind too many inter-related clauses and conditions. Visual statements can be difficult for the receiver for similar reasons: they may contain vocabulary or signals with which the reader is unfamiliar; they may be too long or too complex; they may contain too many inter-related items and conditions for the reader to absorb. So, just as writers must be skilful in selecting words and sentence structures from the verbal code, they must be equally skilful in selecting and handling the elements from the visual code.

THINKING ABOUT THE TASK

Tactics for selecting and handling information applies equally to the choice of visual techniques. As always, aim and audience are the governing factors in this choice, and it is especially important to consider two questions:

- What is the precise function of the table or illustration?
- Will the readers of the paper receive this information more readily in verbal or in numerical/visual form?

We have argued earlier that the way a text is organized and laid out, and the rate at which information should be 'unloaded' or packed into our pages, must be varied according to the function of the text. In a dictionary or a parts list, it is effective to pack together a great deal of information tightly and economically, because these texts are designed for reference, for scrutiny and cross-checking of particular items. We must make it easy for 'readers' to find their way into and around the assembled information, but we do not have to construct a coherent discourse; the entries are not statements in a connected argument.

Tactics of selection and organization are different from those used in a report or an instruction sheet. In just the same way, tactics in using tables and graphic techniques must be related to the precise function of the document as a whole and of the visual items in particular. Distinguish between tables and charts that are to be used for reference, as stores of classified and juxtaposed information, and visual statements that are to be used to make a point in an explanation or argument.

Tables and drawings designed as reference material can be packed tightly in the equivalent of dictionary or parts-list form. They are usually best separated from the main text of a report or paper so that they are not an obstacle to the readers' smooth progress through the argument. Tables and drawings that are designed to make a point as part of an argument should have simple structures and carefully judged information-loads. They should be placed as close as is physically possible to the point in the prose text at which you want readers to take in the information they provide.

For example, providing a mass of information about the enthalpy of methane for reference and for scrutiny of detail. In most circumstances, it would distract the reader if it were part of the text, and it would be best placed in an appendix. A specially drawn graph, based on the same information; but it is a simpler statement designed to make one particular point. It was placed within the prose text of a report, close to the point in the argument at which the visual point was needed. A practical tip: abstractions of information like this can often be made simply by putting tracing paper over a complicated original and inking in the significant lines.

The traced outline can then be photocopied (perhaps even reduced) and included conveniently within a typewritten report or paper. The second important question-will the readers receive the information more easily in verbal or in numerical/visual form-is of particular concern to writers who must communicate to specialists from a wide range of backgrounds.

It is well established that readers will take more information more rapidly from documents if they know what to expect from the document and where in the document to look for it. It is also well established that some people are by nature and training more inclined to be 'verbalizers' and others are more inclined to be 'visualizers'.

Some readers will find it easier to assimilate the verbal statement, 'Output falls to half within the first hour, to a quarter within the next hour, and then stabilises at one tenth for the remainder of the run'; other readers will absorb that information more rapidly if they are shown a simple graph that shows output plotted against time. In writing for engineering and scientific readers, you will probably decide that they will usually be helped by the use of tables and graphic presentation techniques; but *which* technique still requires careful thought. Readers who like block diagrams may be bemused by complex drawings of electronic circuits. In debates with engineers and scientists about the relative effectiveness of different algorithm layouts, we have been surprised to find how powerful is the influence of 'what they are used to'.

THE RESOURCES AND TECHNIQUES AVAILABLE TO THE WRITER

We shall discuss only the best use of resources and techniques usually available to writers who have *by themselves* to produce internal reports and papers, instruction sheets and other similar documents.

If you are fortunate enough to have access to experts who can produce exploded drawings or use airbrush techniques, always involve them as early as possible in your planning and preparation for a report or paper. But most engineers and scientists have to rely on their own resources to produce the graphic presentation of their data. What is the best way of doing this? First, review the 'language' elements available.

The main symbols in visual presentation are:

- Numbers (used mainly in tables);
- Words (used in tables, algorithms, or flow charts);
- Lines (used in graphs and drawings to symbolise Paths, links, a lapse of time;
- Shapes (used in symbolic charts, drawing and photographs).

These symbols constitute the equivalent of the verbal Vocabulary'. This vocabulary is put together into the visual equivalent of sentences and paragraphs, and as in your choice of verbal 'style', it is vital to:

- Consider carefully the length and complexity of the statements you ask your reader to digest;
- Be sure to conform to conventions of 'word order';
- Avoid the visual equivalent of wordiness and waffle;
- Control the use of jargon.

In visual signalling, you also have available important cues that you cannot use in verbal signalling:

- Spatial cues (alignment in columns and rows, grouping);
- Typographic cues (size, design, and weight of type);
- colour cues (shading, colouring, colour of paper as well as of print);
- Ruling (use of lines not as symbols in themselves but as a framework to separate, group and relate information);
- Use of 'white space' to group or emphasize items of information.

Perhaps the greatest advantage of visual presentation is that it is possible to represent three dimensions. Prose restricts information to a one-dimensional linear sequence: visual presentation enables you to show shapes, to show activities going on in parallel, to show movement in varying directions. Your reader can take in all these things 'at a glance', because the human eye can use a span of awareness much wider when looking at visual presentations than when looking at words (focus on any word in this sentence, and notice how much of the surrounding text you can see without changing your point of focus).

By presenting information in tables or in graphic forms, you can often make much more efficient use of your readers' perceptual abilities than by presenting information in prose. But remember that perception and comprehension are not the same. Your readers must not only *perceive* your visual presentations but also *understand* them. So beware of complication and overloading.

Give readers the minimum data needed to make your points, not the maximum data available to justify your existence. And make your visual statements self-sufficient, so that readers can comprehend them without continuous cross-reference to the prose text. Just as it is desirable to coin a new sentence each time you want to say something, it is wise to try to produce a fresh illustration each time you decide you want to make a visual statement. Automatic re-use of prepacked words and phrases frequently produces only approximations to the intended meaning of a statement: likewise, apparently time-saving (and thought-saving!) use of ready-made graphs or photographs frequently presents only an approximation to the point intended. As you work at communication tasks, you will constantly be tempted to trade-off efficiency against convenience. Often, you will be able to use existing visual material very effectively; but sometimes you may be tempted to write a text that fits the available visual material rather than to take extra trouble to produce visual material to suit your text. Resist this temptation.

The great advantage of using visual presentations is that they give all readers the same visual image to look at. But notice that we are not saying that readers will all see the same thing: each illustration must have a caption or heading telling readers what you want them to see in the illustration. Imagine two identical pictures of a boy kicking a ball along the pavement of a busy suburban street.

One caption reads: 'Road-safety training teaches children to stay safely on the pavement'. The other caption reads: 'We need parks to keep our children away from dangerous roads'. Readers see different points made by the same picture in the two illustrations. You might be entertained by taking any drawing or photograph designed for inclusion in a report without its caption, and asking your colleagues to tell you not only what it shows but also what *point* it is making about its content. We suspect you will rarely get a clear or unanimous response.

TABLES

Tables give a systematic and orderly arrangement of items of information. Tabular layout has the particular virtue of juxtaposing items in two dimensions for easy comparison and contrast. Tables eliminate tedious repetition of words, phrases and sentence patterns that can instead be put at the tops of columns or at the sides of rows in the table. Although tables do not make much impact by visual display, it is possible, by careful arrangements, to emphasize and highlight particular items or groups of information. There are several ways of arranging information within a table and no one way is always the best. As usual, we must return to our basic questions: what are we trying to achieve with this table? What is the required emphasis? For whom are we presenting the information? What are the interests and needs of those readers?

Tables can be organized with the information in numerical order, in alphabetical order or in an order which groups items according to common features or common values. Normally, however, readers expect the elements or entities which are being compared to be grouped or listed vertically, and to find variables, qualities or performance details listed horizontally. Readers expect to move from known material on the left to new information on the right; known (or base) information should therefore appear on the left, with explanatory, conversion, or derived material on the right.

We find it helpful to distinguish two broad types of tables: *dependent* tables and *independent* tables. A dependent table is placed in the text and is an integral part of the prose statement. It continues the sentence or paragraph in just the same way as a mathematical or chemical equation that is included in a sentence, and it needs no title or caption because it is a continuous part of the text. It follows that it must be restricted to a small amount of information, probably a maximum of two or three columns and rows, a dozen or so numbers in all. An example of a dependent table. The reader can read through this table as a continuation of the sentence that it completes.

EUROPEAN PRODUCTION REQUIREMENTS

The forecast provided by Production Planning, London was tabled as follows:

Requirement (Mt)	1988	1989	1990
Min	1.9	3.5	4.8
Max	2.9	5.4	7.2

It was explained that these are min-max numbers and that the use of the average would be most realistic. With these numbers plus US requirements, the present plant design capable of 2.5-3.0 Mt with small-scale de-bottlenecking, would be outstripped in 1989. Thus, a European site would provide the added volume plus provide the safety of a second source.

Exploratory discussions on the concept of buying product in Europe and on stock procedures at the sites was accepted without commitment for further study. Technology was via denitrogenation, by the route:

$$NaCl+C_2H_6N_2 \rightarrow 22H_4\ Cl+NaN_2\ +H_2O$$

This process yields a serious loss of nitrogen via salts and it is a very important economic facet of this process that any nitrogen loss is fully recovered. Initially, the raw material is transported to site in single-load tankers to significant points that emerge from the data and to have put the full table in an appendix.

An independent table may be placed physically within the text-be surrounded by it-but should be clearly distinguished from it. In an independent table, you are inviting your readers to look at a visual display of the information separate from their reading of the text; the amount of information being presented will require a conscious step by the reader from the text to the table and back again. Minimize the size of that step if you can, by placing the table as near as possible to the text that discusses it.

Even for non-geriatric beds at Moreton the average length of stay is much longer than at say Widepark where, for example, general surgical patients stay for an average of 8.9 days. This is because the majority of all Moreton patients are old and are kept in after acute treatment is completed, often for social reasons. Thus the atmosphere at Moreton and Woring is very slow compared to a General Hospital. Moreton General Hospital was formerly a workhouse but became a chronic sick hospital in 1944.

After the formation of the N.H.S. many improvements were carried out and a programme of ward up-grading is now virtually finished. There is also a new assessment wing, mainly for "Eastern" patients, which has improved staff morale which is generally low, because the rest of the wards are in three-floor blocks most of which have no lifts. The wards are not very wide but patients do have lockers, though not individual clothing. In general the wards are light and clean and the blocks are arranged as follows:

Ground floor: Patients attending treatment departments such as Physiotherapy

- *Middle Floor*: (sister's office)-Admissions and Patients requiring active nursing.
- *Top Floor*: Long stay, convalescent and social cases awaiting discharge.

It has only been possible to provide day rooms on the ground floors so non-ambulant patients higher up cannot use them. Brownpath Wing, where over 100 male psychogeriatrics live has proved unsuitable for the type of patients because not all significant facts or inferences that you want them to see are also important.

RULING

The design of the ruling in independent tables presents choices: an *open* design, a *semi-closed* design or a *closed* design. An open design is one which has no vertical or horizontal rulings in it at all. A semi-closed design has just some vertical lines and/or some horizontal lines. A closed design has a complete array of both vertical and horizontal lines separating virtually all elements from all others.

Which of these helps you to see most readily the information that the writer is trying to present with particular emphasis? Even if you do not know what information the writer wants to emphasize, it is possible to sense the difference of impact of the various ways of ruling a table. Most readers find an open table is confusing, giving too little help to the eye. A fully closed table is also difficult to use because the apparatus of lines seems to overwhelm the information that is being presented. Most readers prefer a semi-closed design, with some horizontal and/or some vertical lines to help signify the importance of the piece of data.

Are vertical lines or horizontal lines preferable in semi-closed tables? There can be no over-all rule, because the lines in the tables may be doing two separate things. They may be helping the readers' eyes with the simple business of seeing the figures in the table, and they may be stressing the significance of particular groupings. They may be guiding the eye *across* the page or *down*. Most readers are accustomed to looking up and down columns of figures without too much difficulty. They need more help when they have to compare figures in horizontal rows. That might seem to suggest that in semi-closed tables, the normal use of lines should be horizontal.

But you must also take account of the second function of ruling within a table. That function is to stress the significance of particular groupings. It may be that you wish to stress groupings that are horizontal or vertical. This report is based on actual operating conditions and the calculated rates have been demonstrated in the plant. The report reckons to have 31 days shutdown in January for major repairs (motor overhaul, drive and mounting repairs etc.) and a 15 days shutdown in June for part overhaul.

Therefore, all rates include 5% downtime for the two yearly shutdowns, the significance of groups, or more help simply in following the rows of figures across the page. In general, however, the eye more often needs help with horizontals than with verticals. We more often use a ruler, or a finger, to run across a line than down a column. This report is based on actual operating conditions and the calculated rates have been demonstrated in the plant. The report reckons to have 31 days shutdown in January for major repairs (motor overhaul, drive and mounting repairs etc.) and a 15 days shutdown in June for part overhaul.

Therefore, all rates include 5% downtime for the two yearly shutdowns. However, some lines are redundant, these can be removed. Note that the double line under the headings helps the eye to separate heading and content. This method of ruling looks neat, and has the advantage that it can be produced on a typewriter without taking the paper out and ruling it separately. This report is based on actual operating conditions and the calculated rates have been demonstrated in the plant.

The report reckons to have 31 days shutdown in January

for major repairs (motor overhaul, drive and mounting repairs etc.) and a 15 days shutdown in June for part overhaul. Therefore, all rates include 5% downtime for the two yearly shutdowns. In designing a table, you must consider how readers will use it. Is their main objective to find a single item of information in a single 'cell' of the table (for example, the arrival time in Cardiff of the 1400 departure train from London); or is their main objective to compare the lists of figures in two columns (for example, the comparative times at various stopping points for two trains on the journey between London and Cardiff); or is their main objective to appreciate generally the over-all pattern (for example, the existence of faster trains at 'peak' hours compared with 'off-peak' hours)? To help with the first objective, more lines would probably be effective.

To help with the second, fewer lines, emphasizing complete columns rather than individual numbers would probably be better. To help with the third objective, perhaps a bar-chart would be better than a table; at least the table should make use of some means of emphasizing starting and finishing times, perhaps by using heavier print. You can obtain the effect of ruling without the use of lines by using white space to separate groups or blocks of information. When you do this, restrict your groups to blocks of five at the most.

The eye can discern easily the top, bottom and centre rows within a block of five, but once you provide six or more rows in a block, it is difficult for the eye to move through the figures without help. We can 'see' a group of up to five objects (such as marbles on a table) at a glance; six objects tend to be counted as two groups of three, and so on. However, take care if you introduce blocking. Arbitrary arrangement of rows into blocks may suggest a special relationship between the rows in each block, and differences between the blocks.

CLARITY AND MANAGEABILITY

There are blank spaces in some of the columns and rows, and some items are marked simply with dashes. Presumably, the writer wished the blanks to signify something different from the dashes, but it is not clear to readers what a blank space signifies or what a dash means. The principle that emerges is that there should never be blanks or other unexplained signals in a table. If you have no reading (if there was a nil value or if it was not possible to make a measurement for a particular reason) you should place either a nil within the table or some hieroglyphic such as an asterisk or dagger and explain the significance of that hieroglyphic at the foot of the table.

The difference between tables designed to make a point in an argument and tables designed to make available masses of information for scrutiny. It is far too large to be included within a text or even within an argument. You may find, however, that there are occasions on which you feel it is necessary to invite your readers to examine a mass of facts and figures at a central point within a report. In such a case, it may be necessary to use a table. But recognize the overwhelming impact of so much information presented in that way. If possible, provide some small steps by means of which your readers can approach the mass: for example, provide two or three smaller tables in which you separate some of the variables or groups of information, so that the final presentation of all the information seems less daunting.

BAR CHARTS

Bar charts are often better ways of presenting numerical data than tables. Frequently it is necessary to show several different variables or relationships within overall totals. In these circumstances, the use of a table does not make this information as clear as the use of a bar chart. It shows the number of students who have various types of qualifications in different types of higher education.

But the presentation of raw numbers does not make an impact quickly. The figures in the first column are not very different in shape and size. Readers draw information from these numerical signals only after mental addition or subtraction. If, however, the information is presented in bar-chart form, it offers an immediate visual impression of the different proportions of students with various qualifications in various forms of higher education. Notice that it is possible by joining the various levels within the bars to get some of the sense of movement usually associated with the drawing of graphs. Also, note that it is possible to use bar charts horizontally, as well as vertically. If, for example, you are showing braking distances for various types of cars, it is valuable to show these horizontally because the bars reflect the spatial point you are making.

It is helpful for your readers if you label the tops of the bars in your chart either with a number or with an identifying word. Since it is mainly the top of the bar that interests readers, that is naturally the first place they look. The suppression of zero in a chart in order to emphasize some difference in levels.

PIE CHARTS AND SURFACE CHARTS

In drawing pie charts, remember that it is easiest for readers to read clockwise from the twelve o'clock position. Also, it is normally most effective to place larger segments first, provided that does not distort a time sequence.

That is useful for showing proportions within rising figures over a period of time is a surface chart. A surface chart is a cross between a chart and a graph. A visual impression can be made, emphasizing not only development over a period of time but also the proportional changes within the totals over that period of time.

GRAPHS

Graphs need to be composed with as much care as any other type of verbal or visual communication. Unfortunately, it is common to find that little thought is given to choice of scale and to emphasizing the precise point which is to be made. The weaknesses in graphs that occur in too many scientific and technical reports. It is mystifying, designated simply Graph A. As there is no explanatory caption, readers are required to remember what Graph A was supposed to be showing or have to refer back to the text to remind themselves. The line of the graph is scarcely visible, and it is not at all easy to see how many changes of direction there are in the line as it moves forward in time. It may be that the writer's intention was to emphasize that the results scarcely rose above the bottom axis. But it would probably have been better to emphasize the flatness of the graph in general, and the small changes in movement in particular, by choosing a different scale.

What we see here is the equivalent of thoughtless choice of words in making a verbal statement. However, this graph was not designed to make a single point within an argument. It must be seen as a 'reference' graph. Once again, we must distinguish between tactics chosen to make a point during an argument, and tactics used to present masses of inter-related data for readers to scrutinize at greater length. But even so, it would probably help readers if that graph were approached by means of two or more steps presenting smaller elements of the information and gradually building up to the composite package provided.

Visual presentation can be overdone; the inexpert user of charts and diagrams often fails to resist the temptation to try and say too much at a time. The keynote of nearly all successful diagrammatic presentation lies in simplicity of design and absence of cluttering detail. A sequence of logically developed charts is invariably preferable to a single monsterpiece, which in saying everything conveys nothing. How many lines is it possible to accommodate comfortably on a graph? Once again in discussing effective communication, there is no single correct answer. Everything depends upon the precise objective of the graph that you are drawing. But if those lines had begun to move across one another, the load of information would have been too great to absorb.

The different lines are labelled by means of small symbols and a key is provided in the top left corner of the graph. Most readers find this an irritating practice, since they are obliged to move their eyes frequently from the identifying symbols on the lines to the keys in the top corner and back again to ensure that they are not misunderstanding the information being presented. Wherever possible, it is desirable to put the label at the ends of the lines so that the reader does not have to keep moving to and fro across the graph to find identifying information in a key. A graph labelled in this way. Notice, however, that the label for the left-hand curve seems to be in the wrong place. It would be better on the left of the curve. A moment's thought shows that in fact all the labels are on the top right-hand end of the curve; but this 'verbal' logic conflicts with the visual logic of the eye. Visual logic should always take precedence.

FLOW CHARTS

Flow charts use lines to help readers see sequences and movements through a process or a set of facts or possibilities. Lines are used to enable each reader not only to follow a path, but also to ignore information which might be relevant to other readers but is not relevant to him or her. Normally, in creating an algorithm or a flow chart, the writer wishes to make it easier for readers to decide which details, circumstances or conditions relate to their interests and needs.

The information is arranged in a hierarchy, enabling each reader to start by asking the most important overall question, and subsequently to follow a decision-taking sequence through a number of points at which simple decisions between two paths are possible. The paths normally represent a sequence in time or priority in physical or mental operations.

But not all flow charts are algorithms. A conventional circuit diagram can be described as a flow chart, as it shows all the paths or flows in a circuit without necessarily emphasizing any principal flow. But the best circuit diagrams, too, are structured to help the reader recognize groups of operations, sequences, primary and secondary flow, or feedback.

LOGICAL TREES

The simplest type of flow chart is a logical tree (otherwise called a family tree, or a genealogical tree). By reducing the information to a series of questions and comments, the writer has managed to avoid generating dense paragraphs of prose setting out various possibilities, and the actions that should be taken in the light of those possibilities. This enables readers to concentrate on the particular faults they identify in the apparatus before them.

USE OF SYMBOLS

The reader simply by the use of lines. All other information is provided in words. It is possible to use flow charts to reduce the number of words as well. This can be done by introducing pictorial representation into the presentation as well as words. By use of recognizable symbols, the writer has managed to give an impression of the various stages in the process, culminating in the production of the literature and its dispatch from the factory.

Not many flow charts go this far in pictorial representation. Most rely on the use of well-known symbols to add information to that which is written in words within the various elements on the flow chart. Some of the most familiar symbols in use. A circle indicates a starting or finishing point, a diamond or lozenge shape indicates a question and a rectangle indicates an instruction or decision point. Use of conventional symbols, and reliance on readers' recognition of information conveyed not by words but by the use of symbols. However, this practice can become dangerous because some readers may not recognise the significance of the symbols used in the presentation.

Particularly, readers in other countries may not understand symbols that are very familiar to you. Most British readers understand the meaning of a tick as used; in many other countries, the symbol is not used. In some countries, too, a cross (x) customarily signifies a positive response (not, as in Britain, a negative response). For example, in a register of attendees at a meeting in France, the secretary puts a cross by the name of each person present (not, as in Britain, by the name of each absentee).

So, when you use symbols in your illustrations or text, try to choose symbols that are in use everywhere. Avoid the confusion that arises when organizations create different ways of symbolizing a single meaning. Seven ways of symbolizing the earliest and latest times of an event in a Critical Path Analysis network! Of course, the safe way to proceed is to use international standards and to give readers a key to symbols at the start of each document. But remember that your readers may not be using the document as frequently as you are, and extensive use of symbols identified by keys may place heavy loads on your readers' memories.

Emphasis on flow and Functions

A common fault in flow charting is to make all movement or flow seem to be of equal importance. A flow chart in which it is difficult to see the relative importance of different pieces of information and different movements. A simplified and clarified flow chart emphasizing by different weights of line and symbols the main movement and the feedback within the flow. Sometimes flow charts become long and complex if you attempt to show all possible paths, branches and outcomes on a single chart.

One way of reducing complexity is to have a 'family' of charts-a main chart showing an overall flow, indicating branches to lower-level charts that give more detail of specific decision-points or procedures. Another helpful technique for reducing the length of flow charts is to 'bend' them. Block diagrams can be used particularly successfully to indicate the linking of functions or other structural entities in scientific and technical work.

And if the information is not too complicated, it is possible with benefit to superimpose the two functional layouts one upon the other, to produce a flow chart which shows functional blocks with the explanation in words and the circuit diagram all in one presentation.

Skilful use of Lines, Shapes and Tones

In this discussion of graphic presentation techniques, we have not included analysis of the advantages and disadvantages of different types of specialized technical drawing such as orthographic projection, isometric projection and so on. Neither have we discussed the production of illustrations using air-brush techniques, multiple colours and other specialized techniques. However, some of the simple but effective techniques used by professional illustrators *are* available to the producer of reports and papers.

For example, you do not have to be a professional illustrator to use lines, shapes and shading effectively in your presentations. A valuable summary of the tactics the non-specialist illustrator can use to show relationships. Simple photographs, emphasizing size, scale and position can be used effectively in reports and papers at low cost and without specialized help.

A word of Caution

Finally, let us emphasize that although the presentation of factual information in diagrams or even in pictorial charts can ensure that it will be understood and remembered better than when it is presented in a table, much depends on the skill with which the presentation is matched to its aim and audience.

Indeed, for some readers, the inclusion of graphical illustrations in a text may *decrease* accuracy of recall and grasp of an argument over-all. Much seems to depend on the intelligence of the readers and the extent of their training in how to interpret visual presentations.

10

Writing Letters and Memoranda

Letters (and the informal, internal kind of letter we call a memorandum) are the principal day-to-day medium of information exchange. This is not about letter-writing in general, though much of what we say would apply to any letters; it is about letters written to give technical information, the type of letter likely to be written by the scientist or engineer working in an industrial or scientific organization. Other sorts of letters (in particular, sales letters) are not our province.

Every letter carries not only information but also an image of the writer and the organization he or she works for. It is important to be aware of the potency of this image. Consider, for example, the following letter in reply to a customer's query about his account:

Dear Mr Knight,

Re:	55	78	91	99
	38	00	31	00

We are in receipt of your letter received at this Office 14th April 1987 and would advise that according to our records, an exchange of model to colour receiver type 7641 was effected on account 55 78 91 99 from 15th December 1986 and an initial payment of £8.50 was allocated.

However, an annual invoice in respect of previous television was despatched prior to details of exchange of model being completed on the account and a subsequent payment of £72.15 was allocated on 15th December 1986. It would appear that a further remittance of £179.22 was made 13th January 1987 in respect of annual rental for both television accounts and the sum of £86.02 has been transferred to clear rentals on account 38 00 31 00 until 19th April 1988. Two detailed statements are enclosed to assist in clarification and you will observe that account 55 78 91 99 is in fact clear until 23rd February 1987 with a further credit balance of £79.40.

In the circumstances, would you kindly advise whether this balance is to remain on the account or be refunded.

A pre-paid envelope is enclosed for your convenience.

Yours sincerely,

John W. Hunt

Manager, Subscriber Relations Dept.

We wonder what sort of 'subscriber relations' the writer of this letter presides over. Is he hired to make a point of offending customers? Even a tolerant or resigned reader can hardly sense helpfulness in this letter. The writer seems aloof, impersonal, and probably old, crabbed, and bad-tempered. These reactions are a reader's natural response to the tone created by the wording of the letter. But many of the words and phrases are traditional and conventional usage in business correspondence. The writer may be a young, friendly man with a genuine concern for the comfort of his customers, but we cannot, however hard we try, ignore the overtones of aloof detachment. People often argue that letters such as this belong to the age of Dickens; yet this example is real. Admittedly, it is an extreme example, but many of the features of this letter can be found in the less monstrous, but very numerous, examples we all receive. Here is a re-written version of the same letter:

Dear Mr Knight,

Balance of your television rental

Your television rental account is in fact paid until 23rd February 1987. We exchanged the television for a colour set on 15th December 1986, but our invoice was unfortunately sent out before this.

We have received three payments from you:

15th December, 1986	£8.50
15th December, 1986	£72.15
13th January, 1987	£179.22

Because the rentals for the first set were more than covered by these payments, we transferred the balance (£86.02) to the other rental account. This still leaves a credit balance of £79.40. Would you like us to refund this, or will you leave it in credit for future rentals?

To help you follow this rather complicated situation, we are sending copies of the two accounts, that is No. 55 78 91 99 and No. 38 00 31 00. We are sorry for the confusion.

Yours sincerely,
John W Hunt
Manager, Subscriber Relations Department.

The success of this letter derives not just from the friendly tone but also from the directness of style and the clarity of the information. There are no tortuous structures or pompous words, no stylised phrases such as are never spoken aloud by a real person. There is also a careful re-thinking of the information needed. The reader is not overloaded with a mass of detail which may or may not be relevant. The letter is short and to the point, but we do not feel it to be abrupt, unfriendly, or stingy with information. The truth is that the over-elaborate courtesies of the first version (such as 'I trust that this information will suffice') strike readers as hollow and hypocritical.

We learn an important point from the original letter. It was probably not indifference that created the unfortunate tone; rather, it was probably helpfulness which failed to think. No letter-writer actually *wants* to create the impression that this letter creates, but many letter-writers, naturally friendly people in themselves, *do* create just this impression by lack of thought.

COMMUNICATION IS A RELATIONSHIP

When we communicate, we are forming a relationship. Even if we transmit and receive only neutral information, we cannot help making judgements about the other person, and his or her likely intentions.

Because there is a residual unease in person-to-person interactions, inherited from rougher and more insecure times, we have evolved elaborate rituals to reassure each other of good intentions. Thus, in a normal spoken interaction, a great deal of information about attitude and intention is transmitted non-verbally, by facial expression and movement, gesture, position of the body, distance away, use of the eyes, and many other signals. This non-verbal component of the message is vitally important in forming the communicative link.

In a letter there is no face and no smile. Without non-verbal signals to confirm good intentions, the *tone* of the letter is especially important. Judgement of the other person's intentions, of his or her confidence and assurance about what he or she is saying, is a vital part of communication. We perceive the *senders* of messages as well as their information. The perceptions which led 1580 scientists to make judgements about the personal qualities of the report-writer after reading only a few paragraphs also operate when reading a letter. Readers cannot stop themselves making continual judgements of writers' intention and competence, as well as of the information they are receiving.

Nor can writers prevent these normal human perceptions coming into play. That was why the example a few pages ago was so disturbing. Being careful about tone does not mean that letters should be full of racy mateyness, or crammed with lugubrious reassurances. It *does* mean you must select from the resources of the language code very carefully, to guard against possibilities of misinterpretation.

Use the language of everyday human contact. Overformality and impersonal constructions have no associations of friendliness, no familiar context of helpful human interaction. We meet them only in the cold impersonal environments of administrative writing, and they open a door to chilly drafts of indifference.

HELPFUL CLARITY

Choice of language affects the way readers respond to letters. If writers wish to convey the impression of being friendly and helpful, the simple natural rhythms of everyday serious conversation are best. Why, then, do some writers choose a high-flown style? The answer is, we think, that the artificiality of writing to a face they have not seen is as upsetting for the writer as for the reader. Writers feel they must be careful not to offend; finding it difficult to judge the reactions of a silent and invisible reader, they protect themselves by being over-formal. Writers also feel that they must be more explicit in writing, and they reach for the longer, more formalized words.

It is true that the absence of non-verbal signals means letters must be clear; but clarity does not come from long-windedness. Writing needs precision and detail, but it does not need a roundabout, pompous, and over-formalized style. The aim should be to create the impression of an efficient but human organization, which is interested in the reader's problems, and wants to help.

USE PERSONAL PRONOUNS

Avoid impersonal constructions; they give the atmosphere of distant formality which upsets readers. Write 'I suppose', not 'it is apprehended that'. You may feel that using 'I' lays you open to personal responsibility for the information you give; but use of the first person does not increase your responsibility, especially if you write on headed notepaper as an organization's agent. Equally, roundabout, impersonal phrases will not decrease your responsibility, but they will reduce clarity.

Writers are afraid of sounding self-centred if they continually use 'I' or 'we'. So they use a variety of alternatives such as 'the writer', or 'the undersigned', or 'this office'; the reader translates all these as 'I' with the added connotations of impersonality. 'The writer' means, for the reader, 'I, the distant and indifferent writer...'. Use 'we' for communal work or decisions, or write active sentences with the object under discussion as subject.

Thus do not always write: 'I have the parts you ordered ready for collection'. Sometimes write instead: 'The parts you ordered are ready for collection'. Similarly, it is often possible to turn the sentence round so that 'You' becomes the subject of an active sentence. Thus do not write, where there are already several sentences starting with 'I', yet another one: 'I am pleased to tell you that the tests were negative'. Write instead, 'You will be pleased to know that the tests are negative'. A skilful choice from these resources can make a letter varied and interesting, and avoid chilling impersonality.

AVOID LONG, FORMAL WORDS

The temptation to reach out for the long word seems more irresistible than ever in letters. Words and phrases long out of use in normal conversation are dusted off, and ancient formalities are dragged out. Often, writers seem to climb up on to ancient, Dickensian high stools and desks, straighten their backs, clear their throats, and with much dipping and chewing of their quills, scratch and blot their way through copious and fawning formalities. Try to use simple, familiar words instead. They are easier to read, more economical in time and space, but most importantly they have the atmosphere of efficiency and friendliness.

Every entrant into the civil service comes equipped with a vocabulary of common words of precise meaning adequate for all ordinary purposes. But when he begins to write as an official he has a queer trick of forgetting them and relying mainly on a smaller vocabulary of less common words with a less precise meaning. The English language is rich in verbose and unwieldy phrases to replace the plain and serviceable everyday word. Instead of 'about' the writer can say 'in regard to' or 'referring to' or 'in connection with'.

We think writers choose these longer phrases because they feel such wording adds variety and elegance; perhaps they feel that these ceremonious circumlocutions convey a timeless old-world courtesy; perhaps also they hope that if they linger politely over these words, their reader will think they have taken care and trouble over the letter. But whatever the motive, the tactics are mistaken. Such long phrases do not convey respect and courtesy; the simple phrase conveys real helpfulness by sensibly getting on with the job.

LAYOUT OF THE LETTER

The layout of a document is part of a system of signs, a code which reader and writer use more successfully when it is familiar to both of them. For these reasons, letters should follow the standard format which the reader is conditioned to expect. The writer's address, if it is not printed, will be expected in the top right-hand corner. The name and address of the reader will be expected slightly lower down on the left. The references will usually be either below or above the receiver's address; they can also be put in the title line of the letter. Within simple conventions, a letter can follow any form which is a convenient and effective way of communicating the information.

The first impact of the letter is created by the greeting. Many writers always put 'Dear Sir', or even worse 'Dear Sir or Madam', even if they know the name of the person they are writing to. But using first names has become the norm in personal contacts, and is becoming the norm in business letters. If you are not on first-name terms, the best policy is to address your reader by surname. A name is a personal thing, and to use it is a sign of respect. The convention of addressing even friends with a peremptory and military 'Sir!' died with the First World War; to start letters with a uniform 'Dear Sir' suggests indifference to people and their names.

Some companies state that all letters must be addressed to the company. This is an antiquated restriction, and we meet it less and less; but in replying to one of their letters, the sensible thing to do is to accept their requirements, since there is no point in irritating your reader gratuitously. But show that you are replying to the person who wrote to you by clearly marking your letter for the attention of that person. When you are writing to someone whose name you do not know, 'Dear Sir or Madam' is acceptable as a polite form of address, but only then.

When addressing the letter, put the addressee's position in the company as the next line after his or her name. There are two reasons for this. First, if no official position is in the address, the office may think the letter is personal, and leave it unopened when the addressee is away. Second, if the addressee has left, the new holder of the job may send your letter on. This confusion is avoided if the addressee's status is given after his or her name. In most letters, some sort of heading or title-line should come immediately after the greeting. Most people in offices deal with many letters on widely different topics every day, and it helps them to focus their attention on the subject of any particular letter quickly if the topic is clearly stated in a title line. But do not write 'Re: Cotton wool swabs'. The *Re* adds nothing, and most people do not even know what it means (it is in fact Latin for 'the thing' and was used by mediaeval lawyers to give formality to their writing). Just as informative, and simpler is: 'Cotton Wool Swabs'. The title line may also contain the references, if they are informative. Thus the title might be 'Cotton-Wool Swabs: Order C.59487'. It could also contain the date of the letter you are replying to: 'Diesel Generator: your letter of 21st April'. In this way, cumbersome references are kept out of the first sentence.

START WITH THE IMPORTANT POINT

Your first sentence should contain the main point of the letter. Many writers seem to find it difficult to start. They write:

Dear Sir,

Thank you for your letter of 27th April, which we have received. Turning to the matter you mention in your first paragraph, you will be pleased to know that the Diesel Generators are ready...

The opening phrases of this letter are redundant; they have little function other than to clear the writer's throat. Readers must skip over them to get to the meat of the letter, and this is wasteful for reader and writer alike. More importantly, it blunts the impact of the message. Such an opening gives an apologetic and hesitant tone. Start letters, instead, with the key point:

Dear Mr Smith,

The diesel generators are ready...

Many of the stilted phrases of the ugly 'correspondence' style are redundant opening lines:

With reference to your enquiry please find attached...

I am writing to tell you that...

No one could write 'I am not writing to tell you that...'or even 'I am writing not to tell you that...'. Equally silly is the opening: We have received your letter...

The phrase is meaningless because its opposite is unlikely. Much awkwardness in opening sentences is created by the feeling that it is essential to refer at the outset to the date of the letter to which you are replying.

We have already suggested that the date is better in the reference or in the title line; but if you must refer, in the first sentence, to the date of the letter to which you are replying, put it in a more comfortable position, not highlighted at the beginning. Do not write: Thank you for your order of 21st April for diesel generators, which are now ready.

But write: The diesel generators, which you ordered on 21st April, are now ready. The old habit of using Latin in the first sentences of letters is dying out. Writers used to refer to 'yours of 21st. ult.' or 'prox.' or 'inst'. Many readers are not certain what the abbreviations mean, and in any case such Latin tags give an air of stuffy pomposity to a letter. Write clearly by always stating the month itself. Sometimes a letter is little more than a cover-note for something you are sending. The traditional openings for this are stilted and formal.

Do not write 'Please find enclosed...'; it has an unnatural ring to it, and most of the variations of this phrase are not much better. It is simpler and more natural to write: 'Here is the plan you wanted...'

ORGANIZATION

Before ending a letter, make sure all the necessary points are covered. Give information clearly, and in an order which makes it easy for the reader to follow the points through. Do not be afraid to use sub-headings in a letter. They are very helpful to the reader as a signal that he or she is moving to a different topic. If the letter is more than a page long, it can have sub-headings, exactly as in a report.

Check that you have dealt with all the questions you must answer by making brief notes in the margin of the enquirer's letter, and going through them while writing.

ENDING

At the end of your letter, stop. This is obvious advice, perhaps, but many writers add pious and empty courtesies. A customary flourish, by its very weary familiarity, adds nothing; indeed, it detracts from the impression of sincerity. Consider this ending: Meanwhile we should be pleased to have your assurance of immediate delivery of a replacement supply and look forward to being advised of delivery on Monday or Tuesday of next week.

Yours faithfully, The ending has a genuine point to make, but does so in such a verbose way that it is unlikely to succeed. A more effective ending is: Please will you tell us by Tuesday next week when you can deliver.

A second example of a verbose ending which struggles to say something simple, at great length, is: We should be pleased to have confirmation of your understanding of this purchasing agreement between us, which we are sure will be to our mutual advantage.

Such an ending leaves a bad taste: 'We should be pleased to...' sounds pompous. 'Confirmation of your understanding...' means simply 'confirmation'. 'Agreement between us' means simply 'agreement'. 'We are sure will be to our mutual advantage...' sounds like the bland re-assurances of the conman. A better ending is: Please confirm this agreement. Many absurd and uncomfortable phrases are used to end letters. Such endings should be cut out; the best way to finish a letter is with the last factual statement. If an early reply is genuinely needed, then give both a date, and a reason.

Not: The favour of a response in the near future would be appreciated. but: Please reply by the 25th because we make up our monthly orders then.

THE SIGNATURE

It is polite to type your name, or write it in block capitals below the signature. The range and variety of English surnames is amazing. We all feel upset if our name is mis-spelt; we all feel embarrassed if we are unsure about the spelling of a name. To save your reader puzzling over a signature, try also to acquire a legible and neat signature. Finally, it is off-hand to end 'Dictated and signed in his absence by...' It suggests the writer is too busy to deal with letters personally. We know it is sometimes done for legal reasons, but the secretary is as much the organization's agent in law as the manager is. If your letter has to be signed by someone else, the simple explanation 'for' is clearest and politest. When signing letters, it is also polite to put your position or status after the signature. Everyone in the office may know who you are, but the reader may not. It is always courteous to tell your reader in what capacity the letter is written.

TACTICS FOR LETTERS

Not all letters merely report information. In many cases they have to explain failure, repeat requests, refuse information or confess to not having done something. If you have to fulfil one of these tasks, try to report first what you *have* been able to do, then report what you have not been able to do. Reflect on the impression this reply makes:

We have searched our files for the test reports on Batch C467. We think this report must be held at the New York office, and if you write direct to them you may be able to get a copy of it. We are sorry not to be able to help you this time. This letter reports failure to help, but does so in a strategic way. The impression is that the writer has made an effort to find the information, and he or she has thought of the way forward for the reader. Exactly the same information could have been communicated more clumsily:

We do not seem to keep copies of the test reports, such as that on Batch C467 which you requested, though we spent time searching our files. You should write to the New York office. The blame here appears to be put on the reader's shoulders for asking the wrong office. Even the fact that the writer spent time looking for the report sounds like a reproach, whereas previously it sounded like an effort to help. Tactical thinking is vital if you are to convey a good impresion. By using sympathy and understanding for the reader, you can create a good impression and avoid unfortunate misunderstan-dings.

WRITING MEMORANDA

A memorandum may be as long as a short report or as brief as a sentence. The main difference from a letter is the informality and immediacy of the memorandum. Because it is internal, it does not require the apparatus of addresses; because it is informal it does not require a greeting or a farewell; because it is immediate, it does not require a framework of courtesies. But a memorandum cannot be carelessly written. Tone is important; only careful choice of tactics can avoid the threat of misunderstanding. The most important advice is to avoid over-formal language, and to use every-day, clear and direct words and structures. A memo which starts:

The writer apprehends that difficulty has been experienced in achieving monthly targets... will court failure. It would create a better impression written in simpler language: I realise that you have found it hard to meet monthly targets... Elaborate courtesies in memoranda rarely ring true, and in some circumstances invite a cynical reaction. A simple 'please' or 'thank you' is adequate, because its simplicity reinforces rather than detracts from its sincerity. Thus a balanced memorandum to the sales staff might read:

Our sales quota for the month has again been achieved by the middle of the third week. Head Office have commented favourably on our area's performance. Thank you for your efforts.

The original version was less effective: I am very pleased to tell you that our sales quota for the month has already been met, and it is only the middle of the third week. You will be delighted to know that Head Office has commented favourably on this area's performance. Once again, my heartfelt thanks for your very real efforts.

A memorandum is a tool of management, a business device, aiming at convenience and speed. To spin it out with a *multiplicity* of 'pleases' and 'thank-yous' is redundant. Memoranda should briefly state their message, and stop. Most activities are co-operative; few organizations work for the benefit of one person only. It is therefore usually possible to put any request in a form which makes some benefit for the reader clear, and a little thought will make the writer sensitive to the ways in which such tactics can be used. It is well worth while, in terms of co-operation and efficiency, to make the effort to adjust to a reader-centred way of thinking. As an example, here is a memorandum which does its job less than efficiently:

USE OF ENVELOPES

It appears that new envelopes are being used for internal mail and for the London office when, instead, used envelopes, sealed by stapling, would be quite satisfactory or, alternatively, envelopes could be dispensed with and the contents folded and secured by either a paper clip or staple and the recipient's name written on the outside. In the interests of economy, it is suggested that for internal mail or for London office, where practicable, either of the latter two methods should be adopted, care being taken to avoid any confusion or mis-direction by ensuring that any re-used envelopes are clearly addressed and all previous names and addresses obliterated.

Supplies of used envelopes are normally available from Traffic Department. The first impression is unfavourable, because the title line is not helpful in focusing attention on the precise subject. A more informative title would be: 'Economical re-use of envelopes', or 'Saving costs by re-using envelopes'. Next, long sentences (only three for the whole memo), and pompous words ('alternatively', 'dispensed with') build up an atmosphere of directive, insensitive fussing over details. There is no attempt to make the instructions in any way to the benefit of the reader. Nor is there any attempt to soften it with a simple 'please'; it remains blunt and impersonal. We would judge that there would be little saving of envelopes as a result of this memo. But it can be re-written in a simpler, more direct and personal style, adopting the tactics of appealing to mutual benefit:

SAVING COSTS BY RE-USING ENVELOPES

Envelopes are costing our organization a great deal of money. Please re-use envelopes for internal mail as much as possible. Re-used envelopes can also be used for mail for London office; re-stapling old envelopes, or simply folding the message (and stapling or clipping) will do. Please make sure that the old address is crossed out. Traffic Department have plenty of used envelopes. Simplicity and thoughtfulness transform a poor memo into an effective one.

Dictating Letters

Many letters are dictated. This is neither as easy nor as timesaving as it appears. Spoken language is very different from written language; in general it does not have the same sentence structures, uses more and simpler words, and relies on intonation as well as syntax for structure and emphasis. Here is an exact transcription of a spoken talk on a technical subject:

Well if you take one of these animals and put it between two electrical terminals in a laboratory, and create a strong static electricity field, which doesn't hurt the animal at all, it's perfectly lively and unaffected by it, but it will start to discharge electrons; they fan out from the openings of the body, the openings in its external shell, its exoskeleton, and there's an avalanche of electrons moving out and knocking into molecules of gas in the air, nitrogen molecules mostly, and these are excited, and because they're excited, they glow, and so each individual insect, gives out rather a weak light, but if you look at it, in a darkened room, you can see this glow fanning out in all directions.

If you have never seen spoken language written down before, you have probably not thought how radical the differences are. The spoken voice, has an extra 'code', an extra system of signals to communicate with. Intonation, by rising and falling pitch, by varying loudness, and by grouping sounds, is able to communicate the structures and meanings of groups of words. Because of this, spoken language often does not need the same explicit system of grammatical structures which written language uses. Stripped of the ability to use this intonation code, the *writer* has to use the grammar code more fully. It is for this reason that transcribed dictation is often uncomfortable to read. It also tends to be more repetitious (often using the same word with different meanings in the same sentence) and to use long phrases rather than single words. Simply talking into a dictating machine naturally produces the spoken variety of language. Therefore, when dictating, you must learn to reproduce the grammatical explicitness of written language while speaking. Here are three pieces of advice:

A dictated letter often lacks structure and headings. Therefore make a brief note plan of the main points before dictating. Look through these notes, determining the best order and dictate from them, clearly specifying paragraphs and sub-headings. Dictate slowly, using deliberately short sentences. Because spoken language tends to make less use of what we would recognize as a sentence boundary, dictated letters often have long sentences. Sentences which seem short when dictating are frequently of the right length when written down.

Try to dictate in a clipped style. Talking is easy and encourages verbosity and repetition. If you say things briefly, and stop before expanding, repeating or embroidering the point, the written result will be economical and effective as written language. Finally, it is essential to edit dictation. The transcript may have a different tone from that intended. Here is an example of 'raw' dictation, with signs of loquacity and unusual structures in written language.

It was unfortunately issued in this form: Dr Brown used to work with Quintra and has now been appointed Production Manager at this comparatively new plant which so far has not been involved with exterior finishes but is about to do so having developed a range of pretreatment systems and undercoatings for the industry which is likely to expand very substantially over the next few years. He now wishes to introduce new window re-finishing lines and to this end has been sampled with our products.

Evaluation of the other products continues but next week Dr Brown will advise E.C.D. of his requirements. At this stage, demand will certainly be small because in terms of manufacture they have had no previous experience as a company in producing these coatings. When spoken, the oddities of grammar in structures like 'which so far has not been involved...but is about to do so' and 'in terms of manufacture they have had no previous experience...' would go unnoticed. Intonation would supply the structure which the grammar confuses. The letter also has very long sentences, and verbose phrases like 'to this end'. Edit dictation to produce written language: Dr Brown used to work for Quintra.

He has been appointed Production Manager at this new plant. So far it has not produced external finishes, but is about to start. It has developed a range of pretreatment systems and undercoatings for the building industry (which is likely to greatly expand over the next few years). He wants to introduce new window re-finishing lines so I gave him samples of our products.

He will continue to evaluate the other products; but he promises to tell us what his requirements will be next week. They have no previous experience in the company of producing these coatings, so orders will be small.

Clear and Useful Letters

No doubt many readers already follow the suggestions we have made here; but we are still surprised at the number of tortuously phrased and confusing letters.

If writers are careful about adopting a direct and friendly tone, use simple, clear language, thoughtful tactics and a helpful layout, their letters create a favourable impression.

Index

E

F

G

H

I

L

M

N

O

P